About This Book

"[Harry] Oldmeadow skillfully considers the legacy of Black Elk (1863-1950), a Lakota holy man who is best known through poet John Neihardt's 1932 biography *Black Elk Speaks*. . . . Readers interested in Black Elk will find this book an effective synthesis of the scholarship on the mystic's life."
    —*Publishers Weekly*

"This studious, extensively researched and analytically presented account [is] highly recommended especially for public and college library Native American Studies shelves."
    —*Midwest Book Review*

"*Black Elk, Lakota Visionary* merits a place on the shelf of all who are serious about Native American culture. And it should be an essential element of Indian studies curricula in colleges, for it presents Indian spiritual tradition not as an atavistic exercise to appreciate the past, but a source to be drawn upon for rational existence in today's world."
    —**Charles E. Trimble**, Oglala Lakota, Founder of the American Indian Press Association and past Executive Director of the National Congress of American Indians

"This book will oblige readers to reassess Black Elk and his legacy. It is the most authoritative and up to date work I have seen on the subject."
    —**Michael Oren Fitzgerald**, author of *Yellowtail: Crow Medicine Man and Sun Dance Chief* and editor of *The Essential Charles Eastman (Ohiyesa)*

"*Black Elk, Lakota Visionary* studies the debate among scholarly specialists as they reconstruct the history behind the life story and Great Vision of the *wicasa wakan*. Their exchange of views is counterbalanced by an examination of Lakota spirituality in relationship to Western and Eastern religious traditions. Exposure to this discourse will inspire the reader to appreciate the universality of tradition and revelation in Lakota ancestral wisdom and one's place in a world of order with beauty and meaning."
    —**Vivian Arviso Deloria**, former Executive Director of Education for the Navajo Nation and Chairperson of the Navajo Nation Women's Commission

T0019551

"A significant contribution to the Black Elk literature. Especially valuable for new information on Joseph Epes Brown and the composition of *The Sacred Pipe*."

—**Clyde Holler**, author of *Black Elk's Religion: The Sun Dance and Lakota Catholicism* and editor of *The Black Elk Reader*

"*Black Elk, Lakota Visionary* is a wonderful addition to understanding this Oglala holy man's significance in both Native American and United States history. Harry Oldmeadow uses new sources to reassess Black Elk's life, impact, and the controversies with John G. Neihardt, Joseph Epes Brown, and his adoption of Catholicism. . . . Oldmeadow demonstrates how the views of Frithjof Schoun, the pre-eminent Perennialist philosopher, offer a better understanding of Black Elk. All students of Native American history and of Black Elk should be required to read this valuable contribution to the literature."

—**Raymond Wilson**, Fort Hays State University, author of *Ohiyesa: Charles Eastman, Santee Sioux* and *Native Americans in the Twentieth Century*

"Harry Oldmeadow brings together in one volume information that comes from specialists in cultural anthropology as well as rich insights into the human condition from scholars like Mircea Eliade and Frithjof Schuon. Building upon this background, Oldmeadow explores the cultural legacy of Black Elk and the Sioux people. He does so using ordinary language which enables the reader to grasp the rich vision of this holy man and his world."

—**Richard Davies**, Culver Academies, author of *Swords at Culver*

World Wisdom
The Library of Perennial Philosophy

The Library of Perennial Philosophy is dedicated to the exposition of the timeless Truth underlying the diverse religions. This Truth, often referred to as the *Sophia Perennis*—or Perennial Wisdom—finds its expression in the revealed Scriptures as well as the writings of the great sages and the artistic creations of the traditional worlds.

Black Elk, Lakota Visionary: The Oglala Holy Man and Sioux Tradition appears as one of our selections in the American Indian Traditions series.

American Indian Traditions Series

This award-winning series celebrates the unique cultural, spiritual, and artistic genius of the Indians of North America. Classic and contemporary works of scholarship stand alongside collections of the writings and recorded statements of America's first inhabitants. These writings, together with diverse illustrations, testify to an enduring and living legacy.

Black Elk, Pine Ridge Reservation, South Dakota, 1948

Black Elk, Lakota Visionary

The Oglala Holy Man and Sioux Tradition

By
Harry Oldmeadow

Foreword by
Charles Trimble

World Wisdom

Black Elk, Lakota Visionary:
The Oglala Holy Man and Sioux Tradition
by Harry Oldmeadow
© 2018 World Wisdom, Inc.

Most recent printing indicated by last digit below
10 9 8 7 6 5 4 3

Library of Congress Cataloging-in-Publication Data

Names: Oldmeadow, Harry, 1947- author.
Title: Black Elk, Lakota visionary :
the Oglala holy man and Sioux tradition
/ by Harry Oldmeadow ; foreword by Charles Trimble.
Description: Bloomington, Indiana : World Wisdom, Inc., 2018. | Series:
American Indian traditions | Includes bibliographical references and index.|
Identifiers: LCCN 2017057064 (print) | LCCN 2017058288 (ebook) |
ISBN   9781936597611 (epub) | ISBN 9781936597604 (pbk. : alk. paper)
Subjects: LCSH: Black Elk, 1863-1950. | Oglala Indians--Biography. |
Oglala   Indians--Religion. | Lakota Indians.
Classification: LCC E99.O3 (ebook) | LCC E99.O3 B5365 2018 (print) |
DDC 978.004/9752440092 [B] --dc23
LC record available at https://url.emailprotection.
link/?aQIGj4lOvUgMGIEdjJ2U_yJx71H-NPBWzjh2y4RGuH1A~

Cover:
Black Elk praying to the Six Grandfathers on Harney Peak
(renamed Black Elk Peak in August 2016 in honor of the holy man).
His red underwear modestly represents how his body was painted red
during his vision. Photograph by John G. Neihardt.
From the John G. Neihardt (1881-1973) Papers, C3716. Courtesy of the
State Historical Society of Missouri, Manuscript Collection.

Printed on acid-free paper in the United States of America.

For information address World Wisdom, Inc.
P.O. Box 2682, Bloomington, Indiana 47402-2682
www.worldwisdom.com

I saw more than I can tell and understood more than I saw;
for I was seeing in a sacred manner . . .

Black Elk Speaks, 26

The Indian world represents on this earth a value that is irreplaceable;
it possesses something unique and enchanting. . . . It is human
greatness, and at the same time harbors within itself something
mysterious and sacred, which it expresses with profound originality.

Frithjof Schuon, *The Feathered Sun*, 147

If you ever enter into this other world . . . you may never again be
contented with what you have been accustomed to
think of as "progress" and "civilization."

Ananda Coomaraswamy, *Selected Papers I*, 45-46

Mitakuye oyasin.
("All my relatives" or "We are all related")

Lakota saying

Contents

List of Tables

List of Illustrations

A Note on Terminology and Documentation

Some folk find the term "Indian" unacceptable. I find nothing disparaging in it, and nor do many of the people to whom it is applied. A 1995 US Census Bureau survey found that the majority of these people prefer the term "American Indian" to "Native American." As a result, the Smithsonian chose the name "Museum of the American Indian" for their new museum in Washington D.C. I use "Indian" interchangeably with "Native American." I have standardized the use of Lakota and other Indian terms, even within direct quotations: thus, for instance, *wicasa wakan* (holy man) is always rendered this way, however it might appear in different sources. Apart from a few terms which have passed into English currency—"tipi" for instance—Indian words are invariably italicized. Full publication details of all works cited can be found in the list of Sources at the end of this volume. Only such details as are necessary to identify the work in question are supplied in endnotes.

Abbreviations Used in Endnotes

BES   *Black Elk Speaks: The Complete Edition*, by John G. Neihardt. Lincoln: University of Nebraska, 2014.

Holler   *Black Elk's Religion: The Sun Dance and Lakota Catholicism*, by Clyde Holler. Syracuse: Syracuse University, 1995.

Schuon   *The Feathered Sun: Plains Indians in Art and Philosophy*, by Frithjof Schuon. Bloomington: World Wisdom, 1990.

Jackson   *Black Elk: The Life of an American Visionary*, by Joe Jackson. New York: Farrar, Straus & Giroux, 2016.

Reader   *The Black Elk Reader*, edited by Clyde Holler. Syracuse: Syracuse University, 2000.

Sixth G.   *The Sixth Grandfather: Black Elk's Teachings Given to John G. Neihardt*, edited by Raymond J. DeMallie. Lincoln: University of Nebraska, 1984.

S. Pipe   *The Sacred Pipe: Black Elk's Account of the Seven Rites of the Oglala Sioux*, by Joseph Epes Brown. Norman: University of Oklahoma, 1989.

Foreword

My first glance at the manuscript gave me pause as to whether I could do justice to writing a foreword for such a scholarly book. My doubts were quickly relieved as I got to reading, first by the author's assurance in his introduction that "The present volume is addressed to the general reader though I hope scholarly specialists may also discover something of interest in these pages" (p. xvi); and secondly, by the sheer enjoyment of such clarity as I read on.

With that warm opening, author Harry Oldmeadow sets the tone for the enjoyable course one enters the moment one begins to read. The author presents a thorough history of John G. Neihardt's 1932 classic, *Black Elk Speaks*, and the controversy surrounding the book on the part of historians and scholars, as well as academic and political activists. It is a concise, very readable summation of the book and its impact on Western and Eastern religious traditions. It is enlightening with new facts and keen insights from some of the most respected contemporary scholars of philosophy and religious traditions.

The book's content page is outlined like a syllabus of a favored professor; and, indeed, the book is an education in itself for the first-time reader or devoted fan of Neihardt and the Lakota holy man, offering a welcome contextual refresher to the most diligent scholar of *Black Elk Speaks* and the new metaphysical and traditional religious world it has engendered.

At the outset, Oldmeadow gives three related convictions that provided the motivation for his book: (1) "the spiritual heritage of the Plains Indians deserves a more honored and more fully understood place among the world's great religious traditions"; (2) "Black Elk's account of his early life, his Great Vision, and the principal rituals of the Lakota comprise an eloquent expression of that heritage and one of the most radiant spiritual testimonies of our time"; and (3) "the Lakota visionary and his tradition offer the contemporary world profound lessons of the most urgent importance" (p. xiii).

Although the author devotes no words to his own authority in the field, the reader is introduced to the great mind of Oldmeadow, one of the most respected members among those same contemporary scholars he cites to support these convictions.

Oldmeadow opens the door to the world of great thinkers who, through their diverse views and criticisms, have placed Black Elk's teachings amidst those of the greatest visionaries, spiritualists, philosophers, and teachers, and advanced the story of the Lakota holy man into a national and world phenomenon. Among those are such names as Joseph Epes Brown and Frithjof Schuon foremost, Raymond DeMallie, Clyde Holler, Dale Stover, Brian Holloway, Mircea Eliade, Ananda Coomaraswamy, and others. The critics and detractors of Neihardt and Black Elk are not slighted, but are given a full and fair hearing.

In *Black Elk, Lakota Visionary*, Oldmeadow gives us a book that merits a place on the shelf of all who are serious about Native American culture. And it should be an essential element of Indian studies curricula in colleges, for it presents Indian spiritual tradition not as an atavistic exercise to appreciate the past, but a source to be drawn upon for rational existence in today's world. The words of Ananda Coomaraswamy, as quoted in the epigraph page of this book, should inspire all teachers and scholars and embracers of traditional cultures: "If you ever enter this other world . . . you may never again be contented with what you have been accustomed to think of as 'progress' and 'civilization.'"

Charles E. Trimble, Oglala Lakota,
founder of the American Indian Press Association,
past Executive Director of the National Congress of American Indians

Introduction

Crazy Horse, Red Cloud, and Sitting Bull were the most renowned Lakota of the nineteenth century; Black Elk became the most celebrated of the twentieth. Indeed, no other Native American of any tribe has attained the status of Black Elk in the last half-century. Unlike most of the Indians who have a prominent place in the popular American consciousness—Tecumseh, Geronimo, Cochise, Chief Joseph, to name a few—Black Elk was not a great warrior chief but a *wicasa wakan*, a holy man. His life was governed by a mystical vision which he experienced as a boy. The present study explores the life and teachings of Black Elk, focusing on his spiritual experience and his role as a custodian of traditional Lakota wisdom. Three related convictions provide the motive force for the inquiry: first, the spiritual heritage of the Plains Indians deserves a more honored and more fully understood place among the world's great religious traditions; second, Black Elk's account of his early life, his Great Vision, and the principal rituals of the Lakota comprise an eloquent expression of that heritage and one of the most radiant spiritual testimonies of our time; third, the Lakota visionary and his tradition offer the contemporary world profound lessons of the most urgent importance.

Like Socrates, Jesus, and the Buddha, Black Elk himself wrote nothing. His fame rests largely on *Black Elk Speaks*, a recounting of his early life narrated to the Nebraskan poet of the Old West, John G. Neihardt, and first published in 1932. Carl Jung, the Swiss psychologist, was an early enthusiast and compared Black Elk's Great Vision to those of Ezekiel and The Journals of the Wild Liturgies.[1] Largely thanks to Jung's efforts the book was translated into German, although it did not appear in published form until 1955.[2] But generally the book attracted only scattered attention and was soon remaindered. It was not until the counter-cultural ferment of the 1960s that it commanded the interest of activists, seekers, and scholars alike, igniting widespread acclaim. Over the last half-century it has become a classic text, "arguably the single most widely read book in the vast literature relating to North American Indians."[3] Black Elk himself "has acquired the status of a mythological figure": "European Americans have fixed on Black Elk as a primary image by which they feel linked to the traditional world of the native peoples of North America. For them Black Elk represents quintessential Indianness by his nineteenth-century Lakota origins, his association with storied events such as the Battle of Little Big Horn and the massacre at Wounded Knee, and by his status as a visionary. . . ."[4] Less well-known but equally important is *The Sacred Pipe*, first published in 1953. It gives a detailed account of the seven primary rituals of the Lakota, as told to Joseph Epes Brown by the old medicine man in his last years. *The Sacred Pipe* provides an exposition not only of the rites but of the whole spiritual economy of the Lakota and of the wider cultural group to which they belonged, the Plains Indians.

In compiling *Black Elk Speaks*, John Neihardt selected only parts of Black Elk's narration. Describing his own role, Neihardt later said this:

> *Black Elk Speaks* is a work of art with two collaborators, the chief one being Black Elk. My function was both creative and editorial. . . . The beginning and end of the book are mine; they are what he would have said had he been able. . . . And the translation—or rather the transformation—of what was given me was expressed so that it could be understood by the white world.[5]

Elsewhere he wrote, "It was my function to translate the old man's story, not only in the factual sense—*for it was not the facts that mattered most*—but rather to recreate in English the mood and manner of the old man's narrative."[6] Neihardt's role in *retelling* Black Elk's story has come under severe scrutiny in the last few decades.

During the period that Black Elk and Neihardt spent together in 1931, Neihardt's daughter Enid took stenographic notes recording the old man's words, along with testimony from several other Lakota elders who were intermittently present during the interviews. These notes were later transcribed into a typescript. It was only in 1984 that the full text saw the light of day in published form as *The Sixth Grandfather*, edited by Raymond DeMallie.[7] *The Sixth Grandfather* also includes the transcripts of Neihardt's further interviews with Black Elk in 1944. *Black Elk Speaks*, *The Sacred Pipe*, and *The Sixth Grandfather* are three pillars on which any study of Black Elk must be built. We will also examine what arguably constitutes a fourth pillar that must henceforth be taken into consideration in any comprehensive study of Black Elk's life.[8]

The holy man provided not only an account of his own extraordinary experiences but a key with which to unlock the mysteries of the spiritual/religious life of the Plains Indians;[9] in DeMallie's apposite image, *Black Elk Speaks* is "an American Indian Rosetta Stone."[10] Furthermore, as Clyde Holler tells us, "As a living religion, the Lakota wisdom tradition that Black Elk represents also constitutes a deep challenge to Western ways of understanding human life and the cosmos, constituting a uniquely American perspective on ultimate truth."[11]

The popular and scholarly reception of *Black Elk Speaks* is revealing. Dale Stover has identified four phases in its history.[12] The first retelling of Black Elk's narrative by Neihardt and Brown foregrounds the romantic motifs of the "noble savage" and "the vanishing Indian." The counter-culture, the Native American cultural resurgence, and the political activism of the 1960s and 70s provide the context for the second phase in which Black Elk becomes mythologized as "the archetypal Indian" and *Black Elk Speaks* becomes a privileged literary text. Vine Deloria Jr. called it "a North American bible of all Tribes"[13] and "the standard by which other efforts to tell the Indian story are judged."[14] The publication of *The Sixth Grandfather* inaugurates the third period, one marked by scholarly controversies about the genesis, authenticity, and significance of Black Elk's mediated narratives, and about his hitherto obscured and neglected conversion to Catholicism. Lastly, in Stover's schema, comes a postcolonial re-reading of Black Elk and his legacy, rejecting "the hegemonic assumptions of European American discourse" and inviting a new, more respectful and egalitarian dialogue in which Native American agency is more fully recognized. In his introduction to *The Black Elk Reader* (2001) Clyde Holler noted some of these changing perceptions:

> The more we learn about Black Elk, the more controversial he becomes, a development that would hardly have seemed possible recently, youlike ago. In those happy days, practically everyone accepted Frank Fools Crow's assessment of Black Elk as the greatest of the Lakota holy men . . . and Plains anthropologists accepted *Black Elk Speaks* and *The Sacred Pipe* as authentic revelations of aboriginal Lakota consciousness. The situation today, after a little critical scholarship, is somewhat different. Leading anthropologists now question whether these same texts are authentic. . . . Perhaps this is due in part to the fact that the more we learn about Black Elk, the more his romantic image as an old-time Lakota holy man seems compromised by Christianity. In any case, it has become painfully clear that some people greatly prefer the nineteenth-century traditionalist who was constructed by Neihardt and Brown to the real Black Elk, the twentieth century religious leader in dialogue with Christianity.[15]

Who was "the real Black Elk"? This remains the question.

Most commentators have, at the least, treated Black Elk and his testimony with considerable respect. But we should also take note of the dissenters. For instance, John Fire Lame Deer, who himself attained some celebrity as a Native American visionary, dismissed Black Elk as "a catechism teacher" and a "cigar-store Indian,"[16] while William Powers indicts *Black Elk Speaks* as a "fabrication of the white man."[17] Powers asserts that it belongs with "other books written by white men for a white audience" in which "the ideas, plots, persons, and situations of these books have been constructed to conform to the expectations of a white audience."[18]

The present volume is addressed to the general reader, though I hope scholarly specialists may also discover something of interest in these pages. It is neither a full-dress biography, nor a history, nor a systematic account of Lakota religious life. Rather, its foremost aims are to contextualize Black Elk's life in his culture and period, to explore the meaning and significance of his Great Vision, to reassess the role of John Neihardt and Joseph Brown in the light of later scholarship, to draw attention to important recently published documents that shed light on Black Elk's relationship to Catholicism, to re-examine Black Elk's personal beliefs in the last years of his life, to assess his role in the revival of traditional rites, and finally, to reflect on the lessons that we might most profitably draw from the *wicasa wakan*. In this context the Lakota understanding of the natural order—or more precisely, their "metaphysic of virgin nature"—is of paramount significance. As Theodore Roszak remarked nearly half a century ago,

> How embarrassing it is for western society to have come so far in its rational, empirical study of nature, only to discover that the most basic principles of environmental intelligence have slipped through the mesh of science like water through a sieve. Even more to our chagrin: we now advance (fitfully) toward ecological sophistication only to find there the footprint of our "primitive" brothers and sisters who long ago possessed whole the wisdom we now piece laboriously together.[19]

The eminent scholar and Sufi philosopher, Seyyed Hossein Nasr, provides a window onto traditional understandings of the natural order when he writes, "On the highest level virgin nature can be contemplated as a theophany which possesses its own metaphysical message and spiritual discipline. Nature reveals the One and Its multiple qualities. It prays and invokes."[20] No doubt this kind of claim will puzzle many readers; if the following inquiry illuminates Nasr's statement and shows how Lakota culture was pervaded by this truth it will have served a noble end.

Mircea Eliade, a trailbreaker in the study of archaic traditions, provides one of the guidelines for the present study: "The scholar has not finished his work when he has reconstructed the history of a religious form or brought out its sociological, economic or political contexts. In addition he must *understand its meaning*."[21] This is no easy task and to imagine that it can be accomplished by the mere accumulation of data or by the application of theories and analytic techniques which lay claim to some sort of "objectivity" is to pursue the unicorn. As Frithjof Schuon has observed,

> There is in fact a sphere which by definition is beyond the reach of ordinary science . . . but which is the basis of every [traditional] civilization: this is spirituality—the knowledge of Divine Reality and of the means of realizing It, in some degree or other, in oneself.[22]

Elsewhere Schuon issues a caution which students of primal cultures would do well to ponder:

> Modern science . . . can neither add nor subtract anything in respect of the total truth or of mythological or other symbolism or in respect of the principles and experiences of the spiritual life. . . . We cannot be too wary of all the attempts to reduce the values vehicled by tradition to the level of phenomena supposed to be scientifically controllable. The spirit escapes the hold of profane science in an absolute fashion.[23]

This stricture applies not only to the "hard" sciences but to those so-called "social sciences" which ape their procedures—most notably in the present context, ethnography, anthropology, and sociology.

My researches into the life and teachings of Black Elk have drawn heavily on the work of scholars who have been working this terrain over the last half-century. As Holler notes, "Black Elk stands at the intersection of many scholarly disciplines"—anthropology, literature, religion, philosophy, history, and postcolonial studies. The accent of the present work is on Black Elk and Lakota culture from a religious and spiritual perspective, but I have harvested the insights of scholars working from a variety of viewpoints. It is a pleasure to acknowledge a substantial debt to several writers and to express my gratitude for such invaluable works as Joseph Epes Brown's *The Spiritual Legacy of the American Indian* (1972); *Black Elk's Religion: The Sun Dance and Lakota Catholicism* (1995) by Clyde Holler; two studies by Michael Steltenkamp, *Black Elk: Holy Man of the Oglala* (1993) and *Nicholas Black Elk: Medicine Man, Missionary, Mystic* (2009); *The Black Elk Reader* (2000), edited by Clyde Holler; Brian Holloway's *Interpreting the Legacy: John Neihardt and "Black Elk Speaks"* (2003); the complete and annotated edition of *Black Elk Speaks* (2014); and Joe Jackson's *Black Elk: The Life of an American Visionary* (2016). These works are familiar to anyone with a serious interest in Black Elk and Lakota religion. However, there is another book, little known, which gives us the most profound non-native account of the spirituality of the Plains Indians: *The Feathered Sun: Plains Indians in Art and Philosophy* (1990) by Frithjof Schuon.

For many years my own work has been informed by the writings of Schuon, the pre-eminent exponent of the Perennialist, or Traditionalist, perspective associated with such figures as René Guénon, Ananda Coomaraswamy, and Titus Burckhardt. Joseph Brown himself, greatly influenced by Schuon, belonged to this school which seeks to explicate the universal wisdom at the heart of the world's diverse religious traditions and behind their variegated forms. It was to this group that Seyyed Hossein Nasr referred when writing, "there are those whose vocation it is to provide the keys with which the treasury of wisdom of other traditions can be unlocked, revealing to those destined to receive this wisdom the essential unity and universality and at the same time the formal diversity of tradition and revelation."[24] These thinkers elucidate the metaphysical axioms and cosmological principles which constitute the *sophia perennis;* they affirm the mystical convergence of integral traditions in what Schuon has called "the transcendent unity of religions." Schuon's contribution to the understanding of Native American traditions has been neglected in academic quarters, partly because the whole Perennialist outlook issues an implacable challenge to the assumptions and purposes of contemporary scholarship. Schuon himself developed close relations with several prominent Indian leaders, including Benjamin Black Elk, the holy man's son. He also spent time with different Plains groups during the late 1950s and early 60s. One of the purposes of the present work is to adopt a Perennialist perspective in the study of Black Elk and to bring the work of Frithjof Schuon's writings on the Indians to wider attention. Frequent reference is made throughout to *The Feathered Sun*, but a more deliberate consideration of Schuon's contribution appears in the final chapter.

Finally, I would like to make mention of Michael Fitzgerald, student of Joseph Brown, a friend and associate of Frithjof Schuon, the author of several important works on Indian subjects, a generous friend of Native Americans, and a tireless advocate for the preservation of their ancestral ways. Without him the present work could not have come to fruition.

1

Nomadic Peoples and the Mark of Cain

And he said, "What hast thou done?
The voice of thy brother's blood crieth unto me from the ground."
Genesis 4:10

Well, it is as it is. We are prisoners of war while we are waiting here.
But there is another world.
Black Elk[1]

The Destruction of the Nomadic Peoples

Ruminating on the destruction of the traditional and largely nomadic culture of Tibet, the Perennialist author Marco Pallis wrote this:

> One can truly say that this remote land behind the snowy rampart of the Himalaya had become like the chosen sanctuary for all those things whereof the historical discarding had caused our present profane civilization, the first of its kind, to come into being. . . . The violation of this sanctuary and the dissipation of the sacred influences concentrated there became an event of properly cosmic significance, of which the ulterior consequences for a world which tacitly condoned the outrage or, in many cases, openly countenanced it on the plea that it brought "progress" to a backward people, have yet to ripen.[2]

Similar considerations may be applied in more or less analogous cases, whether we think of the fate of the American Indians, the Australian Aborigines, the Inuit, the Bedouin, the Gypsies, the Amazonians, the Bushmen of the Kalahari, or any other nomadic culture which has been razed by the juggernaut of modernization. In *The Reign of Quantity* the French metaphysician René Guénon observes that it is only in these latter days, marked by the ever-accelerating "solidification" of the world, that "Cain finally and really slays Abel"[3]—which is to say that the sedentary civilizations destroy the nomadic cultures. Moreover,

It could be said in a general way that the works of sedentary peoples are works of time: these people are fixed in space within a strictly limited domain, and develop their activities in a temporal continuity which appears to them to be indefinite. On the other hand, nomadic and pastoral peoples build nothing durable, and do not work for a future which escapes them; but they have space in front of them, not facing them with any limitation, but on the contrary always offering them new possibilities.[4]

No doubt it was with similar reflections in mind that Frithjof Schuon remarked that "traditions having a prehistoric origin are, symbolically speaking, made for 'space' and not for 'time.'"[5] George La Piana also alludes to the symbolism of the Biblical story in writing, "Cain, who killed his brother, Abel, the herdsman, and built himself a city, prefigures modern civilization, one that has been described from within as a 'murderous machine, with no conscience and no ideals.'"[6] It follows from these observations that the slaying of Abel—the violent extirpation of the primordial nomadic cultures—not only drastically contracts human possibilities, but is actually a cosmic desecration. Since the genocidal vandalisms of the nineteenth century a great deal has been written about the destruction of the indigenous cultures of North America. There have also been many attempts, with varying degrees of success, to elucidate and to reanimate at least some aspects of their ancestral ways of life. But many writers on these subjects are quite impervious to the deeper significance of the events they seek to explain.

During the span of Black Elk's life most European accounts of the American Indians were steeped in racist assumptions and triumphalist attitudes much easier to discern from our present vantage point than they were at the time. It was only some twenty-odd years after Black Elk's passing that the tide began to turn with new efforts to understand the history of Indian-white encounters through the eyes of those who had been apparently vanquished. Dee Brown's *Bury My Heart at Wounded Knee* (1970) was one of the vanguard works. The counter-culture of the late 1960s and 70s also sponsored, among its more serious-minded participants, an interest in ways of life and modes of consciousness which stood at odds with the dominant ethos of "progress," competitive individualism, and acquisitive materialism. The resurgence of interest in *Black Elk Speaks*, the appearance of such works as *Touch the Earth* (1973), the rediscovery of the poignant photographic legacy of Edward Curtis, and the nascent A.I.M. (American Indian Movement) were other signs of the times.[7] The time-worn narrative about the "red savages," the "taming of the wilderness," the "march of civilization," the "manifest destiny" of the European settlers, and the dying out of a "stone-age people," had been mythologized and deeply embedded in popular culture, most obviously perhaps through Hollywood. It was now seen to hide a long and shameful history of European rapacity, hypocrisy, treachery, and murderous violence. Figures like Crazy Horse, Red Cloud, and Sitting Bull were now seen by many Europeans as well as by Native Americans as culture-heroes. Speeches and utterances from nineteenth century Indian leaders were integrated into the discourse about Indian-European relations; Sitting Bull, Chief Joseph, and Chief Seattle were among those most frequently cited. Here is one well-known passage from Sitting Bull which struck a resonant note:

> What treaty that the whites have kept has the red man broken? Not one. What treaty that the white man ever made with us have they kept? Not one. When I was a boy the Sioux owned the world; the sun rose and set on their land; they sent ten thousand men to battle. Where are the warriors today? Who slew them? Where are our lands? Who owns them? What white man can ever say I stole his land or a penny of his money? Yet, they say I am a thief. What white woman, however lonely, was ever captive or insulted by me? Yet they say I am a bad Indian. What white man has ever seen me drunk? Who has ever come to me hungry and unfed? Who has ever seen me beat my wife or abuse my children? What law have I broken? Is it wrong for me to love my own? Is it wicked for me because my skin is red? Because I am a Sioux; because I was born where my father lived; because I would die for my people and my country?[8]

No doubt there were many bloody acts carried out by Indians—hardly surprising—but no dispassionate student of the history of the West can doubt that the conflict was, in general terms, between an invading force determined to subjugate and if necessary destroy the indigenous peoples and cultures and, on the other side, scattered bands of primarily nomadic peoples who were desperately trying to defend their homelands and their way of life. As Helen Hunt Jackson observed in 1880, "It makes little difference where one opens the record of the history of the Indians; every page and every year has its dark stain. The story of one tribe is the story of all, varied only by differences of time and place; but neither time nor place makes any difference to the main facts. Colorado is as greedy and unjust in 1880 as Georgia was in 1830, and Ohio in 1795; and the United States Government breaks promises as deftly now as then, and with an added ingenuity from long practice."[9] The invaders came armed not only with more powerful technology but with the moral conviction that these lands, and all they contained, were theirs to take by right of their superior civilization as well as "right by might."

It is not the purpose of the present work to rehearse the blood-stained history of the West, nor to recount the ways in which the lust for land, gold, and other resources was dressed up in all manner of ideological vestments whether of the social-Darwinian, evangelical Christian, or "manifest destiny" variety. Nor need we linger over the exemplary story of the Lakota as it unfolded from Black Elk's childhood down to the present time. Anyone with even a passing interest in the Lakota will be familiar with the pivotal moments and the melancholy symbols of this history: Red Cloud's War, the Fort Laramie Treaty of 1868 (violated within four years because of the discovery of "the yellow metal that makes white men crazy"), the coming of the "Iron Horse," the Battle of Little Big Horn (Custer's Last Stand), the death of Crazy Horse,[10] the flight to Canada, the slaughter of the buffalo, the Dawes Act, the Ghost Dance movement, the killing of Sitting Bull, the Wounded Knee Massacre, reservations, repression of native customs and ceremonies, assimilation, demoralization, degradation, despair. Alongside the military and political campaigns went the efforts of Christian missionaries to eradicate "heathen" beliefs and practices, and legislative programs of forced cultural repression which made it illegal for Lakota people to practice their traditional rites, even for children to speak their own language, wear their customary garb, or to grow their hair long. Here is the Secretary of the Interior, Henry M. Teller, writing in 1882 to the Commissioner of Indian Affairs, urging him to take action against traditional practices:

I desire to call your attention to what I regard as a great hindrance to the civilization of the Indians, viz., the continuance of the old heathenish dances, such as the sun-dance, the scalp-dance, &c.... Another great hindrance to the civilization of the Indians is the influence of the medicine men, who are always found with the anti-progressive party. The medicine men resort to various artifices and devices to keep the people under their influence . . . using their conjurer's arts to prevent the people from abandoning their heathenish rites and customs.[11]

In similar vein, the Indian agent on the Pine Ridge reservation, V. T. McGillycuddy, called the medicine men "barbarism personified," "one of the principal obstacles in the way of civilization."[12] The policy of repression and "assimilation," implemented in 1884, continued for nearly five decades. A tribal historian who was awarded the Presidential Medal of Freedom tells a story repeated many times across the West:

> In 1884, the Secretary of the Interior issued the so-called "Secretary's Order" to "de-tribalize" the Indian people and make them into white men as soon as possible—a unilateral cultural assimilation process. . . . The boarding school was set up about 1890 at Crow Agency. . . . The Crow children were required to be taken to that school and left there, including very young kids, 5, 6, 7 years old. The Indian agent would send out his Indian policemen to collect the children. . . . They were ruthless because they had to try to please the agent and, of course, they get paid, so they were his men, his Gestapo. . . . And there [the children] would become like slaves; they were mistreated and some were even killed there. At the boarding school the children were also forbidden to speak their native language. If they were caught speaking the Crow language they made the children chew a strong soap. The kids also couldn't play any Indian games—they were forbidden to follow anything to do with the traditional culture. If they violated any of these rules they were not allowed to visit their parents on weekends or to go home for family visits. A lot of children died mysteriously. . . . The "Secretary's Order of 1884" also prohibited the Indians from practicing all activities related to their culture, including all traditional ceremonies. . . . The Crow people were afraid to even put on their native costumes; they were told to wear overalls, white man's outfits— told to start becoming white men. Our people were forced to become farmers and to give up their traditions.[13]

Alongside the military campaigns, the destruction of the buffalo, and the devastating programs of cultural suppression and assimilation, successive waves of introduced diseases—smallpox, measles, scarlet fever, typhoid, flu, cholera, diphtheria, venereal disease, and tuberculosis—killed large parts of the Indian population.

Historians, both white and Indian, have largely repaired the historical record, though the task is by no means complete. Integral to the revision of the Eurocentric historiography of the Plains peoples have been those many native testimonies which have appeared since the first publication of *Black Elk Speaks* in 1932. One may mention such works as Luther Standing Bear's *Land of the Spotted Eagle* (1933), *Black Hawk: An Autobiography* (1955) (ed. Donald Wilson), *Two Leggings: The Making of a Crow Warrior* (1967) (ed. Peter Nabokov), *Lame Deer, Seeker of Visions* (1972) (ed. Richard Erdoes), Thomas Mails' *Fools Crow* (1979), Michael Fitzgerald's *Yellowtail: Crow Medicine Man and Sun Dance Chief* (1991), and Charles Eastman's *Living in Two Worlds: The American Indian Experience* (2010) (ed. Michael Fitzgerald).[14]

Despite more open-minded attitudes and a more sympathetic understanding of the Indians, many Americans are still lamentably ignorant about the continent's indigenous peoples, and racist prejudices and jaundiced stereotypes—sometimes more subtle than in days gone by—persist. Ideas and attitudes which were once almost universal amongst the whites are buried deep in the collective psyche and not simply swept away by good will or shallow political pieties. No, the problem is much more recalcitrant. Even amongst better-educated Americans, who are painfully aware of the injustices of the past and free of at least the crude forms of racial prejudice, there remains one massive obstacle to a proper understanding of Indian culture, an impediment just as likely to face the historian, the anthropologist, and the sociologist as "the man or woman in the street": the deeply entrenched belief in "progress" and the often unacknowledged or camouflaged notion that the prevailing way of life of the modern West (liberal democracy, the rule of law, capitalism, materialist science, industrial technology, the nuclear family) is, when all is said and done, an "advance" on the "backward" cultures of yesteryear. The idea of "progress" is one of the most potent shibboleths of modernity, a kind of pseudo-myth. It comes attired in many alluring guises, often hand-in-hand with its sinister accomplice, social evolutionism, and finds applications in many fields. So pervasive is this idea in the modern climate, so much taken for granted, that it has become almost invisible, rather like the smog to which urban dwellers become inured. No doubt the unprecedented barbarisms of the twentieth century have caused some disenchantment but the tenacity of the idea is quite bizarre. "Progress" has a long and sordid pedigree in Western thought, and many brutalities and infamies have been justified in its name—the obliteration of the nomadic cultures is but one of them, the rape of nature another. Surveying the many literary representations of Native Americans, the Italian scholar Elémire Zolla exposes the malignant effects of this siren song:

> The history of the many images of the Indian that appear in the course of American literature sets a whole series of works and authors in an unusual, revelatory perspective. It is also extremely instructive, for it shows us the (quite simple) stylistic means by which a program of genocide can be facilitated. It also shows us that the chief culprit, *the actual agent of the slaughter, was the idea of progress,* which by its very nature demands the elimination of everything that it decrees old, obsolete, out of date and nostalgic, while at the same time it represses the love, so congenial to man, of that delicate, wise patina that time deposits on the things of this world. . . . The idea of progress has not only justified and promoted the slaughter—at times physical, at times spiritual, depending on the circumstances—but it has even removed it from consciousness.[15]

By way of illustrating a progressivist view, let us briefly consider the attitude of most non-Indian commentators to the issue of literacy: It is simply assumed that literacy marks a step up from non-literacy, that peoples who read and write are more "civilized" than those who do not. Now—let it be said plainly—there is no doubt that in the modern world literacy is to be preferred to illiteracy, and that those without it face serious disadvantages. But this does *not* preclude the possibility—hardly ever taken seriously by modern scholars—that in some fundamental sense non-literate societies constitute a richer cultural mode, that the mythopoeic understanding of the world might be deeper than the abstracted, rationalistic, philosophical-scientific perspective which, historically, succeeds it. As Joseph Brown observed many years ago,

> With our own overemphasis on mental activity we are apt to think that the Indian, without any written language, lacks something important or necessary in not possessing a scho-

lastic or dialectic type of doctrinal presentation. However such a "lack" may have prevented *us* from understanding the completeness and depth of their wisdom, it represents for the Indians a very effective type of spiritual participation in which the essential ideas and values, reflected by the world of forms and symbols are spontaneously and integrally *lived*.[16]

In this light the move from non-literacy to literacy might well be seen as a degradation or diminution, a *deprivation*. And, crucially, what is lost is the power of memory, both individually and collectively. Then, too, there is the intervention of texts which mediate our experience of the world and factitiously structure the workings of the mind. Nearly a century ago Paul Radin observed that, "The disorientation in our whole psychic life and in our whole apperception of the external realities produced by the invention of the alphabet, the whole tendency of which has been to elevate thought and thinking to the rank of the exclusive proof of verities, never occurred among [primal] peoples."[17] As Huston Smith remarked of the American Indians, "the invisibility of their texts, which is to say their myths, leaves their eyes free to scan for other sacred portents, virgin nature and sacred art being the prime examples."[18] Even Plato, often credited with the Greek move from a mythological to philosophical mode of understanding, and with the triumph of literacy over the archaic oral tradition, recognized the dangers inherent in this apparent "advance":

> This invention [of letters] will produce forgetfulness in the minds of those who learn to use it, because they will not exercise their memory. Their trust in writing, produced by external characters which are no part of themselves, will discourage the use of their own memory within them. You have invented an elixir not of memory, but of reminding; and you offer your pupils the *appearance of wisdom, not true wisdom*, for they will read many things without teaching, and will therefore seem to know many things, when they are for the most part ignorant and hard to get along with, since they are not wise but only wiseacres.[19]

Plato goes on to say that the wise man, "*when in earnest, will not write in ink*" but will sow the seeds of wisdom directly into the souls able to receive them. We hardly need add that this is precisely how Lakota culture functioned. In this respect it shared a great deal not only with other non-literate cultures but with some of the more ancient literate traditions such as that of India.

> From the [Hindu] point of view a man can only be said to know what he knows by heart: what he must go to a book to be reminded of, he merely knows of. . . . From the earliest times, Indians have thought of the learned man, not as one who has read much, but as one who has been profoundly taught. It is much rather from a master than from any book that wisdom can be learned.[20]

The "education" which was forcibly imposed on the American Indians, far from being one of the "benefits" conferred by "civilization," is properly seen as one more instrument of cultural genocide. As Ananda Coomaraswamy noted many years ago, "there is no necessary connection between literacy and culture, and . . . to impose our literacy . . . upon a cultured but illiterate people is to destroy their culture in the name of our own."[21] It is also worth dwelling on Coomaraswamy's remarks about the "proselytizing fury" which destroyed non-literate and nomadic cultures the globe over:

> What lies below this fury, of which our punitive expeditions and "wars of pacification" are only more evident manifestations? It would not be too much to say that our educational activities . . . are motivated by an *intention* to destroy existing cultures. And that is not only, I think, because of our conviction of the absolute superiority of our *Kultur*, and *consequent contempt and hatred for whatever else we have not understood* (all those for whom the economic motive is not decisive), but grounded in an unconscious and deep-rooted envy of the serenity and leisure that we cannot but recognize in people whom we call "unspoiled."[22]

These observations, made in 1949, remain sharply pertinent today.

Studying Primal Cultures
Much of the early literature concerning the religious life of the Native Americans came from anthropologists who were tyrannized both by the prejudices of the age and by the limitations of their discipline. Some of these persist down to the present day; think, for instance, of

the unhappy associations of the word "myth." There are still plenty of folk (anthropologists among them) who apparently share the view of the nineteenth century folklorist Andrew Lang, who pronounced that myths were "a product of the childhood of the human race, arising out of the minds of a creature that has not yet learned to think in terms of strict cause and effect"[23]—mythology as a kind of befuddled proto-science. True, recent anthropologists have abandoned many of the grosser racist and evolutionist assumptions of their predecessors, but they all too often have succeeded only in replacing earlier prejudices with those more characteristic of our own time, whilst still retaining a naïve faith in the capacity of a rationalistic and materialistic pseudo-science to grasp the mysteries of a complex spiritual tradition. Not for nothing has Mircea Eliade written of the "religious illiteracy" of so many scholars of so-called "primitive" religious traditions.[24] Also instructive are the words of the Australian anthropologist, W.E.H. Stanner, written over forty years ago, concerning the scholarly litera-ture on the Australian Aborigines: "It is preposterous that something like a century of study, because of rationalism, positivism, and mate-rialism, should have produced two options: that Aboriginal religion is either (to follow Durkheim) what someone called 'the mirage of society' or (to follow Freud) the 'neurosis of society.'"[25]

Whilst intellectual fashions amongst ethnologists and anthropolo-gists have changed over the last century, the one constant in the pat-tern of study has been an intransigent reductionism which refuses to treat primal traditions in their own terms or, indeed, in terms appro-priate to any religious tradition.[26] The influential theories of Freud, Durkheim, and Levy-Bruhl and their epigones, are all variations on the reductionist theme. Victor Frankl: "Reductionism is today a mask for nihilism. Contemporary nihilism no longer brandishes the word nothingness; today nihilism is camouflaged as *nothing-but-ness*. Human phenomena are thus turned into mere epiphenomena."[27] This pitfall can only be bypassed when religious phenomena are studied *as such*, as Eliade so often reminded us:

> A religious phenomenon will only be recognized as such if it is grasped at its own level, that is to say, if it is studied as something religious. To try to grasp the essence of such a phe-nomenon by means of physiology, psychology, sociology, eco-nomics, linguistics, art or any other study is false; it misses the one unique and irreducible element in it—the element of the sacred. Obviously there are no purely religious phenomena. . . .

But it would be hopeless to try and explain religion in terms of any one of these basic functions. . . . It would be as futile as thinking you could explain *Madame Bovary* by a list of social, economic, and political facts; however true, they do not effect it as a work of literature.[28]

Too often anthropologists and other commentators fall prey to the delusion that the accumulation of empirical data and the pursuit of "objective scientific analysis" will yield understanding. As T.S. Eliot memorably asked, "Where is the wisdom we have lost in knowledge? Where is the knowledge we have lost in information?"[29] Sally McCluskey has noted how "scientific accounts of Indian religion tend to pile rite on rite, folk tale on folk tale, and to compound the confusion with rising tides of footnotes pointing to analogues, sources, and parallel practices noted in the Fiji Islands. Religion becomes a jumble of disparate details united only by the compiler's belief in the ubiquity of Corn Gods."[30] With no less asperity, Frithjof Schuon remarked on the oft-made claim that the Native American had no conception of a Supreme God: "What incomprehensions of this sort reveal more than anything, is that scientific 'specialization'—the knowledge of cranial shapes, languages, puberty rites, culinary methods, and so forth—does not amount to the intellectual qualification enabling one to penetrate ideas and symbols."[31] This observation is especially germane to the study of the religious life of primal peoples, whose cosmology is comprised of symbolic understandings and whose spiritual life is rooted in a metaphysic of nature. Walking Buffalo (Stoney):

> We were lawless people, but we were on pretty good terms with the Great Spirit, creator and ruler of all. You whites assumed we were savages. You didn't understand our prayers. You didn't try to understand. When we sang our praises to the sun or moon or wind, you said we were worshipping idols. Without understanding, you condemned us as lost souls just because our form of worship was different from yours.
>
> We saw the Great Spirit's work in almost everything: sun, moon, trees, wind, and mountains. Sometimes we approached him through these things. . . . I think we have a true belief in the supreme being, a stronger faith than that of most whites who called us pagans. . . . Indians living close to nature and nature's ruler are not living in darkness.[32]

For good reason Charles Eastman (Ohiyesa) observed that "the religion of the Indian is the last thing about him that a man of another race will ever understand."[33]

These admonitions notwithstanding, anthropologists and other scholars did accumulate a vast amount of information about traditional Indian life even if the data in question were often only superficially understood (or, in the religious domain, not misunderstood altogether!). It must also be acknowledged that some anthropologists have been acutely aware of the dangers of reductionism in the study of indigenous cultures, and that some have made, and continue to make, an invaluable contribution to the literature on Native Americans.[34] But it comes as no surprise that comparative religionists, less inhibited by materialistic/functionalistic assumptions and more attuned to the realm of the sacred, have often been able to give us much more insightful interpretations of the spiritual and religious life of indigenous peoples; in this context one might mention such figures as Åke Hultkrantz, Mircea Eliade, James Cowan, and Joseph Epes Brown.[35]

A more adequate understanding of Indian cultures *necessarily* entails a radical questioning of the modern worldview and at least a provisional acceptance of the idea that Indian ways of understanding, far from being "childish," "naïve," or "outmoded," actually constitute a wisdom of which the modern world has long been bereft. Perhaps we might then more fully understand the words of Luther Standing Bear when he said,

> The man who sat on the ground in his tipi meditating on life and its meaning, accepting the kinship of all creatures and acknowledging unity with the universe of things was infusing into his being the true essence of civilization. And when native man left off this form of development, his humanization was retarded in growth.[36]

The need to interrogate our Eurocentric assumptions in the study of the Native Americans (and, by implication, other primal cultures) was noted by Joseph Brown in his Preface to the 1971 edition of *The Sacred Pipe*: "We are still very far from being aware of the dimensions and ramifications of our ethnocentric illusions. Nevertheless, by the very nature of things we are now forced to undergo a process of intense self-examination; to engage in a serious re-evaluation of the premises and orientations of our society."[37] This is an on-going project, one that must be "radical" in the proper sense: going to the root of things.

Leaving aside the relatively small corpus of works written or narrated by Indians themselves, much of the most illuminating material about their tradition, and indeed about indigenous peoples in various parts of the world, has come from non-academic writers who have lived with the people in question, closely observed their way of life, and through their *existential engagement* come to a deeper understanding than could be provided by any amount of book-learning.[38] The Laubins' fine book *The Indian Tipi* (1957), which owed much to Black Elk,[39] furnishes one example of this genre. It should also be remembered that none of the three non-native authors whom I will argue are indispensable to a study of the Lakota—John Neihardt, Joseph Brown, and Frithjof Schuon—came to their understanding of the Native Americans in the lecture-hall or library but through direct personal experience and a vital involvement with their everyday life. Indeed, one may be forgiven for thinking that more often than not a formal academic study of the Indians may actually construct rather than demolish barriers to understanding.

We can conclude this chapter with some cautionary words from William Paden about the study of religion: "Religions do not all inhabit the same world, but actually posit, structure, and dwell within a universe that is their own. They can be understood not just as so many attempts to explain some common, objectively available order of things 'out there,' but as traditions that create and occupy their own universe. Acknowledging these differences in place, these intrinsically different systems of experiencing and living in the world, is fundamental to the study of religion."[40] Nowhere is this truer than in the study of primal cultures such as those of the Native Americans.

It is with these reflections in mind that we come to a reconsideration of Black Elk and the Lakota tradition for which he was such an eloquent spokesman. In this alternative story the Thunder Beings, the Grandfathers, the Sacred Hoop, the Red Road, and the Flowering Tree take on a more lasting significance than the pell-mell doings of the myriad soldiers and settlers, cowboys and buffalo-hunters, legislators and bureaucrats, miners and missionaries, the generals and presidents who populate the linear and horizontal histories written by non-natives.

2

The World of the Lakota

The traditional Indian was one of the freest men that can be
imagined, and at the same time one of the most bound: the vast
prairie, the forests, and the mountains belonged to him; practically
speaking, his vital space knew no limits; yet at no moment could
he depart from his religious universe and the role which
this imposed upon him.
Frithjof Schuon[1]

A long time ago my father told me what his father told him, that
there was once a Lakota holy man, called Drinks Water, who
dreamed what was to be, and this was long before the coming of
the *Wasichu*s. He dreamed that the four-leggeds were going back
into the earth and that a strange race had woven a spider's web all
around the Lakotas. And he said: "When this happens, you shall live
in square gray houses, in a barren land, and beside those square gray
houses you shall starve." They say he went back to Mother Earth
soon after he saw this vision, and it was sorrow that killed him. . . .
Sometimes dreams are wiser than waking.
Black Elk[2]

The Material and Social Culture

Before turning directly to Black Elk it will be as well to sketch in the
broad contours of traditional Lakota culture. First, a general description in the current academic *lingua franca*: the Lakota, comprising
seven sub-tribal groups including the Oglala, were one of three tribes
within the larger grouping of the Sioux, which includes the Dakota
and Nakota people.[3] The Plains Indians included such tribes as the
Blackfeet, Crow, Arapaho, Cheyenne, Pawnee, Comanche, and Kiowa
as well as the Sioux. The Lakota, also known as the Tetons, roamed
over the prairies and plains between the Mississippi-Missouri River
and the Rocky Mountains, but their ancestral homelands were in what
is now North and South Dakota. They regarded the Black Hills of
South Dakota as a sacred precinct, protected by the Treaty of Laramie
(1868) but desecrated within a few years by the white invaders seeking
to plunder its gold; it was none other than General George Armstrong
Custer who led a military expedition into the Black Hills in 1874 to

investigate reports of a gold discovery there.[4] Lakota numbers actually increased over the course of the nineteenth century and contemporary estimates put the current population at about 70,000, most of whom live in reservations in the western region of South Dakota.[5]

Plains Indian culture, in this lexicon, can be described as a nomadic, equestrian, warrior, hunter-gatherer society in which tribal members were highly mobile within clearly understood geographical boundaries, and in which social dynamics were governed by complex kinship systems and by principles of reciprocity and exchange. The web of beliefs and practices which might loosely be called "religious" is best described as mythologically-based and embedded in a ritual-ceremonial complex rooted in a sacramental relationship with the land itself.[6] Indian religion can also be described as "primal," which is to say that it is prehistoric in origin, non-literate, and one in which the distinction between "religion" and "culture" at large has no meaning.[7] Indeed, most tribes had no equivalent to the English term "religion." The features which Hilton Deakin has identified as characteristic of primal societies apply specifically to the Plains Indians: such cultures are ethnocentric, non-universal, non-missionizing; they are intimately related to the natural world by a perceived spiritual kinship; they emphasize the existence of psychic and supernatural powers which are accessible to the human world, particularly through the shaman/medicine man, and through ritual; and they experience the world as saturated with spiritual powers.[8] Such cultures are governed by sacred myths which leave them indifferent to the linear and chronological conception of history as understood in the modern West.[9] The Indian worldview is underpinned by a "visionary geography" which constitutes an ordered and meaningful world and which situates both the individual and the community in relation to the whole cosmos.[10]

> The Indian world signifies first and foremost the reading of the primordial doctrine in the phenomena of Nature—each man reads what he can understand—and the experiencing of Nature as the holy, primordial Home that everywhere manifests the Great Spirit and everywhere is filled with Him; and this consciousness gives the Red Man his dignity, composed of reverence for Nature and of self-dominion.[11]

Historians and anthropologists have identified six defining characteristics of the Plains Indians, distinguishing them from other groupings such as the south-western peoples (Hopi, Pueblo, Navaho, and others): nomadism (which largely precluded the development of agriculture); dependence on the buffalo (almost extinct by the end of the nineteenth century); the centrality of the horse (a comparatively recent development); the tipi; the warrior ethos; and, perhaps most importantly in the present context, the Sun Dance.[12] Mother Earth was benign and generous, and the Indians lived in a reciprocal and cooperative relation with the land itself. Chief Luther Standing Bear:

> We did not think of the great open plains, the beautiful rolling hills, and winding streams with tangled growth, as "wild." Only to the white man was nature a "wilderness" and only to him was the land "infested" with "wild" animals and "savage" people. To us it was tame. Earth was bountiful and we were surrounded with the blessings of the Great Mystery. Not until the hairy man from the east came and with brutal frenzy heaped injustices upon us and the families we loved was it "wild" for us. When the very animals of the forest began fleeing from his approach, then it was that for us the "Wild West" began.[13]

Mircea Eliade has provided a useful schema for the broad classification of worldviews: archaic, historical, and modern.[14] "Archaic" refers to nomadic, non-literate cultures informed by an orally-transmitted mythology and a cyclic view of time; "historical" applies to the sedentary civilizations in which sacred texts and a strong sense of linear history are foregrounded; and "modern" describes those societies in which the sense of the sacred has been largely eclipsed by secular/materialist ideas and values. Under these categories we can situate the primal traditions as "archaic," the major religious traditions as "historical," and the profane and humanistic culture of the post-medieval West as "modern." It must be stressed that Eliade's schema is in no way evolutionary; indeed, in many respects it is counter-evolutionary. Eliade was a seminal figure in opening up new vistas in the study of archaic religions, largely through his inquiry into the conceptions of sacred space and sacred time as well his more localized and intensive study of phenomena such as "shamanism" (a problematic term to which we will return).

We are not here concerned with providing any account of Lakota culture as a whole beyond what is necessary to understand Black Elk's life and testimony. Many sources are available for those readers interested in the material culture and social organization of the Lakota.[15]

Nonetheless, it may be useful to offer the following shorthand table of some of the salient differences between traditional Lakota culture and that of the modern West.

TABLE 1:

Traditional Lakota and
Modern Western Culture Compared

	Lakota	Modern West
Worldview	mythological spatially-oriented cyclical time animistic symbolic & archetypal spiritual religious panentheistic	historical temporally-oriented linear, chronological time materialistic empirical & "factual" scientific humanistic theistic/atheistic
Relation to "Nature"	reciprocal cooperative holistic ecological synthetic sacramental nature "transparent"	exploitative combative fragmentary industrial analytic profane nature "opaque"
Social Order	semi-nomadic/nomadic customary equilibrium homogeneous communitarian hierarchical "natural"	sedentary, urban legalistic, bureaucratic change, "progress," dynamism pluralistic individualistic egalitarian artificial

Cosmology and Spirituality

Lakota spirituality starts and finishes with an awareness of *Wakan-Tanka*—the Great Spirit, the Great Mysterious, the Great Holy—who is envisaged in both transcendent and immanent aspects, as is made perfectly clear by Black Elk's insistence that,

> We should understand that all things are the work of the Great Spirit. We should know that He is *within all things*; the trees, the grasses, the rivers, the mountains, all the four-legged animals and the winged peoples; and even more important we should understand that *He is also above all these things and peoples*.[16]

This passage refutes the threadbare claim that the Indians were "pantheists" and "nature-worshippers"; their outlook is more precisely defined as panentheistic. As Ella Deloria noted, "it was an error to say the [Indians] actually worshipped rocks, trees, the four winds, and other manifestations of nature. They are not themselves *Wakan*, but *Wakan* is in all things."[17] Joseph Brown was one of the first Europeans to grasp some of the subtle distinctions in the Lakota conception of *Wakan-Tanka*:

> *Wakan-Tanka* as grandfather is the Great Spirit independent of manifestation, unqualified, unlimited, identical to the Christian Godhead or to the Hindu *Brahma-Nirguna*. *Wakan-Tanka* as father is the Great Spirit considered in relation to His manifestation, either as Creator, Preserver, or Destroyer, identical to the Christian God, or to the Hindu *Brahma Saguna*.[18]

The Great Spirit as Creator orders the cosmos through the seven directions (the four cardinal points, zenith, nadir, and the center where they all meet). The Great Spirit also manifests in the Sky and Earth, indeed in *all* natural forms, but especially in the supernal phenomena of wind, lightning, and thunder, and in the animals which, being anterior to man, are intermediaries between *Wakan-Tanka* and human beings. The eagle and the bison occupy a privileged place in this symbolic repertoire.[19] All phenomena are permeated by spiritual energy or power (*wochangi*) which can be transmitted to people primarily through visions and rites; the natural order, as a whole and in its parts, is *wakan*—a multivalent term which has been variously translated as "sacred, holy, consecrated, powerful, mysterious."[20] It is to the Great Spirit as Creator—the source of all that is *wakan*—that the

Indian prays and to whom ceremonial life is directed. As Ohiyesa the Santee reminds us, "In the life of the Indian there was only one inevitable duty—the duty of prayer—the daily recognition of the Unseen and Eternal. His daily devotions were more necessary to him than daily food."[21] More recently Chief Thomas Yellowtail has tersely observed that, "People think other things are more important than prayer, but they are mistaken."[22] The Indians lived in the truth of Emerson's claim that "the happiest man is he who learns from nature the lesson of worship."[23] As Frances Densmore noted in her famous study, *Teton Sioux Music*, "In old times the term *Wakan-Tanka* was not used in ordinary conversation, because it was held too sacred to be spoken except with due reverence and at a proper time."[24]

Lakota cosmology posited three inter-related realms or dimensions in a vertical hierarchy; each realm can be conceptualized from a variety of viewpoints. Allowing for a somewhat schematic and abstracted representation, and for the use of some anachronistic Western terminology, we might construct an explanatory diagram something like Table 2 opposite.

Although in general terms this table can be regarded as hierarchical, this comes at the cost of some crude over-simplifications; for instance, Earth as Mother and Grandmother cannot be equated or paralleled with gross matter; or, to flag another anomaly, the status of animals is complex as in some respects they are above humankind—they were created before man and are thus closer to the Creator—whilst in other respects they are below because "it is the two-legged men alone who, if they purify and humiliate themselves, may become one with—or may know—*Wakan-Tanka*."[25] As Benjamin Black Elk and others have made clear, Lakota cosmology can also be envisaged as a three-tiered system of circles inscribed with a cross marking the four directions, and with a vertical axis running through the three levels.[26] Of course, the Lakota themselves did not envisage things in this abstract and diagrammatic fashion; they had no need of such thinking: rather, "Religious concepts and values are given substance through the direct visual or pictorial image and through the symbol, which includes the auditory word or echo, all of which have reference to the forms, forces, and voices of nature."[27]

The polyvalent symbolism of the center and the circumference and of the cross (six-armed as well as four) is, of course, universal, and is found in sacred architectural forms from the Hindu temple to the Christian cathedral to the Indian sweat lodge, the tipi, and Sun Dance lodge—each an *imago mundi*.[28] Circles—temporal as well as spatial—

TABLE 2:

Lakota Cosmology

Metaphysical Realm	Cosmological Realm	Psychological Realm	Physical Realm
The Absolute The Real The One —immutable, infinite, eternal	*Wakan-Tanka* (Great Spirit, Great Mysterious) —Grandfather (*Tunkashila*) (God as Beyond-Being) —Father (*Ate*) (God as Creator) Heaven	Spirit The world of the ancestors	The Pure Non-material, non-temporal, non-spatial
The "relatively Real" The intermediary realm	Human Domain The human being as axial and microcosmic, and as vice-regent (thus the human links the three domains)	Soul/psyche The world of spirits and psychic forces (both "white" and "black"); dreams and visions; animals as intermediaries	Subtle matter (still conditioned; i.e., within time and space)
The relative, the provisionally real, the world of appearances and "shadows"	Earth —Grandmother (*Unchi*) (potentiality) —Mother (*Ina*) (the creative principle)	The body	Gross matter in flux; time and space

were everywhere in the Indian world. In an oft-quoted passage, Black Elk observed:

> Everything the Power of the World does is done in a circle. The sky is round, and I have heard that the earth is round like a ball, and so are all the stars. The wind, in its greatest power whirls. Birds make their nest in circles, for theirs is the same religion as ours. The sun comes forth and goes down again in a circle. The moon does the same and both are round. Even the seasons form a great circle in their changing, and always come back again to where they were. The life of a man is a circle from childhood to childhood, and so it is in everything where power moves. Our tepees were round like the nests of birds, and these were always set in a circle, the nation's hoop, a nest of many nests, where the Great Spirit meant for us to hatch our children.[29]

The Lakota worldview rests on a consecrated geography in which the world of nature is *revelatory* or *hierophanic*; the natural order is itself a sacred text, "an open book containing an inexhaustible teaching of truth and beauty."[30]

> The world of nature was their temple, and within this sanctuary they showed great respect to every form, function, and power. That the Indians held as sacred all the natural forms around them is not unique. . . . But what is almost unique in the Indians' attitude is that their reverence for life and nature is *central* to their religion: each form in the world around them bears such a host of precise values and meanings that taken altogether they constitute what one would call their "doctrine."[31]

Nature itself was at once a scripture, a sanctuary, a theophany. Ohiyesa:

> There were no temples or shrines among us save those of nature. Being a natural man, the Indian was intensely poetical. He would deem it sacrilege to build a house for Him who may be met face to face in the mysterious, shadowy aisles of the primeval forest, or in the sunlit bosom of virgin prairies, upon dizzy spires and pinnacles of naked rock, and yonder in the jeweled vault of the night sky![32]

The *Wicasa Wakan* and Shamanism

The term *wicasa wakan* has been variously translated as "holy man," "medicine man," "priest," "shaman." The essential function of the *wicasa wakan* is the deployment of certain powers (often, but not necessarily, including those of healing), primarily through the exact performance of rites and ceremonies, and through an arcane knowledge of psychic and cosmic energies. One of the areas of expertise of many medicine men is in the use of herbs and other natural remedies, as was the case with Black Elk. The powers in question are beyond the reach of ordinary folk and only accessible to the *wicasa wakan* because of an arduous initiation, usually through visions and a lengthy apprenticeship. Thus the terms "holy man" and "priest" are less confusing than "medicine man," which for some readers no doubt conjures up the idea of a "primitive" doctor, bereft of medical science, fumbling about with superstitious practices.[33] The term "priest" also has certain connotations and associations which render it problematic. However, all of these translations can be used if we keep these considerations in mind, also remembering that in the Indian idiom "medicine" generally refers to power; thus the medicine man is one with access to both physical and psychic powers.[34]

The term "shaman" is also somewhat loosely used in writings about the American Indians. We need not here enter into the technical and somewhat abstruse scholarly debate about precisely what constitutes "shamanism." However, Arthur Versluis gives us a useful working definition which holds good for the *wicasa wakan*:

> Shamanism is essentially indigenous visionary spirituality, in the practice of which the shaman either undergoes a visionary journey through the cosmos, or calls spirits to him in order to heal or accomplish other benefits for the tribal people. . . . A shaman is, in general, "called" by the spirits to his vocation, and is then initiated into the shamanic tradition by a practicing shaman.[35]

In his commanding study of shamanism, Mircea Eliade called it "a technique of religious ecstasy";[36] the shamanic initiation entails a radical change in the state of consciousness, "a temporary derangement of the future shaman's spiritual equilibrium," one which gives access to hitherto closed realms and dimensions of reality.[37] Shamanism, says Eliade, is "at once mysticism, magic, and 'religion' in the broadest sense of the term."[38] Black Elk's Great Vision furnishes us with a dramatic instance of this "temporary derangement"—in his case one which he did not seek but which came to him unbidden at a young age.

On the vexed question of shamanistic "magic" it is helpful to consider these words from Frithjof Schuon:

> Behind every sensible phenomenon there lies in fact a reality of animic order that is independent of the limitations of space and time; it is by getting in touch with these realities, or these subtle and suprasensorial roots of things, that a shaman is able to influence natural phenomena or to foretell the future. All this may sound strange, to say the least of it, to the modern reader whose imagination now bears different imprints and responds to different reflexes than did that of medieval or archaic man; his subconscious, it must be avowed, is warped by a mass of prejudices having intellectual or scientific pretensions. Without going into details, one need only recall, in the words of Shakespeare, that "there are more things in heaven and earth than are dreamt of in your philosophy."[39]

Quite so!

The shaman's privileged vocation is hazardous, lonely, and heroic; the initiatory "soul flight" is full of perils and encounters with "hostile disincarnate entities," while the use of volatile powers requires a discriminating wisdom on the part of the practitioner if he is not unwittingly to unleash destructive forces. In working for the benefit of his people, as well as harnessing the beneficent powers of the universe, the *wicasa wakan* exposes himself to the menacing forces of darkness.[40] This is one reason for the careful preparations for any vision quest, and the need to integrate visionary experience into daily spiritual practice. As Chief Yellowtail observed, "When a person is on a vision quest, he must have certain attitudes and intentions for his prayers to be sincere, and then he must carry these over into daily life; unless you remember to carry on your prayer continually during every day of your life, you will not have learned one of the most important purposes of the vision quest."[41]

Black Elk Speaks, and indeed the holy man's whole life, is the story of his valiant commitment to the Great Vision of his childhood and to the visionary spirituality of which he became a steadfast custodian. Our study of Black Elk will throw into sharp relief the pivotal role of the *wicasa wakan* in the spiritual life of the Lakota, and more generally, the Plains Indians.

The Sacred Pipe and the Seven Rites

In *The Sacred Pipe* Black Elk recounted the myth of the coming of the sacred pipe and expounded the seven principal rituals of the Lakota. Here a brief description of each will suffice, but before doing so let us highlight the role of myths in the Indian worldview. We need not here detain ourselves with the sometimes absurd theories which have been fashionable at different times over the last century, but only remind ourselves that a myth is an allegorical narrative, often concerned with the origins of things—their coming into being—and conveying teachings which are *metaphysical* (concerning the degrees of reality which lie beyond time and space), *cosmological* (concerning the visible universe), and *anthropological* (concerning the human domain). In the apt words of a Hindu-Christian mystic, a myth is "a complex of signs and meanings which symbolize a reality so rich that it cannot be expressed directly in logical terms."[42] We might also recall Ananda Coomaraswamy's insistence that, "The myth is the penultimate truth, of which all experience is the temporal reflection. The mythical narrative is of timeless and placeless validity, true nowhere and everywhere. . . . Myth embodies the nearest approach to absolute truth that can be stated in words."[43] Moreover, "To have lost the art of thinking in images is precisely to have lost the proper linguistic of metaphysics and to have descended to the logic of 'philosophy.'"[44] Remember too this declaration from Carl Jung: "No science will ever replace myth, and a myth cannot be made out of any science. For it is not that 'God' is a myth, but that myth is the revelation of a divine life in man. It is not we who invent myth, rather it speaks to us as a Word of God."[45] Likewise Joseph Campbell: "myth is the secret opening through which the inexhaustible energies of the cosmos pour into human cultural manifestation."[46]

A ritual is a prescribed and time-honored sequence of symbolically charged actions and gestures, performed at auspicious times; rituals are frequently concerned with re-enacting mythic narratives, with entering sacred time and space, with participating in the creative activity of the divine powers, and with initiation into new modes of being.[47] Rituals, properly speaking, are always religious. As with myth,

> Ritual is not just archaic, prescientific language but a form of language in its own right, a form of expressive action. It "says" things that cannot be said as effectively in any other medium. It focuses, displays, enacts, creates, remembers, transforms. Ritual time sanctifies the important moments in life. It defines the calendar and hence temporality. It governs—annually,

daily, or whenever needed—the critical points of a world's concerns. It intersects ordinary time with enduring symbols and with alternating moments of purification and celebration, quietude and vigor.[48]

The gift of the sacred pipe is one of the foundational myths of the Lakota and provides a template for their ritual life. *Black Elk Speaks* opens with this story, recounted in more detail in *The Sacred Pipe.* "Very many winters ago," a divine and mysterious *wakan*-woman, White Buffalo Cow Woman (Pte San Win), came to the Lakota "in a very strange and wonderful manner." She conferred on them the gift of the sacred pipe, teaching them the symbolic meanings which it embodies and instructing them in its ceremonial use. Something of the pipe's multiple meanings can be seen in the Buffalo Woman's instructions to Standing Hollow Horn, the leader of the Lakota:

> Behold this and always love it! It is *lela wakan* [very sacred].
> . . . With this you will, during the winters to come, send your
> voices to *Wakan-Tanka*, your Father and Grandfather. . . .
> With this sacred pipe you will walk upon the Earth; for the
> Earth is your Grandmother and Mother, and She is sacred. . . .
> The bowl of the pipe is of red stone; it is the Earth. Carved
> in the stone and facing the center is this buffalo calf who rep-
> resents all the four-leggeds who live upon your Mother. The
> stem of the pipe is of wood and this represents all that grows
> upon the Earth. And these twelve feathers . . . are from *Wanbli
> Galeshka*, the Spotted Eagle, and they represent the eagle and
> all the wingeds of the air. All these peoples, and all the things
> of the universe, are joined to you who smoke the pipe—all
> send their voices to *Wakan-Tanka*, the Great Spirit. When
> you pray with this pipe, you pray for and with everything. . . .
> These seven circles which you see on the stone have much
> meaning, for they represent the seven rites in which the pipe
> will be used.[49]

Thus the pipe is a microcosm, a condensation of the entire universe, in which the six powers and directions are concentrated in the center, and in which all creatures and all created things are unified. The Calumet is a veritable compendium of Lakota cosmology and is integral to many of their ceremonies. Black Elk tells us that it "means more than any man can understand."[50]

✧ *Purification* (*Inipi*), the sweat-lodge ceremony, is performed prior to any other and is of fundamental importance in the spiritual life of the Lakota. During *inipi* the four elements of earth, air, fire, and water cooperate in the physical and psychic purification of the participants, bringing about spiritual renewal. The sweat lodge, like the sacred pipe, is a synthetic symbol of the universe itself: for instance, the fire (which heats the rocks and turns water into steam) signifies the transforming power of *Wakan-Tanka* "which gives life to all things"; it is also "as a ray from the sun, for the sun is also *Wakan-Tanka* in a certain aspect."[51] Black Elk:

> These rites of the *Inipi* are very *wakan* and are used before any great undertaking for which we wish to make ourselves pure or for which we wish to gain strength; and in many winters past our men, and often our women, made the *Inipi* even every day.... Now that we have neglected these rites we have lost much of its power; it is not good, and I cry when I think of it. I pray often that the Great Spirit will show to our young people the importance of these rites.[52]

✧ *The Keeping of the Soul* facilitates the journey of the dead person's soul from this life to the next. As Black Elk observed, the ritual is also a salutary reminder of the presence of death:

> It is good to have a reminder of death before us, for it helps us to understand the impermanence of life on this earth, and this understanding may aid us in preparing for our own death. He who is well prepared is he who knows that he is nothing compared with *Wakan-Tanka* who is everything; then he knows that world which is real.[53]

The Native Americans, living among the vicissitudes of nature, were keenly aware of the ephemerality of life, nowhere more beautifully expressed than by Crowfoot of the Blackfeet: "What is life? It is the flash of a firefly in the night. It is a breath of a buffalo in winter time. It is the little shadow which runs across the grass and loses itself in the sunset."[54]

✧ *Crying for a Vision* (*Hanblecheyapi*), "solitary communion with the Unseen," is the most exalted form of prayer and a rite of passage in which youths were sent into the wilderness to fast, meditate, and pray for the visitation of a spirit-being ("spirit friend," "vision person," "vision guide"), often in the form of an animal, who would become their guardian and the formative influence in shaping their personal vocation and destiny. Any vision induced by solitary invocation, by "lamenting," would only become efficacious once it had been related to a wise elder who would decipher its meaning and the imperatives which it disclosed. Emblematic of the Vision Quest was the "medicine bundle," usually comprising such things as animal bones, skin, rocks, and herbs, gathered together under the direction of the vision guide.

An Oglala Lakota has provided us with the following description of the ritual:

> When a man cries for a vision, it is nearly like the Sun Dance. . . . He takes a pipe filled with tobacco to the lodge of a holy man. . . . Then the holy man takes the pipe and smokes it. . . . And then the holy man says, "When a man cries for a vision, from that time on he can think nothing bad. Try to live well! My friend, later, in this way, I will prepare you". . . . Now he builds a sweat lodge . . . [and] everything is well covered with a blanket of sage. Now the vision quester goes into the lodge, it is said, and they cover the door: then they pray very earnestly. . . . So the holy man instructs the vision quester . . . "stand with a strong heart! In this way you will become *wakan*." Saying this, he instructs him, it is said, "Pray to inquire wisely and well into everything!" . . . Now the vision quester wraps the robe around himself with the fur side out, and until the sun rises, he stands looking east, pointing with the pipe that he holds, praying as hard as he can. All night long he stands in this way, it is said. At last the dawn seems to be visible, and so he stands, rejoicing greatly, it is said.[55]

✧ *The Sun Dance* (*Wiwanyag Wachipi*) was performed yearly by the whole community, over several days, and is the central tribal act of collective sacrifice, prayer, worship, renewal, and celebration; it was, in Ella Deloria's words, "the whole of life."[56] Frank Fools Crow, Black Elk's nephew, called the Sun Dance "the highest expression of our religion."[57] It involved the symbolic offering of bodies (fasting from food and water for the duration) to *Wakan-Tanka* through a complex dance around a sacred tree, the *axis mundi* joining Heaven and Earth. Like the sacred pipe, the Sun Dance comprises a kinetic encyclopedia of Lakota cosmology. This can be illustrated by Black Elk's explanation of just one of the Dance's manifold symbolic aspects. Here is the holy man explaining the significance of the lodge's twenty-eight posts and the poles connecting the circumference to the center (the tree):

> We are really making a universe in a likeness, for, you see, each of the posts . . . represents some particular object of creation, so that the whole circle is the entire creation, and the one tree at the center, upon which the twenty-eight poles rest, is *Wakan-Tanka*, who is the center of everything. . . . I have already explained to you why the numbers four and seven are sacred; then if you add four sevens you get twenty-eight. Also the moon lives twenty-eight days . . . [and] each of these days of the month represent something sacred to us: two of the days represent the Great Spirit; two are for Mother Earth; four are for the four winds; one is for the Spotted Eagle; one for the sun; and one for the moon; one is for the Morning Star; and four for the four ages; seven are for our seven great rites; one is for the buffalo; one for the fire; one for the water; one for the rock; and finally one is for the two-legged people. . . . You should also know that the buffalo has twenty-eight ribs, and that in our war bonnets we usually use twenty-eight feathers. You see, there is a significance for everything, and these are things that are good for men to know, and to remember.[58]

The outward purposes of the Sun Dance included sanctifying the vows and spiritual aspirations of the participants, enhancing the well-being of the tribal community, and the renewal of the whole created order. In this context we should take note of Mircea Eliade's remarks concerning the cosmic responsibility of primal peoples:

> It would be wrong to believe that the religious man of primitive and archaic societies refuses to assume the responsibility for a genuine existence. On the contrary . . . he courageously assumes immense responsibilities—for example, that of collaborating in the creation of the cosmos, or of creating his own world, or of ensuring the life of plants and animals, and so on. But it is a different kind of responsibility from those that, to us moderns, appear to be the only genuine and valid responsibilities. It is a responsibility on the cosmic plane, in contradistinction to the moral, social, or historical responsibilities that

are alone regarded as valid in modern civilizations. From the point of view of profane existence, man feels no responsibility except to himself and to society.[59]

On a more mystical plane the Sun Dance is the reunion of the heart (the ebb and flow of the dancers inwards and outwards from the cosmic tree symbolizing both breathing and the beating of the heart, as does the incessant drum beat which accompanies the dance) and the sun (variously associated in the ritual with a buffalo skull and with the eagle). As Frithjof Schuon has observed,

> The inward and invariable intention is to be reunited with the Solar Power, to establish a link between the sun and the heart. . . . The sun is the Heart of the Macrocosm, the human heart is the sun of the microcosm that we are. The visible sun is only a trace of the Divine Sun, but this trace, being real, is efficacious and allows the operation of "analogical magic," so to speak.[60]

Describing a Shoshone-Bannock-Crow Sun Dance which he witnessed in 1959, Frithjof Schuon has left us with a vivid picture of this awesome rite:

> The opening of the Sun Dance was one of the most powerful things I have ever witnessed. . . . In the darkness an extraordinarily powerful, rapid drumming began, and at the same time a monotonous, wild, and thrilling singing; it was like a war cry, and yet was not of this world. . . .
>
> The consonance of all these impressions—the Sun Dance Tree under the starry sky, the flickering fire, the thunderous drumming, the powerful singing, whose melody cascaded from high to low, the wonderful and timeless figures and faces—resulted in a truly grand and majestic image, indeed as powerful a one as senses and imagination can grasp.[61]

✧ *The Making of Relatives* (*Hunkapi*) entailed the burning of sweet grasses, smoking, eating buffalo meat, and the ritual exchange of tobacco and corn; it created, sanctified, or consolidated three types of relationships: personal, tribal, and between people and the earth. Reflecting on this ritual Black Elk had this to say:

I wish to mention here, that through these rites a three-fold peace was established. The first peace, which is the most important, is that which comes within the souls of men when they realize their relationship, their oneness with the universe and all its Powers, and when they realize that at the center of the universe dwells *Wakan-Tanka,* and that this center is really everywhere, it is within each of us. This is the real Peace, and the others are reflections of this. The second peace is that which is made between two individuals, and the third is that which is made between two nations. But above all you should understand that there can never be peace between nations until there is first known that true peace which, as I have often said, is within the souls of men.[62]

✧ *Preparing a Girl for Womanhood* was a rite of passage for adolescent girls, taking place immediately after the first menstruation, instructing her in the new duties of womanhood. "She should realize that the change which has taken place within her is a sacred thing, for now she will be as Mother Earth and will be able to bear children, who should also be brought up in a sacred manner."[63]

✧ *The Throwing of the Ball* comprised a game with a ball of buffalo hair, played by four teams and with four goals, one at each quarter. Anyone could participate. The game symbolically rehearsed the course of a person's life and concerned the maintenance of the right relationship with *Wankan-Tanka.* Black Elk told Joseph Brown that the understanding and practice of this rite had fallen away so that "there are only a few of us today who still understand why the game is sacred, or what the game originally was long ago."[64]

Hitherto our description of Lakota culture has been from the outside, as it were, somewhat in the manner of the scientist examining a dead specimen on the laboratory bench. The life of Black Elk and his evocative testimony in *Black Elk Speaks* will take us closer to the living heart of the Lakota tradition.

3

A Sacred Voice is Calling:
The Life of Black Elk

Behold, a sacred voice is calling you . . .
Black Elk[1]

If it were only the story of my life I think I would not tell it; for
what is one man that he should make much of his winters, even
when they bend him like a heavy snow? So many other men have
lived and shall live that story, to be grass upon the hills. It is the
story of all life that is holy and it is good to tell.
Black Elk[2]

Early Years and Visions
The Little Powder River flows through southeast Montana and north-
east Wyoming, draining the high plains to the west of the Bighorn
Mountains. In September 1865, the riverside was the site of a minor
encounter in the campaign of the US Army to conquer the Sioux,
Cheyenne, and Arapaho Indians who had long wandered this territory.
Scholars dispute the date of Black Elk's birth, putting it anywhere
between 1857 and 1866; the most plausible of these datings are 1863
and 1866.[3] In any event, somewhere along the banks of the Little
Powder, White Cow Sees gave birth to a baby boy, named Kahnigapi
("Choice").[4] Later he was named after his father, Hehaka Sapa (Black
Elk), a medicine man and cousin of the famed warrior and visionary,
Crazy Horse.[5] They belonged to the Oglala, one of seven bands of the
Lakota,[6] and the name Black Elk now ran through four generations.
The boy's father was wounded in the Battle of the Hundred Slain, a
pyrrhic victory in Red Cloud's War of 1866-1868.[7] General William
Tecumseh Sherman responded to this battle with these words: "We
must act with vindictive earnestness against the Sioux, even to exter-
mination of men, women, and children. Nothing less will reach the
root of the case."[8] Black Elk recalled this period of his childhood:

> I had never seen a *Wasichu* [non-native] then, and did not
> know what one looked like, but every one was saying that
> the *Wasichu*s were coming and that they were going to take

33

our country and rub us all out and that we should all have
to die fighting. . . . Once we were happy in our country and
we were seldom hungry, for then the two-leggeds and four-
leggeds lived together like relatives, and there was plenty for
them and for us. But the *Wasichus* came . . .[9]

One of the greatest of the Lakota leaders, Red Cloud, voiced a
moving elegy for the old ways:

My sun is set. My day is done. Darkness is stealing over me.
Before I lie down to rise no more, I will speak to my people.
Hear me, my friends, for it is not a time for me to tell a lie.
The Great Spirit made us, the Indians, and gave us this land
we live in. He gave us the buffalo, the antelope, and the deer
for food and clothing. . . .

    We fought our enemies and feasted our friends. Our
braves drove away all who would take our game. . . . Our
children were many and our herds were large. Our old men
talked with spirits and made good medicine. Our young men
herded the horses and made love to the girls. Where the tipi
was, there we stayed, and no house imprisoned us. No one
said, "to this line is my land, to that is yours." In this way our
fathers lived and were happy.[10]

Black Elk's childhood was a time when, in the words of the contemporary Jesuit priest-explorer, Pierre DeSmet, the Lakota were
subject to "the incessant provocations and injustices on the part of the
whites. . . . When the savages raise the hatchet to go on the warpath,
it is because they are pushed to the limit of endurance, and then the
blows that they deal are hard, cruel, and terrible. . . . It is always true
that if the savages sin against the whites it is because the whites have
greatly sinned against them."[11]
    Apart from the depredations of the invaders, this was still the
traditional world of the Lakota, "a sacred world in which the Lakota
people lived in daily interaction with the seen and unseen spirit forces
that comprised their universe."[12] Black Elk's childhood marked the
final years of the disappearing nomadic life of the Plains Indians. As
Clyde Holler has written,

Given the way in which he remembers it, we may suppose that
Black Elk's early years were happy years, relatively unmarked

by overt oppression. As a young boy he must have experienced at least the afterglow of the glory days of the Lakota, when they enjoyed hegemony over a large portion of the Plains, which was supplied with an abundance of food in the form of the buffalo. Despite this abundance, life was not necessarily easy for the Lakota. They had plenty of enemies, and shortages of food were common during the harsh Plains winters. But the summers were devoted to festivals, togetherness, and feasting—and to the Sun Dance—and at least some of Black Elk's evident nostalgia for the old free days of the Lakota must be attributed to the fact that he actually lived them.[13]

But these years were clouded by the intermittent wars with the US Army. Indeed, as a boy Black Elk witnessed the last great military triumph of the Indians, the Battle of the Greasy Grass (Battle of Little Big Horn, 1876) where "Long Hair" (General George Armstrong Custer) was killed and his army routed. After observing some of the fighting, Black Elk ventured onto the battlefield when the shooting had stopped. He came across a wounded soldier from Major Reno's command, whom, on the order of a Lakota warrior, he scalped and shot.[14] Soon after the battle Black Elk's people moved to the Bighorn Mountains in Wyoming where they joined Crazy Horse's band. Crazy Horse and Sitting Bull, two of the Indian leaders, were now high on the list of "hostiles" being pursued by the army. Crazy Horse was captured and killed at Fort Robinson in September 1877. Black Elk and his people fled to Canada where they remained for about three years, living on the Frenchman River before returning south. By mid-1881 many of the Lakota had found their way onto the Pine Ridge reservation in South Dakota.

It was at the age of four or five, playing alone, that Black Elk began to hear voices: "It was like someone calling me, and I thought it was my mother, but there was no one there. This happened more than once, and always made me afraid, so that I ran home." In the following year the boy experienced the first of his remarkable visions:

It was when I was five years old that my Grandfather made me a bow and some arrows. The grass was young and I was on horseback. A thunder storm was coming from where the sun goes down, and just as I was riding into the woods along a creek, there was a kingbird sitting on a limb. This was not a dream, it happened. And I was going to shoot at the kingbird with the bow my Grandfather made, when the bird spoke and said: "The clouds all over are one-sided." Perhaps it meant that all the clouds were looking at me. And then it said: "Listen! A voice is calling you." Then I looked up at the clouds, and two men were coming there, headfirst like arrows slanting down; and as they came they sang a sacred song, and the thunder was like drumming. I will sing if for you . . . "Behold, a sacred voice is calling you; All over the sky a sacred voice is calling."[15]

The crucial event of Black Elk's childhood occurred when he was about nine years old. His family was traveling to the Rockies for the yearly Sun Dance when the boy fell ill with swollen limbs and face, and lapsed into a semi-conscious state. During a near-fatal illness of twelve days, mostly more or less unconscious and prostrate, he experienced the Great Vision which he later recounted in such graphic detail to John Neihardt:

I am sure now that I was then too young to understand it all, and that I only felt it. It was the pictures I remembered and the words that went with them; for nothing I have ever seen with my eyes was so clear and bright as what my vision showed me; and no words that I have ever heard with my ears were like the words I heard. I did not have to remember these things; they have remembered themselves all these years. It was as I grew older that the meanings came clearer and clearer out of the pictures and the words; and even now I know that more was shown to me than I can tell.[16]

In the vision Black Elk is visited by the Thunder Beings whom he had encountered as a very young boy, and taken to the Grandfathers, spirits "kind and loving, full of years and wisdom, like revered human grandfathers."[17] The Grandfathers transport him to the center of the world, the axis of the six sacred directions:

And while I stood there I saw more than I can tell and understood more than I saw; for I was seeing in a sacred manner the shapes of all things in the spirit, and the shape of all shapes as they must live together like one being. And I saw that the sacred hoop of my people was one of many hoops that made one circle, wide as daylight and as starlight, and in the center grew one mighty flowering tree to shelter all the children of one mother and one father. And I saw that it was holy.[18]

Becoming a *Wicasa Wakan*

The vision disclosed Black Elk's vocation as medicine man, visionary, and spiritual leader of his people but, as he later told Neihardt, "a man who has a vision is not able to use the power of it until after he has performed the vision on earth for the people to see."[19] In the years after his vision Black Elk was often troubled by fearful dreams and further visions of the Thunder Beings. He describes his disturbed state when he is about sixteen, after the death of Crazy Horse and the flight to Canada:

> A terrible time began for me then, and I could not tell anyone, not even my father and mother. I was afraid to see a cloud coming up; and whenever one did, I could hear the thunder beings calling to me: "Behold your Grandfathers! Make haste!" I could understand the birds when they sang, and they were always saying: "It is time! It is time!" The crows in the day and the coyotes at night all called and called to me: "It is time! It is time! It is time." Time to do what? I did not know. Whenever I awoke before daybreak and went out of the tepee because I was afraid of the stillness when everyone was sleeping, there were many low voices talking together in the east, and the daybreak star would sing this song in the silence: "In a sacred manner you shall walk! Your nation shall behold you!"[20]

As Black Elk dolefully says later in his narrative, "It is hard to follow one great vision in this world of darkness, and of many changing shadows. Among those shadows men get lost."[21] In his prodigious study of shamanism, Mircea Eliade states that, "The shaman begins his new, his true life [i.e., after his visionary 'soul flight'] by a 'separation'—that is . . . by a spiritual crisis that is not lacking in tragic greatness and in beauty."[22] Such was the case with Black Elk. It was not until seven or eight years after the Great Vision that he was released from these fearful perplexities by recounting his vision to the medicine man, Black Road, and other tribal elders who were "astonished by the greatness of his vision."[23] This recalls the Gospel passage where we are told that when Jesus visited the temple as a twelve-year old and talked with the elders, "all who heard him were amazed at his understanding" and that thereafter "Jesus increased in wisdom and in stature, and in favor with God and man."[24] So it seems to have been with Black Elk.

The young Black Elk was instructed to publicly re-enact the first part of his Great Vision. In springtime 1881, with the help of Black Road and Bear Sings, he performed the Horse Dance Ceremony at Fort Keogh in Montana.

> After the horse dance was over, it seemed that I was above the ground and did not touch it when I walked. I felt very happy, for I could see that my people were all happier. . . . The fear that was on me for so long was gone, and when thunder clouds appeared I was always glad to see them, for they came as relatives now to visit me. Everything seemed good and beautiful now, and kind. Before this the medicine men would not talk to me, but now they would come to me and talk about my vision.[25]

Soon after, Black Elk also told of his "Dog Vision," which he had experienced some time after the Great Vision and, again under instruction from the elders, he performed the *heyoka* ceremony.[26] "By acknowledging the vision in this manner before his people, Black Elk at last put himself in harmony with the spirit world and publicly announced his spiritual calling."[27] Thenceforth he was esteemed as a *wicasa wakan*, a holy man with remarkable powers. In the following years Black Elk practiced as a healer, an expert in herbal medicine, and a practitioner of the "ceremonial magic" of the "transparent stones," the *yuwipi* rite in which the healer is bound up in blankets to pray and sing in total darkness to summon spirits for the healing of the participants.[28]

As a young man Black Elk became a *heyoka* ("trickster," "holy fool")—one who has been visited by the Thunder Beings/lightning and who must thereafter humble himself by playing the fool: "they have sacred power," Black Elk tells us, "and they share some of this with all the people, but they do it through funny actions."[29] The *heyoka* is an "upside down man" whose acts are contrarian: he shivers when it is hot, laughs when he is sad and so on, sometimes attracting the mirth and ridicule of simple folk who do not understand his behavior. But as Schuon explains,

> He is considered to have received mysterious powers and may end by being deeply respected as being apart and out of the

common run. . . . The behavior of the *heyoka* amounts to an initiatory language, comprehensible only to sages, as well as being a sacrificial vocation, that of being a "walking dead man" and called upon to re-establish inwardly the bridge between the world of matter and that of the spirit and immortality.[30]

Heyoka ceremonies (described in *Black Elk Speaks*) and the presence of the trickster in Indian life also testify to the importance of paradoxical humor and its integration into religious life. Black Elk remarks,

> You have noticed that the truth comes into the world with two faces. One is sad with suffering, and the other laughs; but it is the same face, laughing or weeping. When people are already in despair, maybe the laughing face is better for them; and when they feel too good and are too sure of being safe, maybe the weeping face is better for them to see. And so I think that is what the *heyoka* ceremony is for.[31]

Across the Big Water

In 1886 Black Elk, along with several of his friends, joined the traveling Wild West show of the celebrated army scout and former Indian fighter, "Buffalo Bill" Cody (whom Black Elk called Pahuska—"Long Hair"). He wanted, he said, "to see the great water, the great world and the ways of the white men":[32] "I thought I ought to go because I might learn some secret from the Wasichu that would help my people somehow. . . . Maybe if I could see the great world of the *Wasichu*, I could understand how to bring the sacred hoop together and make the flowering tree [of his vision] to bloom again at the center of it."[33] The show moved throughout the West in wagons and on the "iron road," and played for three months at Madison Square Garden before traveling across the Big Water by "fireboat" to London where the troop sang and danced for "Grandmother England" (Queen Victoria) and witnessed the Jubilee celebrations. Black Elk thought her a fine woman and wondered whether "if she had been our grandmother, it would have been better for our people."[34] The monarch, for her part, remarked, "I have traveled widely and have seen many countries and peoples, but I have never seen better-looking people than these."[35] Black Elk reports her as saying, "You are beautiful people, and if you belonged to me, I would treat you better."[36] While in London, Black

Elk, and many others in Cody's troupe, visited the Tower of London, enjoyed a production at the Lyceum Theatre, attended services in Westminster Abbey, and met Prime Minister Gladstone and the Prince and Princess of Wales. The show enjoyed tremendous success in England and, in Cody's words, made "a barrel of money."[37] In London alone, 2.5 million tickets for the show were sold. It enjoyed similar success in Birmingham and Manchester.

The Wild West show returned to America soon after, but Black Elk and two others missed the ship. They joined another touring outfit, Mexican Joe's Western Wilds of America Show, and spent a year performing in Germany, France, and Italy, before returning to England to play in Birmingham, Liverpool, Sheffield, and Manchester. During an illness and near-death experience in Paris, after he had left Mexican Joe's show, Black Elk had a vision of riding on a cloud over his homelands in the Black Hills and the Pine Ridge Reservation to which he soon after returned, only to discover that both his brother and sister had died, soon to be followed by his father. His return to America was paid for by his former employer, "Buffalo Bill," the one-time Indian fighter whom Black Elk had come to like and admire.[38]

The Ghost Dance and Wounded Knee

Back at the Pine Ridge Reservation where the surviving Oglala now lived, Black Elk, after being initially skeptical, became one of the leaders of the Ghost Dance, a messianic and millenarian movement which incorporated not only native myths but Christian motifs as well. It was launched in Nevada by Wovoka (aka Jack Wilson) whom Black Elk describes as "a sacred man among Paiutes who had talked to the Great Spirit in a vision, and the Great Spirit had told him how to save the Indian peoples."[39] The Ghost Dance, it was believed, would usher in a *wanikiye* ("savior," sometimes directly identified with Jesus[40]), reunite the living with past generations, recruit the spirits of the dead in the fight against the white invaders, bring back the buffalo herds, and herald a new era of peace and prosperity. The movement also promoted clean and honest living, and inter-tribal cooperation. In a period of deprivation and despair, the movement exerted a potent appeal and gave a sense of hope to many Native Americans, including Black Elk, who was related to three of the Lakotan Ghost Dance leaders, Good Thunder, Short Bull, and Kicking Bear. For many Indians the Ghost Dance replaced the Sun Dance, which had been outlawed, along with native healing practices, in 1883. Black Elk himself was stunned by the close resemblance of the Ghost Dance to his own vision many years before:

> This was to remind me to get to work at once and help to bring my people back into the sacred hoop, that they might again walk the red road in a sacred manner pleasing to the Powers of the Universe that are One Power. . . . I believed my vision was coming true at last, and happiness overcame me.[41]

The movement swept like prairie fire across the West in 1889 and 1890. As Joe Jackson has pointed out, "no other tribe embraced the Ghost Dance as fully as the Lakota, and no other Lakota band converted in such numbers as the Oglala of Pine Ridge."[42] Amongst its immediate effects was a stiffening of Lakota resistance to the Dawes Act of 1887. This act authorized the President to divide tribal lands and assign allotments to individual Indians, and to sell or give away the so-called "excess land" on the reservations under the terms established by the Homestead Act of 1862, which included the great "land rushes."[43] Henry Teller, whom we have already met as the Secretary of the Interior, but who was now back in his post as senator from Colorado, was surely right in criticizing the Act as "a policy to despoil the Indians of their land and make them vagabonds on the face of the earth."[44]

On December 15, 1890, Sitting Bull was killed while being arrested in his home on the Standing Rock Reservation in North Dakota. The death of this heroic leader, one of the architects of the victory at Little Big Horn and a rallying point for the Indian resistance, was a dismal symbol of the fate awaiting the old ways.[45] In fear of further reprisals, a Hunkpapa band fled Standing Rock and traveled south to the Cheyenne River Reservation where they joined Big Foot's band of Minneconjou. The consolidated group then fled to the Pine Ridge Reservation to seek the protection of the famous Lakota Chief Red Cloud. The Seventh Cavalry, Custer's old unit, arrested Big Foot's band and escorted them to Wounded Knee Creek, where they were surrounded by a much larger detachment of soldiers with artillery. Simmering tensions erupted on the following day, December 29, 1890, when soldiers attempted to disarm the encircled Indians. The result was what one historian has characterized as "mostly a battle, partly a massacre, and entirely a tragic blunder"[46] where up to three hundred Sioux, many of them women and children, were slaughtered or later died from their wounds.[47] Twenty-five soldiers were killed at Wounded Knee. Twenty were subsequently awarded the Medal of Honor.

Black Elk's role in these events remains somewhat shadowy, but we know that he had urged militant action and armed resistance to the US army, he led several Ghost Dances, and he spent a good deal of time making the "ghost shirts" which adherents believed would protect them against the bullets of the white soldiers.[48] He probably supported the breakout to the Black Hills which helped trigger the violent intervention of the army at Wounded Knee. Black Elk himself only arrived in the ravine, where "the Hotchkiss guns turned Wounded Knee into a lake of blood,"[49] in the last stage and was involved in subsequent skirmishes when he was wounded in the hip.[50] He also rescued a baby orphan who was adopted by his future father-in-law.

In the face of official repression and intimidation, the Ghost Dance movement soon faded from public view though some underground attempts were made to keep it alive. However, as Clyde Holler has made clear, Black Elk retained more faith in the Ghost Dance than Neihardt's narrative suggested. Some sixty years after Wounded Knee there were many Lakota elders, including Black Elk, who believed that the Ghost Dance could and should be revived.[51] But Wounded Knee marked the end of Indian military resistance. A "malaise of the spirit" now gripped the Lakota.[52] Scattered groups of Indians found some hope in the sporadic "Peyote Cult,"[53] but most Lakota were demoralized and often despairing. The decade following Wounded Knee was marked by intensified missionizing activity and new government regulations aimed at eradicating the old ways.

In his later years, Black Elk recalled Wounded Knee in this now-famous passage:

> I did not know then how much was ended. When I look back now from this high hill of my old age, I can still see the butchered women and children lying heaped and scattered all along the crooked gulch as plain as when I saw them with eyes young. And I can see that something else died there in the bloody mud, and was buried in the blizzard. A people's dream died there. It was a beautiful dream. . . . The nation's hoop is broken and scattered. There is no center any longer, and the sacred tree is dead.[54]

A more heart-breaking epitaph can scarcely be imagined. This is the most frequently quoted of the many memorable passages in *Black Elk Speaks*. The fact that we now know that this was a poetic intervention by Neihardt rather than words directly spoken by Black Elk does not diminish its power.[55] Wounded Knee became an evocative emblem of the fate of the Indians at the hands of the American military. Dee Brown's "Indian History of the American West," *Bury My Heart at Wounded Knee* (1970), spearheaded the historical revision of the whole sorry story of nineteenth century Indian-European relations. Wounded Knee was to be the site of another violent conflict in 1973.[56]

There has been much debate and controversy about Wovoka and about the role of the Ghost Dance in hastening the destruction of the Indian cultures. For the moment, suffice to note Schuon's observations:

> The features of the Ghost Dance which made it so special and so tragic arose out of the physical and psychological conditions prevailing at that moment. The despair of the Indians transposed [Wovoka's] prophecies into the immediate future and conferred on them a combative tone quite out of keeping with the pacific character of the original message; nonetheless, it was not the Indians who provoked the conflict.[57]

Catholic Catechist

Black Elk had little to say about the years between 1890 and 1904, but it seems that during this time he concentrated on his role as a healer, diviner, *yuwipi* practitioner, and sometime *heyoka*. He also worked for some years as a clerk in the Manderson store. In 1892 Black Elk married his first wife, Katie War Bonnet, with whom he had three children. Katie was a Catholic and all three children (William/Never Showed Off, John/Good Voice Star, and Ben) were baptized. After the death of Katie (variously put at 1901 and 1903) he married Between Lodge (who later became Anna Brings White), a widow with two daughters. The couple had three more children (Lucy, Henry, and Nick Jr.) and remained together until her death in 1941. As well as the loss of Katie, Black Elk suffered many bereavements during his life: a brother and sister in the late 1880s, his father in 1889, son William in 1895, sons John and Henry in 1909 and 1910, Anna Brings White's daughters Agatha and Mary in 1910, his mother in 1915, his second wife Anna in 1941.[58] As one of his biographers has observed, these personal tribulations were rarely mentioned in the old man's reminiscences to Neihardt.[59]

As a condition of belonging to Buffalo Bill's Wild West show, Black Elk had been nominally baptized in the Episcopalian Church in 1886. During his travels in Europe and in the years following, Black Elk had been exposed to various Christian influences and had shown some interest in the Christian faith. During the 1890s many Native Americans joined Christian denominations, some no doubt as a matter of expediency while others were fervent converts. Catholic missionaries—Jesuit priests and brothers and some Franciscan nuns—had arrived in Pine Ridge during the late 1880s when Black Elk was touring with Buffalo Bill and Mexican Joe. As Joe Jackson has observed,

> Unlike Protestant missionaries, whose approach to conversion was all-or-nothing, the Jesuits were more likely to mold Catholic doctrine to Sioux culture. The symbolism of the Sacred Pipe as a focus for all that was holy was easily transferred to the Cross; the Sioux idea of the Great Spirit and watchful Grandfathers was not that different from a Catholic God, Trinity, and host of angels. Ritual sacraments were central to both religions. Pain and suffering—their acceptance and endurance—were the nexus of both Catholic and Lakota identity.[60]

In 1904, sometime after Katie's death, Black Elk formally converted to Catholicism.[61] According to the account of his daughter Lucy, the catalyst for his conversion was an episode during which Black Elk was treating a seriously ill boy in his tent when a Jesuit priest, "Short Father," who had baptized the boy, arrived to administer the last rites. The priest abruptly gathered together Black Elk's sacred accessories and flung them out of the tent, took the medicine man by the scruff of the neck and hurled him out too, intoning "Satan, get out." By Lucy's report, Black Elk was demoralized by this incident and felt that the priest's powers were superior to his own.[62] Several scholars have cast some doubt over Lucy's account, pointing out that Black Elk himself told a remarkably similar story about an incident which had taken place in 1902, but in which the priest (probably Father Aloysius Bosch) is fatally thrown from his horse soon after.[63] In another speculation about Black Elk's conversion the motive force is the final illness of his wife Katie, who had long urged him to become Catholic.[64] In any event, it is clear that Father Joseph Lindebner of the Holy Rosary Mission instructed Black Elk in the Catholic faith and baptized him on December 6, 1904, the feast day of St. Nicholas; thus the new convert was given the name Nicholas. (For the rest of his life he was almost universally known as "Nick" Black

Elk.) Over the next decade he rarely performed the traditional Lakota religious and healing ceremonies.[65] He learned to read the Bible and write letters in Lakota, choosing never to become literate in English.[66]

Black Elk became a catechist and preacher, later traveling to Nebraska and Wyoming in this role. Over the years he attended church regularly, helped prepare people for baptism, conducted prayer meetings, visited the sick and the imprisoned, buried the dead, organized events such as the Sioux Catholic Congress for Native American Catholics, was caretaker of the St. Agnes Chapel in Manderson, and was active in the St. Joseph Society. As a member of the St. Joseph Society he had to demonstrate an understanding of basic Christian dogmas, attend Mass regularly, say Confession at least four times a year, defer to priests and bishops, baptize his children as Catholics, abjure alcohol and gambling, and abandon Lakota "superstitions." Black Elk was a popular and charismatic preacher and gave talks in places as far-flung as New York (where he addressed the inmates of Sing Sing Prison), Boston, Washington, Chicago, Lincoln, and Omaha. One of the "Black Robes" (Jesuits) credited Black Elk with four hundred conversions and declared him "the most prominent" of all the catechists.[67] Black Elk was paid a small stipend which he supplemented by raising cattle. His work for the church also entitled him to free housing. He remained active in church work until 1928 when he moved from Oglala back to his one-room log cabin in Manderson.

When, many years after Black Elk's death, Michael Steltenkamp spent time on the Pine Ridge Reservation, he was astonished to find that "Black Elk's prestige in the reservation community was not attributable to the popularity of his two books. Prestige he had, but it was the result of his very active involvement with priests in establishing Catholicism among his people."[68] During these years many Lakota, including members of his own family, were seemingly unaware of *Black Elk Speaks* and *The Sacred Pipe*.[69] In marked contrast, Fools Crow, perhaps the most celebrated and honored Lakota Sun Dance chief of the twentieth century, presented a different picture when he summarized Black Elk's role in preserving their ancestral traditions:

> My uncle, the renowned Black Elk, has earned a place above
> all of the other Teton holy men. We all hold him the highest.
> I have never heard a bad word about him, and he never said
> a bad word about anyone. All he wanted to do was love and
> serve his fellow man. . . . In the Indian custom, he was also a
> father to me. I stayed with him quite often, and sometimes

for long periods of time. We also made a few trips together and over the years talked about many things. I learned a great deal about *Wakan Tanka*, prophecy, and medicine from him.[70]

These divergent observations provide an introduction to the fierce controversy surrounding Black Elk's conversion to Catholicism. There are three distinct schools of thought, arguing that his conversion was: (a) no more than an expedient stratagem and that he remained true to the ancestral ways; (b) deep and sincere, entailing a repudiation of his old beliefs; or that (c) he somehow blended and reconciled Lakota tradition and Christianity. Much ink has been spilt in this debate; we shall return to it in some detail later.

The second half of Black Elk's earthly sojourn was lived out quietly and in relative obscurity in South Dakota, first in Oglala and then in Manderson. He rarely traveled after being afflicted with tuberculosis in 1912, and his eyesight, seriously damaged by an accident when he was young and later affected by glaucoma, deteriorated over the years.[71] In 1933 he suffered broken ribs and other complications as the result of a wagon accident, his condition being so serious that last rites were administered. He suffered from various infirmities over the last two decades of his life but was able to participate each summer in the Duhamel Sioux Indian Pageant, held nine miles south of Rapid City at the Sitting Bull Crystal Caverns (so named at Black Elk's suggestion), and opening in 1934 or 1935. The pageant was conceived by Black Elk, who was also the principal performer. It was modeled on the Indian segments of Buffalo Bill's Wild West show, but this time rather than glorifying the feats of Indian warriors the show introduced non-native folk to Lakota rituals and spiritual life.[72] "Black Elk's long-term participation in the Duhamel pageants . . . demonstrates his traditional leadership and power, illustrates his desire to teach, and shows the holy man adapting new contexts to traditional ends."[73] He also conducted actual healings and dance ceremonies amongst the pageant participants, prompting Bud Duhamel to remark, "Old Nick was no fake. He was a true medicine man."[74] Black Elk also found much joy in his grandchildren. Joseph Brown wrote of him, "He loves children, & when they are about they are all over him—he is kindly, gentle, with a most marvelous sense of humor."[75] When Brown once asked Black Elk about his special relationship with young children, he replied, "I who am an old man am about to return to the Great Mysterious and a young child is a being who has just come from the Great Mysterious; so it is that we are very close together."[76]

A Low Point for Sioux Culture and a New Start

The first half of the twentieth century was in many respects a nadir for traditional Sioux culture, a time which would later be recognized as also the starting point for the revival of the sacred rites of the Sioux. The Indian Reorganization Act of 1934 repealed both the Dawes Act and the Secretary of Interior's Orders of 1884, allowing American Indians to openly practice their traditional culture once again. However, the U.S. government's policy of forced cultural assimilation proved to be very effective. As a result of the fifty-year legal prohibition on traditional public ceremonies, many of the sacred rites were forgotten or lost. Almost all of the spiritual leaders of the 1880s and '90s had passed on to the "Other Side Camp," so that despite the lifting of legal restrictions, many tribes had no practical means by which to renew or reestablish their sacred rites. Some tribes who had lost their rites were obliged to adopt some from others fortunate enough to retain them. As Michael Fitzgerald has noted, "the first half of the twentieth century was an incredibly difficult period for all American Indians and the time immediately after World War II was in many ways a low point for the preservation of the ancestral spiritual traditions of the Plains Indians."[77]

From our perspective the most momentous events of these years were Black Elk's encounters with John Neihardt in 1932 and Joseph Brown in 1947, generating those works from which his later fame largely derived. As we shall subsequently learn, the providential meeting with Brown also provided the practical support that allowed Black Elk to play an indispensable role in revitalizing the sacred rites of the Lakota. Much less well known was Black Elk's extraordinary relationship with Frithjof Schuon, a man whom he never actually met in the flesh. Later in this study our attention will be fixed on the crucial role of these figures in preserving the spiritual legacy of which the *wicasa wakan* was such a faithful guardian. For now we will make do with a few quick brush-strokes.

The Encounter with John G. Neihardt and *Black Elk Speaks*

John Gneisenau Neihardt was born in a farm shack in Sharpsburg, Illinois, in 1881. After John's father abandoned the family, they moved first to Kansas City, Missouri, and then to Wayne, Nebraska, to live with relatives in a one-room sod house. Despite some early illness, Neihardt was physically tough and in his youth trained as a boxer and wrestler. In time he became a newspaper editor, poet, critic, historian, ethnographer, philosopher, and later an academic. He was a voracious reader and accumulated a personal library of some 5,000 books.[78] Above all he understood himself as an artist "who believed art was the conduit to spirituality and the 'higher values,' who distrusted institutional religion but was reverent. He believed in the visionary and paranormal."[79] He had an abiding interest in the European settlement of the West, and in the culture and fate of the indigenous peoples.[80] He traveled extensively through the West, but his interests extended beyond his native country, evident in his very first publication, *The Divine Enchantment*, a poetic rendition of some ancient Hindu myths. (He was later embarrassed by this work and destroyed whatever copies he could find.) His home during his early adult years was Bancroft, Nebraska, where he settled with his wife Mona (née Martinson), a student of the great sculptor, August Rodin. They married in 1908 and had four children, two of whom, Enid and Hilda, were to assist Neihardt in his great work with Black Elk. Neihardt traveled two thousand miles down the Missouri by open boat,[81] conducted extensive researches throughout the Plains and the Rocky Mountains, encountered many Indian tribes, and nurtured particularly close relationships with the Omaha. Later in life he lived in Branson and Columbia, Missouri, before spending his final years in Lincoln, Nebraska. After the publication of *Black Elk Speaks* he completed *The Song of the Messiah* in 1935. He returned to work on the *St. Louis Post-Dispatch* before being employed by John Collier as the director of the Bureau of Information within the Bureau of Indian Affairs. Neihardt visited Black Elk again 1944, gathering material for *When the Tree Flowered*, in which he aimed to depict the whole way of life of the Sioux in the days before the Indian Wars. In 1921 the Nebraska legislature elected Neihardt the state's poet-laureate, a position he held until his death in 1973. He was showered with many literary awards and honors, but it was only in the last few years of his life that Neihardt became widely-known as the author of the recently reprinted *Black Elk Speaks* and as a guest on the Dick Cavett Show.[82]

Neihardt's many publications run to some twenty-five volumes across several genres—journalism, epic poems, short stories, novels, plays, travelogues, philosophy. His best-known works are *The Song of the Indian Wars* (1925), *Black Elk Speaks* (1932), *The Song of the Messiah* (1935), *A Cycle of the West* (1949), the *magnum opus* on which he worked for thirty years, and *When the Tree Flowered* (1952), the second of his books dealing with the Sioux.[83]

In 1930 Neihardt was in Missouri researching the Ghost Dance movement for *The Song of the Messiah*, and looking for "long hairs" who still remembered the old days. His investigations led him to the South Dakota Pine Ridge Agency where he was told of an old "unre-constructed" Indian, Black Elk.[84] Hilda Neihardt later described her father at this time:

> He was not a large man, but he was very strong, very intense, with wavy blond hair that had darkened to a sandy brown and bright blue eyes that revealed his enthusiasm for the job he had undertaken. With a background of some thirty years of friendship with the Omaha and Sioux peoples, during which he had gained an appreciation for them and for their cultures that was rare indeed in those times, he was ideally suited for the task at hand. That Black Elk had intuitively known this about Neihardt on their first meeting proved to be the remarkable beginning to this whole story.[85]

Black Elk had earlier been quite adamant in refusing a request from writers Eleanor Hinman and Mari Sandoz to tell them his story.[86] He was much more sympathetic to Neihardt. At their first meeting Black Elk told the poet, "There is much to teach you. What I know was given to me for men and it is true and it is beautiful. Soon I will be under the grass and it will be lost. *You were sent to save it*, and you must come back so that I can teach you."[87] The two soon formed a close friendship and an "inexplicable rapport,"[88] the old Indian naming Neihardt "Flaming Rainbow." Henceforth Black Elk referred to Neihardt as "son" or "nephew," and Neihardt called the old man "uncle." Neihardt himself had, during a fever at the age of eleven, experienced a powerful vision which he related to Black Elk and which he later incorporated in his poem "The Ghostly Brother."[89] As DeMallie observes, "The mystic in Neihardt and the mystic in Black Elk were kindred souls."[90] Their interactions were marked by "intuitive under-standing and spiritual kinship" and by "a growing awareness of their joint calling."[91] Here is Neihardt's account of his initial meeting with the old Lakota:

> He [Black Elk] struck me as being a bit uncanny in his intu-itions; not that he favored me, but that he seemed to know what was inside the visitor. He told me—the sphinx-like old chap—that as he sat there, he felt in my heart a very strong

will to know the things of the other world and that a spirit, which stood behind me, had forced me to come to him that I might learn a little from him. In spite of the sound of this statement, he was very modest, modest as a man may be who is sure of what he knows and that what he knows is worth knowing. . . . He seemed to be expecting me and welcomed me as though he had seen me often.[92]

Black Elk addressed the following words to Neihardt: "You are a word-sender. The earth is like a garden and over it your words go like rain making it green and after your words have passed the memory of them will stand long in the West like a Flaming Rainbow."[93] Of the providential encounter of Neihardt and the Oglala holy man, Frank Waters has written this:

> It may seem strange that [Black Elk] told this vision to a white man, a member of the race that had ruthlessly crushed underfoot the proud Sioux nation during its imperial march across the North American continent. Yet the Powers Above which mysteriously prescribe the successive rise and fall of nations and civilizations, often pick unwitting agents and spokesmen to further the ever-evolving consciousness of mankind towards transcendent completeness.[94]

Neihardt conducted many long and detailed conversations with Black Elk about his early life. Also present throughout most of Black Elk's narration were his son Ben, who translated his father's words into English,[95] Neihardt's daughters Hilda and Enid, who recorded Ben's translation, and one of Black Elk's closest and most trusted friends, Stephen Standing Bear,[96] whose presence was for Black Elk a guarantor of the veracity of his account. (It was Standing Bear who provided the illustrations for the first edition of *Black Elk Speaks*.) Several other Lakota elders were also intermittently present, among them Fire Thunder, Chase in the Morning, and Holy Black Tail. Neither Ben nor any of Black Elk's friends had ever previously heard him describe his Great Vision. In 1911, Charles Eastman had written that "sometimes an old man, standing upon the brink of eternity, might reveal to a chosen few the oracle of his long-past youth."[97] Such was the case here. As DeMallie observes, "It was as if something long bound up inside the old man had broken free at last, an impulse to save that entire system of knowledge that his vision represented and that for more than twenty-five years he had denied."[98] Black Elk was "tying together the ends of his life."[99] Neihardt exclaimed to his daughters that "I just cannot *believe* the beauty and the meaning of what is coming out of the old man's head. I know of no other vision in religious literature that is equal to this."[100] Soon after, Neihardt wrote to his friend Julian House, describing the Great Vision as "a marvelous thing, vast in extent, full of profound significance and perfectly formed. If it were literature instead of a dance ritual, it would be a literary masterpiece."[101] It now became Neihardt's sacred duty to capture "the beauty and meaning" of Black Elk's testimony; in so doing he and Black Elk would indeed create "a literary masterpiece." As Brian Holloway has so persuasively observed, "What Neihardt sought in presenting Black Elk (and others) was to give readers a glimpse of a total, powerful, ineffable world—a world that could not be described simply by the everyday language of history and observation but that could be accessed through the medium of poetry and other arts that, Neihardt believed, served as conduits to enhanced consciousness."[102]

The transcription taken from Enid's stenographic notes formed the basis for *Black Elk Speaks,* which Neihardt wrote in an inspired frenzy between June and October 1931.[103] Much controversy has attended the role of Neihardt in creating *Black Elk Speaks,* a subject to be explored later. The book itself draws directly only on a portion of Black Elk's reminiscences, which did not see the light of day in complete form until the publication of *The Sixth Grandfather: Black Elk's Teachings Given to John G. Neihardt* (1984). This volume included Neihardt's interviews with Black Elk in 1944 when the poet again visited the holy man, this time in search of material for *When the Tree Flowered.*

In May 1931, after Black Elk had completed his long and exhausting reminiscences over sixteen days,[104] the holy man, his son Ben, Neihardt, and his daughters traveled to the Black Hills and climbed Harney Peak,[105] the center of the world to which Black Elk had been transported in his Great Vision. There the old man prayed to Grandfather *Tunkashila,* the Great Spirit, concluding with these words:

> With tears running, O Great Spirit, Great Spirit, my Grandfather—with running tears I must say now that the tree has never bloomed. A pitiful old man, you see me here, and I have fallen away and have done nothing. Here at the center of the world, where you took me when I was young and taught me;

here, old, I stand, and the tree is withered, Grandfather, my
Grandfather. . . . In sorrow I am sending a feeble voice, O Six
Powers of the World. Hear me in my sorrow, for I may never
call again. O make my people live.[106]

Black Elk's prayer on Harney Peak would form the final chapter of
Black Elk Speaks, "a prose poem of lamentation for the dead and for
a vanished age."[107]

Joseph Epes Brown and *The Sacred Pipe*

Black Elk's encounter with Joseph Brown was no less significant than
that with Neihardt, but it has received much less attention. Amongst
the several reasons for this comparative neglect is the fact that Brown,
unlike Neihardt, was a shy and private person who shunned the
public limelight. Until recently there was very little in the public
domain about Brown's life, but today we can turn to four recent new
sources: first, the biographical sketch presented by the editors of the
2007 commemorative edition of Brown's *The Spiritual Legacy of the
American Indian: With Letters While Living with Black Elk*; second,
a batch of letters written by Brown to various correspondents in the
late 1940s and early '50s (excerpts of which appeared in *The Spiritual Legacy*, and some of which are reproduced here in Appendix I);
third, newly discovered and unpublished letters written by Brown in
the 1940s, excerpts of which also appear in Appendix I; and fourth,
Michael Fitzgerald's recent article "New Light on Black Elk and *The
Sacred Pipe*."

Joseph Epes Brown (1920-2000) was born in Connecticut and
spent parts of his childhood and youth in South Carolina, Maine,
and New Mexico, developing what became a lifelong interest in the
spiritual heritage of the American Indians.[108] He was a conscientious
objector during World War II. In the post-war years he came under the
influence of the great Perennialists, René Guénon, Ananda Coomaraswamy, and Frithjof Schuon, and later undertook formal studies in
anthropology and comparative religion, including a doctorate at the
University of Stockholm under the guidance of the eminent Swedish
scholar Åke Hultkrantz. In 1970 Brown created the first university
program in Native American Religious Studies at Indiana University,
Bloomington.

As Fitzgerald has revealed, the origins of Brown's long journey
to the remote camp in Nebraska where he found Black Elk can

be found in an "informal reading group" established during World War II by four young spiritual seekers—Brown, Whitall Perry, John Murray, and Lester Kanefsky—who were working as conscientious objectors in a U.S. Forest Service camp.[109] Their studies led them to the Ramakrishna-Vivekananda Center in New York City where they became friendly with Swami Nikhilananda and Gerald Heard, thence to Ananda Coomaraswamy in Boston and René Guénon in Cairo, and finally to the works and person of Frithjof Schuon (about whom more presently) and the Sufi *tariqah* (spiritual order) of which he was the *shaykh*.[110] In late 1946 Frithjof Schuon, living in Lausanne, asked John Murray to send him books on Native American traditions; one of the books Murray forwarded was the now out-of-print *Black Elk Speaks*. Schuon was deeply impressed and, believing that the holy man had more to impart, asked Murray if he knew anyone who might be able to find Black Elk. Murray discussed Schuon's request with his close friend, Joseph Brown, who took up the quest after completing his studies at Haverford College. Equipping his old Ford truck as a traveling home, and with some assistance from Neihardt,[111] Brown set out to find the old man:

> It was not until 1947, after months of travel, that I was able to find him living with his family in a little canvas tent in a migrant potato-picking camp in Nebraska. I well remember him as he sat on an old sheepskin hide, ill and pitiful, with his almost totally blind eyes staring beyond that which surrounded him. . . . We smoked in silence until finally, with a soft and kindly voice, he spoke in Lakota. Translated by his son, he surprised me by saying that he had anticipated my coming, was glad that I was there beside him, and asked if I would remain with him, for there was much that he would like to tell me before, as he said "he would pass from this world of darkness into the other real world of light." I therefore returned with him to his log cabin on the reservation, living with him and his generous family for almost a year. . . . Every day he talked for several hours until the veil of silence fell in which one could sense that he was so absorbed within the realities of which he was speaking that words no longer had meaning. Indeed, the greater part of what I learned from Black Elk was not what he said, valuable as this was, but what he was from his very being, which seemed to hover between this world of forms and the other world of the spirit.[112]

Brown was adopted by Black Elk and named "He Who Walks with the Sacred Pipe." Brown later gave an amusing but instructive account of their initial conversations:

> When I first came to live with Black Elk, I was eager to hear him talk about religious matters. All he talked about, though, was animals. Because of my academic background, I kept wondering when he was going to get serious and talk real theology. When was he going to talk metaphysics? When was he going to speak the kind of language I had become accustomed to from Thomas Aquinas? He never did. This was puzzling to me, because I knew he was a man of great sanctity who had experienced the Great Mysterious frequently through his visions. Finally, it occurred to me that, in talking about animals and birds, the wind and the four directions, he was talking about what non-Natives call "religion." He was, indeed, speaking a sacred, metaphysical language, but it was phrased in terms of living realities in the immediacy of one's experience.[113]

Black Elk's detailed account of the central rituals of the Lakota, hitherto little-known in the white world, was recorded in *The Sacred Pipe* (1953), the second of the three indispensable texts in the study of the ancestral ways of the Lakota. If *Black Elk Speaks* provided an enthralling narrative and recaptured something of the holy man's astounding visions, Brown's book provided a more coherent account of Lakota metaphysics, cosmology, and ritual life. As Frithjof Schuon remarked, as valuable as *Black Elk Speaks* was, "for the doctrine one has to refer to *The Sacred Pipe*, all the more as this book is strictly faithful, word for word, to the account given by the Indian author."[114] Brown went on to write several other books which have been enormously influential in repairing the widespread ignorance about the spiritual life of the American Indians. Most notable of these is *The Spiritual Legacy of the American Indian* (1982).[115]

A Note on Frithjof Schuon and *The Feathered Sun*

Anyone with even a passing interest in Black Elk and Lakota tradition is familiar with *Black Elk Speaks* and many know of *The Sacred Pipe*. But there is a third book, written by an author who had a mystical connection with Black Elk: *The Feathered Sun* (1990) by Frithjof Schuon (1907-1998).[116] Schuon was a Swiss-German writer, poet, artist, and metaphysician, the author of more than twenty-five books covering all of the world's major religious and sapiential traditions, and the pre-eminent exponent of the Perennialist school which focuses on the metaphysical and cosmological principles which inform all of the world's integral traditions, not only those of East and West but also from the primordial and non-literate cultures such as those of the American Indians. Huston Smith, doyen of recent comparative religionists, called Schuon "the most important religious thinker" of the last century.[117]

Perennialists, or Traditionalists as they are sometimes called, affirm the providential necessity of the distinctive formal elements which define each tradition, whilst at the same time avowing their convergence in "the transcendent unity of religions." For this reason the adherents of this school are also sometimes called universalists— but this form of universalism must be sharply distinguished from any proposals for a synthesis or distillation of the different traditions in some kind of "super-religion" such as championed by the likes of Aldous Huxley. Joseph Brown was fully committed to this Traditionalist, or Perennialist, perspective. As Seyyed Hossein Nasr has noted,

> In fact Brown was the link between Black Elk and Schuon who was himself so deeply attracted to the Native American traditions. For years it was Brown who through letters and journeys to Lausanne [where Schuon lived] would speak of the Native Americans to Schuon and would create possibilities of exchange between Schuon and that world, exchanges that were to play an important role in the last period of the latter's life.[118]

Schuon spent two summers with the Plains Indians, in 1959 and 1963, and knew Ben Black Elk as well as leaders such as Last Bull and Thomas Yellowtail. Along with his magisterial essays on Indian subjects, gathered together in *The Feathered Sun*, Schuon completed many striking paintings on Indian themes, some of which are reproduced in the same volume. Both Schuon and his brother Erich, a Trappist monk (Father Gall), were significant figures in Black Elk's last years. But we will leave that story for later. For now all that need be said is that the study-from-the-inside of the religious culture of the Lakota, and more generally of the Plains Indians, inaugurated by Neihardt and extended by Brown, culminated in *The Feathered Sun*, a masterly conspectus of Indian metaphysics, cosmology, and religious life.

Black Elk's Celestial Epitaph

In the spring of 1948, after Joseph Brown's final departure, Black Elk fell and broke his hip, and was thereafter confined to a wheelchair. In the same year he suffered a stroke and was hospitalized. The holy man died at Manderson, South Dakota, on August 17, 1950, and was buried at St. Agnes Mission Chapel. Some time before crossing to the further shore he had told Joseph Brown, "You will know when I am dying, because there will be a great display of some sort in the sky." His daughter Lucy also recalled her father, in his last days, saying, "I have a feeling that when I die, some sign will be seen. Maybe God will show something. He will be merciful to me and have something shown which will tell of his mercy." Many of those at the old man's wake report that there was indeed a dazzling celestial display that night. From the testimony of William Siehr, a Jesuit brother at Holy Rosary Mission:

> When we came back from the wake, the sky was lit up, and you could see those flames going into midair. It was something like light played on a fountain which sprays up. . . . They weren't stars or meteors, but rather, well, they were beams or flashes. And there was variation of color effect in there—the whole horizon seemed to be ablaze. That's the first and only time I ever saw anything like it.[119]

We need not be surprised by these signs of Heaven's favor, often appearing at the passing of the great saints and sages. Indeed, just a few months before Black Elk's death the departure of the great Indian master, Ramana Maharshi, had been marked by astronomical signs. The French photographer Henri Cartier-Bresson was one of many who witnessed a luminous comet or shooting-star which appeared over Mt. Arunachala at the precise moment of the Maharshi's death.[120]

4

The Sacred Hoop and the Flowering Tree: Black Elk's Great Vision

And while I stood there I saw more than I can tell and I understood
more than I saw; for I was seeing in a sacred manner the shapes
of all things in the spirit, and the shape of all shapes as
they must live together like one being.
Black Elk[1]

Nothing I have ever seen with my eyes was so clear and bright as
what my vision showed me; and no words that I have ever heard
with my ears were like the words I heard. I do not have to remember
these things; they have remembered themselves all these years.
Black Elk[2]

Archetypes, Symbols, and Spiritual Realities

No consideration of the place of visions in Indian life can penetrate the
realities in question without some understanding of the universal doctrine of archetypes, to be found in all traditions though the language
in which it is clothed may speak not of archetypes but of "essences,"
"universals," "Divine Ideas," "lights" and so on.[3] Plato gave the
doctrine its paradigmatic European expression, but there is nothing
peculiarly Occidental about it.[4] By way of introduction, consider the
following sample of quotations:

> Things in every instance involve universals. . . . If there were
> no universals we could not speak of things as things. (*Kung-sun
> Lung*)[5]

> For the good and beautiful things in the world could never
> have been what they are, save that they were made in the
> image of the archetype, which is truly good and beautiful.
> (*Philo*)[6]

> A form is made in the resigned will according to the platform
> or model of eternity, as it was known in God's eternal wisdom
> before the times of this world. (*Jacob Boehme*)[7]

Every form you see has its archetype in the divine world, beyond space; if the form perishes what matter, since its heavenly model is indestructible? (*Rumi*)[8]

The Sages have been taught of God that this natural world is only an image and a copy of a heavenly and spiritual pattern; that the very existence of this world is based upon the reality of its celestial archetype. (*Michael Sendivogius*)[9]

All forms of being in this corporeal world are images of pure Lights, which exist in the spiritual world. (*Suhrawardi*)[10]

Formulations of this kind could be catalogued more or less indefinitely, but their burden is clear enough. Meister Eckhart provided a succinct statement of the doctrine: "Form is revelation of essence."[11] Everything that exists, whatever its modality, necessarily participates in universal principles, uncreated and immutable essences contained, in Guénon's words, in "the permanent actuality of the Divine Intellect."[12] Consequently, all phenomena, no matter how ephemeral or contingent, "translate" or "represent" or "reflect" these Divine Ideas in their own fashion at their own level of existence. Indeed, as Abu Bakr Siraj Ed-Din has stated, "If a world did not cast down shadows from above, the worlds below it would vanish altogether, since each world in creation is no more than a tissue of shadows entirely dependent on the archetypes in the world above."[13] Without participation in the Immutable, these shadows, these material forms, would be "a pure nothingness."[14] The fact that natural phenomena necessarily *participate* in the higher orders of Reality confers on them a sacred quality: "The sacred is the incommensurable, the transcendent, hidden within a fragile form belonging to this world."[15] Black Elk relates that "Crazy Horse dreamed and went out into the world where there is nothing but the spirits of things. That is the real world that is behind this one, and everything we see here is something like a shadow from that world."[16] This is not necessarily evidence of a surreptitious Platonic influence smuggled into the narrative by Neihardt, as several critics have averred,[17] but a universal principle expressed in the vocabulary of the Plains Indians. Elsewhere, in his account of the Horse Dance, the *wicasa wakan* says:

I looked about me and could see that what we then were doing was like a shadow cast upon the earth from yonder

vision in the heavens, so bright it was and clear. I knew the
real was yonder and the darkened dream of it was here.[18]

The analogies between the archetypes and the transitory material
forms of this world, "this changing and ephemeral multiplicity,"[19] give
to phenomena certain *qualitative* significances which render them
symbolic expressions of higher realities. A Buddhist lama stated the
principle precisely: "If we look at the world with . . . the eyes of the
spirit we shall discover that the simplest material object, nay anything
that is formed, be it by man or by nature, is a symbol, a glyph of a
higher reality and a deeper relationship of universal and individual
forces."[20] The same idea is implicit in Mircea Eliade's claim that *homo
religiosus* is also, necessarily, *homo symbolicus*.[21] Consider, too, Carl
Jung's insight that, "A view which interprets the symbolic expression
as the best possible formulation of a relatively *unknown* thing, which
for that reason cannot be more clearly or characteristically expressed,
is *symbolic*."[22]

A symbol may generally be defined as a reality of a lower order
which analogically shares the reality of a higher order of being. It follows that a properly constituted symbolism rests on the inherent and
objective qualities of phenomena and their relationship to spiritual
realities. Far from being a contrived and more or less arbitrary construct a symbol is, in Nasr's words,

> an aspect of *the ontological reality of things* and as such is inde-
> pendent of man's perception of it. The symbol is *the revelation
> of a higher order of reality in a lower order through which man*
> can be led back to the higher realm. To understand symbols
> is to accept the hierarchic structure of the Universe and the
> multiple states of being.[23]

Thus the science of symbolism is a kind of objective analogue of the gift
of "seeing God everywhere," that is, the awareness of the transparency
of phenomena and of the transcendent dimension which is present in
every cosmic situation.[24] The Hindu saint Ramakrishna, who could
fall into ecstasy at the sight of a lion, a bird, a dancing girl, exempli-
fied this gift—though in his case, Schuon adds, it was not a matter
of deciphering the symbolism but of "tasting the essences."[25] Eliade,
approaching the whole question from a different angle, has noted
how, for *homo religiosus*, everything in nature is capable of revealing
itself as a "cosmic sacrality," as a hierophany, whereas for our secular

age the cosmos has become "opaque, inert, mute; it transmits no message, it holds no cipher."[26]

The traditional and modern understandings of symbolism are radically different. In his classic study of the Gothic cathedral, Otto von Simson elucidated the "symbolist vision" which informed it:

> For us the symbol is an image that invests physical reality with poetic meaning. For medieval man, the physical world as we understand it has no reality except as a symbol. But even the term "symbol" is misleading. For us the symbol is the subjective creation of poetic fancy; for medieval man what we could call a symbol is the only objectively valid definition of reality. Maximus the Confessor . . . actually defines what he calls "symbolic vision" as the ability to apprehend within the objects of sense perception the invisible reality of the intelligible that lays beyond them.[27]

This is altogether consonant with Coleridge's definition of symbolism: "A symbol is characterized . . . above all by the translucence of the Eternal through and in the Temporal. It always partakes of the Reality which it renders intelligible; and while it enunciates the whole, abides itself as a living part of the Unity of which it is representative."[28] This understanding was shared by the Plains Indians though, of course, the idiom in which it found expression was quite different to that of Western theological discourse.

For our purposes the key lesson to be drawn from these general considerations is that visions, properly speaking, provide access to the archetypal realm and thereby unveil hitherto obscured spiritual *realities*. Discussing the outlook of archaic peoples, Eliade remarks that they want to live

> *in* the sacred or in close proximity to consecrated objects. . . .
> For man of all pre-modern societies, the *sacred* is equivalent to a *power*, and, in the last analysis, to *reality*. The sacred is saturated with *being*. Sacred power means reality and at the same time enduringness and efficacy. . . . Religious man deeply desires to *be*, to participate in *reality*, to be saturated with power.[29]

Visions will occur wherever the sense of the sacred remains alive—in other words, in all traditional worlds. This is because "The sense of the sacred is also the innate consciousness of the presence of God: it is to feel this presence sacramentally in symbols and ontologically in all things."[30] Only when this is properly understood can we begin to understand the place of visionary experience in Indian life.

Visions in Indian Life

The Plains Indians regarded visions as the royal road to knowledge and wisdom. The vision was the crucible in which a man's identity and vocation were forged—thus the cardinal significance of the Lakota rite of crying for a vision which was at one and the same time a purification, a prayer, a rite of passage, and an initiation, consummated by the "telling of the vision" to the elder/s who expounded its meaning for the benefit of both the visionary and the community as a whole. As we have already seen, the vision quest entailed various austerities and ascetic disciplines, practiced in solitude in the wild, in the hope of being visited by a spirit guide who would communicate to the aspirant the knowledge that would set him on his life's path. As Thomas Merton observed many years ago,

> The practice of "fasting for a vision" was once almost universal among North American Indians for whom it might almost be said that a certain level of "mysticism" was an essential part of growing up. . . . The Indian based his life on a spiritual illumination beyond the ordinary conscious level of psychic experience. . . . Such visions were taken for granted as a normal part of life in an archaic culture. They were an essential component in the concept of a mature human personality.[31]

In the "lamenting" the individual prayed for a vision; it was a quest, an act of solicitation. But visions could also come uninvited, often in late childhood, as they did with Black Elk and with White Bull, the Lakota warrior and nephew of Sitting Bull.[32]

Reviewing *Two Leggings: The Makings of a Crow Warrior* (1967), Merton wrote,

> What strikes us immediately is the concept Two Leggings has of biography. What is man's life? It consists primarily in a series of visions. His life is his "medicine." His autobiography is in some sense a description of the way his medicine bundle

was put together over the years. And the medicine bundle is the concretization of his spiritual and warlike "career."[33]

So it was with Black Elk, though in his case his calling was not that of the warrior but of the seer and healer. Visions could not only disclose a vocation but reveal a sacred name, inaugurate a new rite, bring healing. Black Elk explained "lamenting" to Joseph Brown this way:

> Every man can cry for a vision, or "lament"; and in the old days we all—men and women—"lamented" all the time. What is received through the "lamenting" is determined by the character of the person who does this, for it is only those people who are very qualified who receive the great visions, which are interpreted by our holy man, and which give strength and health to our nation.[34]

Crying for a vision tempered a man's character through prayer, making him more constantly mindful of the Creator. As Thomas Yellowtail tells us:

> Some men might seek different kinds of medicine power or understanding. They may want to be able to heal or doctor people. They may seek the answer to a question that is bothering them or their family or tribe. And above all, a man may want to pray in this way because this is a way to come closer to Acbadadea [the Creator]. In this rite each man awakens in his heart the knowledge of the Maker of All Things Above. A man may pray for any of those things because they would be helpful to him, his family, and his tribe, but a man must pray for virtue and the correct understanding with which to face life.[35]

The vision quest was informed by the belief in "a multitude of differentiated spirit beings or sacred powers" associated specifically with natural forms and forces (animals, trees, directions, wind, thunder, rain, and the like), or with a pervasive "life force or animating principle" with subtle qualities which could be transferred to human beings. Furthermore, these sacred mysteries tended "to coalesce into an ultimate unity expressed through polysynthetic terms such as the Lakota *Wakan-Tanka*."[36] Claude Lévi-Strauss, the influential French anthropologist, at least partially understood this view of the natural order when he wrote of "a metaphysical philosophy common to all the Sioux from the Osage in the south to the Dakota in the north, according to which things and beings are nothing but materialized forms of creative continuity."[37] Ohiyesa explained it in more concrete terms:

> The elements and majestic forces in nature, Lightning, Wind, Water, Fire, and Frost, were regarded with awe as spiritual powers, but always secondary and intermediate in character. We believed that the spirit pervades all creation and that every creature possesses a soul in some degree, though not necessarily a soul conscious of itself. The tree, the waterfall, the grizzly bear, each is an embodied Force, and as such an object of reverence.[38]

Black Elk recalled that Crazy Horse received his knowledge and power through lamentation which he practiced "many times a year," receiving visions of the Rock, the Shadow, the Badger, the Spotted Eagle, and a dancing horse (from whence came his name), taking into himself the qualities and powers of these forms. Joseph Brown:

> The Indian actually identifies himself with, or becomes, the quality or principle of the being or thing which comes to him in a vision, whether it be a beast, a bird, one of the elements, or really any aspect of creation. In order that this "power" may never leave him, he always carries with him some material form representing the animal or object from which he has received this "power."[39]

In the Indian outlook everything in the natural order is in some sense "animated." What does this mean? Schuon:

> It means, in principle and metaphysically, that whatever be the object envisaged, there springs from its existential center an ontological ray, made up of "being," "consciousness," and "life," whereby the object in question is attached, through its subtle or animic root, to its luminous and celestial prototype; from this it follows that in principle it is possible for us to attain the heavenly Essences by taking any thing whatever as starting point.[40]

This provides a key not only to the place of visions in Indian life but to the metaphysic of Nature which governs the whole tradition; the "polysynthetic animism" of the Indians, rooted in "this acute consciousness of the homogeneity of the world of phenomena," explains what Schuon calls their "spiritual naturism" and accounts for their "refusal to detach themselves from Nature and to become engaged in a civilization made up of artifices and servitudes, and carrying within itself the seeds of petrifaction as well as of corruption."[41]

The Great Vision

One day on the Little Bighorn River, when Black Elk is about nine years old, he hears a voice calling him, telling him that the Grandfathers are awaiting him: "It is time now; they are calling you."[42] The boy collapses and his limbs and face become badly swollen. Through the opening in the top of the tipi where he has been laid, Black Elk sees the Thunder Beings whom he had encountered in a vision several years earlier. He is taken up into the cloud world. Over the next twelve days he remains in an unconscious or semi-conscious state. His family fear for his life and summon one of the tribal medicine men, Whirlwind Chaser, the uncle of Black Elk's friend, Standing Bear. During this period Black Elk experiences the Great Vision, the spiritual watershed of his life.

In the cloud world Black Elk is greeted by a bay horse; "Behold me! My life-history you shall see." The horse wheels to the four cardinal points: in each direction there are twelve horses—black in the west, white in the north, buckskin in the south, and in the east sorrel. The bay horse tells Black Elk that he will take him to a council of Grandfathers. The sky then fills up with countless dancing horses which "changed into animals of every kind and into all the fowls that are, and these fled back to the four quarters of the world." Inside a tipi with a rainbow-door Black Elk finds the six Grandfathers, the Powers of the World, "older than men can ever be—old like hills, like stars." One of them says in a kindly voice, "Come right in and do not fear."

Each of the Grandfathers, associated with one of the six directions, has a gift and a special message for Black Elk about his future role. The first Grandfather (of the West) gives Black Elk a wooden cup of water which contains the sky (the power of life and healing) and a bow and arrows (the power of destruction). The Grandfather then runs to the West and turns into an emaciated black horse. The second Grandfather (North) tells Black Elk he will make a nation live and gives him a herb which revives the starving black horse who resumes the form of the first Grandfather. He also gives him "the power of the white giant's wing, the cleansing wind." The second Grandfather then runs to the north and becomes a white goose. The third Grandfather (East) shows Black Elk the Morning Star with two men flying beneath it, and gives him a peace pipe with a spotted eagle carved on the stem. He points out a red man who is transformed into a buffalo which in turn looks towards the sorrel horses which also become buffalo. The next Grandfather (South) gives Black Elk a flowering stick with birds in its branches: this is the living center of the nation. Black Elk sees in the shade of the flowering stick a village of people in the shape of a hoop; the stick, or tree, stands at the intersection of a red road running north-south, and a black road going from east to west. The red road, says the Grandfather, is good and brings blessings, the black road is the source of trouble and strife. This Grandfather transforms into an elk as do the buckskin horses in the south. The fifth Grandfather (Sky) turns into a Spotted Eagle and tells Black Elk of his special relationship with birds and his power to destroy enemies.

The encounter with the sixth Grandfather (Earth) is described by Black Elk this way:

> The sixth Grandfather was about to speak, he who was the Spirit of the Earth, and I saw that he was very old, but more as men are old. His hair was long and white, his face was all in wrinkles and his eyes were deep and dim. I stared at him for it seemed I knew him somehow; and as I stared, he slowly changed, for he was growing backwards into youth, and when he had become a boy, I knew that he was myself with all the years that would be mine at last. When he was old again, he said: "My boy, have courage, for my power shall be yours, and you shall need it, for your nation on earth will have great troubles. Come."[43]

Taking with him the gifts of water, bow and arrows, wind, a herb, the pipe, and a white wing, and accompanied by a formation of black, white, sorrel, and buckskin horses, Black Elk rides to a river where he sees a blue man enveloped in flames and dust. "The dust was floating all about him in the air, the grass was short and withered, the trees were wilting, two-legged and four-legged beings lay there thin and panting, and wings too weak to fly." Riders from the four directions attack the man but are unable to kill him; the task is completed by

Black Elk with his lightning spear. The dead man then turns into a turtle. Black Elk's feat is acclaimed by all of creation. "You see, I had been riding with the storm clouds, and had come to earth in the form of rain, and it was drought that I had killed with the power that the Six Grandfathers gave me."[44]

Black Elk now returns to earth and to his village where all the people are dying. But a voice tells him that the flowering stick, the pipe, and the white wing will revive them: "Give them now the flowering stick that they may flourish, and the sacred pipe that they may know the power that is peace, and the wing of the white giant that they may have endurance and face all the winds with courage." He plants the stick in the middle of the hoop; it turns into a tree under which all beings can live in peace and happiness. The Daybreak Star rises and all the people and the spirits of the dead walk with Black Elk along the red road, "a good nation walking in a sacred manner in a good land." This ghostly procession must now make four ascents, each steeper and more perilous than the last. After the first the people turn into animals; after the second they are fearful and restless, and leaves fall from the tree; the third ascent puts the people on the black road and the hoop of the nation is broken; the fourth ascent reveals horrific sights of suffering and starvation. Black Elk sees a man painted red and holding a lance; the man turns into a buffalo and near him a flowering herb with four blossoms springs up to replace the tree at the center of the hoop. Birds sing and the people are rejoicing. Black Elk tells us that the four ascents were the "generations I should know."

In the next phase of the vision Black Elk sees fighting, gunfire, and smoke with his people in retreat. Administering the power of his herb he transforms an emaciated horse into a beautiful stallion, "the chief of all horses." In a spectacle both "beautiful" and "terrible," the horse snorts lightning and summons a vast collection of prancing horses from the four directions. The horse sings:

> His voice was not loud, but it went all over the universe and filled it. There was nothing that did not hear, and it was more beautiful than anything can be. It was so beautiful that nothing anywhere could keep from dancing. The virgins danced, and all the circled horses. The leaves on the trees, the grasses on the hills and in the valleys, the waters in the creeks and in the rivers and the lakes, the four-legged and the two-legged and the wings of the air—all danced together to the music of the stallion's song.[45]

These horses are entrusted to Black Elk by the Grandfather of the West. Under the power of the stallion's song all created beings dance and Black Elk's people are restored to peace and plenty.

Black Elk is then taken to the center of the earth by two winged men, escorted by sixteen riders from the four directions. There he sees the "whole hoop of the world":

> And while I stood there I saw more than I can tell and I understood more than I saw; for I was seeing in a sacred manner the shapes of all things in the spirit, and the shape of all shapes as they must live together like one being. And I saw that the sacred hoop of my people was one of many hoops that made one circle, wide as daylight and as starlight, and in the center grew one mighty flowering tree to shelter all the children of one mother and one father. And I saw that it was holy.[46]

The winged men give him a sacred herb to plant. Before returning to the six Grandfathers, Black Elk sees a horned man amidst flames; the man is transformed into a gopher, then a deadly "soldier weed" and finally a skeleton.[47]

Black Elk returns to the six Grandfathers who again confer on him gifts and powers, and give him further instructions about saving his people. One of them says to Black Elk: "Grandson, all over the universe you have seen. Now you shall go back with power to the place from whence you came, and it shall happen yonder that hundreds shall be sacred, hundreds shall be flames."[48] The Grandfathers return to their directions and the rainbow sets in the east. After leaving the tipi a voice instructs him to look back where he sees a Spotted Eagle and where the rainbow tipi had stood, "the tall rock mountain at the center of the world." Black Elk finds himself alone, back on earth, walking towards his family's village where he enters the tipi and sees his parents tending a sick boy, himself. Whirlwind Chaser tells the parents that the boy has a sacred duty to perform and that he has the power of lightning. The parents attribute his cure to Whirlwind Chaser, who is rewarded with their best horse, but Black Elk knows that it was the work of the Grandfathers. He is sad that his parents "didn't seem to know that I had been so far away."

Reading the Vision

Black Elk's polyvalent vision can be read in several ways: an apocalyptic prophecy about the tragic destiny of his people; a spiritually transformative "hero's journey" through a series of trials and tribulations; a foretelling of his own life; a mystical panorama displaying the inter-relatedness of all natural forms, and the kinship of the living, the dead, and the yet unborn; a dynamic cosmic mandala revealing the multiple and hierarchical states of being and a *coincidentia oppositorum*; mythopoeic allegory carrying metaphysical, cosmological, anthropological, and moral teachings; a mystery play; a map of the psyche, a *mysterium coniunctionis*; a compendium of symbols both Lakotan and universal; a homage to the Lakotan tradition in which the Grandfathers might be seen as "the people" as a whole. In being all of these things it is also a condensation of the esoteric wisdom of the Lakota and indeed of the integral spirituality of the Plains Indians. And perhaps this is where its ultimate significance lies.

The Great Vision has been subjected to all manner of analyses and interpretations by scholars and commentators coming from a variety of vantage points. Many of these have sought to accommodate Black Elk's vision in disparate theoretical categories—historical, psychological, literary, postcolonial, and so on. This has often been a matter of trying to straitjacket the greater (the vision) in the lesser (this or that theory). Then, too, there have been more local and intensive inquiries into particular aspects of Black Elk's narrative. We might mention, for instance, Julian Rice's inquiry into the significance of the horses or Robert Sayre's explication of particular and specifically inflected Lakota symbols.[49] Others have scrutinized the vision chapter of *Black Elk Speaks* as a literary document, concentrating on Black Elk's storytelling technique and/or the ways in which Neihardt edited, embellished, and inflected the narrative, foregrounding some aspects and eliding others. Yet others, like Michael Steltenkamp and Damien Costello, have excavated the account for Christian influences and allusions. Some critics accent the presence of symbols and motifs which are found all over the globe; one simple example: the Flowering Tree bears an obvious resemblance to the Holy Sycamore of the Egyptians, the Tree of Life of the Judaic tradition, Odin's Yggdrassil in Norse myth, the Ceiba of the Mayans, the Vedic Banyan tree, and the Bodhi Tree under which Siddhartha attained enlightenment—to mention only a sample. Frank Waters finds in Black Elk's vision, "all the arcane meanings of the world's ancient myths."[50]

What is the vision's "message"? R. Todd Wise places the various commentaries into three groups, who respectively read it as (a) a non-universalistic Lakotan teaching (Julian Rice, Raymond DeMallie), (b) a veiled Christian message (Michael Steltenkamp, Damien Costello, Lucy Looks Twice), or (c) a Christian-Lakotan message with universal implications (Clyde Holler, Hilda Neihardt, Todd Wise).[51] Raymond DeMallie observes that

> Black Elk never stated succinctly what he considered the meaning of the vision; he left this to Neihardt to interpret. In one sense the meaning is that the powers of the Lakota universe exist and have the ability to aid mankind in all endeavors, to protect people from disease and from their enemies and to bring joy and contentment. These powers were not simply replaced by the Christian God whom Black Elk came to accept; instead, they represented an alternate approach to the unknowable, another path to the "other world." Therefore the vision was good and true and important to save for mankind.[52]

For Neihardt, the Great Vision revealed "the unity and holiness of all life and the brotherhood of man."[53] To put my own cards on the table, I think it is best understood as a universalist Lakota *theoria*, incidentally (and understandably) bearing traces of Christian imagery; its universalism derives not from any "syncretism" but from the fact that the vision fathoms the depths of this *particular* tradition (the primordial heritage of the Plains Indians) and *thereby* discloses the *sophia perennis* which is the inheritance of all humankind and which is beyond all forms. We cannot too often be reminded that, "Truth does not deny forms from the outside but *transcends them from within*."[54]

It is not my intention to rehearse or evaluate various understandings of the vision but only to offer a few general and provisional remarks. As a starting point we might recall the words of William James in *Varieties of Religious Experience* (1902):

> Our normal waking consciousness, rational consciousness as we call it, is but one special type of consciousness, whilst all about it, parted from it by the filmiest of screens, there lie potential forms of consciousness entirely different. We may go through life without suspecting their existence; but apply

the requisite stimulus, and at a touch they are there in all their completeness. . . . No account of the universe in its totality can be final which leaves these other forms of consciousness quite disregarded. How to regard them is the question. . . . At any rate, they forbid our premature closing of accounts with reality.[55]

Most of the scholarly accounts of the Great Vision provide illuminating insights (though these are often highly localized) and offer some guidance to readers who, having been transported into a strange and wondrous realm, perhaps stunned by the power of Black Elk's experience, feel disoriented and confused, and so seek clues to the vision's meaning. Nonetheless, *any* analysis is in some sense an impertinence, rather in the manner of those who seek to "psychoanalyze" a saint. "I saw more than I can tell and I understood more than I saw," declared Black Elk. Like all transformative encounters with the Numinous, ultimately his Great Vision remains ineffable.[56] In *Black Elk Speaks*, the *wicasa wakan* and John Neihardt captured something of the grandeur, the mystery, the beauty, the power of the vision. But, like a great work of art, or—to chance a more hazardous comparison— like a sacred scripture, the holy man's vision is what it is, no doubt amenable to various readings but in the end standing beyond analysis, beyond commentary, and quite out of reach of the sophistic contrivances of any deconstructionism. Indeed, to dissect it is to violate its integrity, to rob it of its vitality, unwittingly to turn it into a corpse from which the spirit has departed. Some of those who have made confident asseverations about Black Elk's visions would profit from a little more of what Keats called "negative capability"—"that is, when a man is capable of being in uncertainties, mysteries, doubts, without any irritable reaching after fact and reason."[57]

Like the world's revealed Scriptures, a vision such as Black Elk's is not without its paradoxes and ambiguities; its "meaning" is not easily quarried and indeed in some senses it must remain both elusive and inexhaustible. Frithjof Schuon's words on the Koran and other sacred texts might just as easily be applied to Black Elk's vision:

The seeming incoherence of these texts . . . always has the same cause, namely the incommensurable disproportion between the Spirit on the one hand and the limited resources of human language on the other: it is as though the poor and coagulated language of mortal man would break under the formidable pressure of the Heavenly Word into a thousand fragments, or as if God, in order to express a thousand truths, had but a dozen words at his disposal and so was compelled to make use of allusions heavy with meaning, of ellipses, abridgements, and symbolical syntheses.[58]

If we take Black Elk's vision to be, among other things, a profound testament concerning spiritual realities beyond the purview of any profane science or any rationalistic analysis—analysis, after all, is a form of decomposition—then our posture should be one of *receptivity*. It might be salutary to remind ourselves that Black Elk did not *create* his vision, he *received* it; he did not *author* the vision but only *transmitted* it. In some respects it may be said that a great deal of the recent scholarly discourse has obsessively focused on Black Elk and on Neihardt as individuals, missing the overarching truth that each man was an instrument of larger forces which are not to be accounted for in the categories of "biography" or of an impudent "psychoanalysis." Also germane are Mircea Eliade's observations nearly half a century ago about the study of religious phenomena:

> The majority of historians of religion *defend themselves* against the messages with which their documents are filled. This caution is understandable. One does not live with impunity in intimacy with "foreign" religious forms. . . . But many historians of religion end by *no longer taking seriously the spiritual worlds they study;* they fall back on their personal religious faith, or they take refuge in a materialism or behaviorism *impervious to every spiritual shock.*[59]

Considering Black Elk's vision, and groping towards an understanding of its perennial meaning and significance, we would do better to take up the attitude recommended by Karl Barth for those studying the Bible: "we must trust ourselves to reach eagerly for an answer which is really much too large for us, for which we are not fully ready, and of which we do not seem worthy, since it is a fruit which our own longing, striving, and inner labor have not planted."[60] We might, in this context, also ruminate on the words of another saintly figure who, like Black Elk, lived much of his life on the frontier between two religious traditions, Swami Abhishiktananda (Fr. Henri Le Saux): "spiritual experience . . . is the meeting place of the known and the unknown, the seen and the not-seen, the relative and the absolute."[61]

There are several traditional tests by which the higher orders of mystical illumination can be distinguished from lower-level psychic experiences of one kind and another (including the drug-induced) and from their simulacra: the mystical experience entails a loss of ego-identity and the dissolution of the knower-known dichotomy; it leaves the mystic in a state of adamantine certitude about the reality of what has been "seen";[62] it leads to a radical and enduring self-transformation, altering forever the trajectory of a life; it often leaves the person with certain powers—though these must never be pursued or valued as an end in themselves. Black Elk's Great Vision meets all these criteria.

Lastly, a few thoughts about Lakota cosmology in the context of the Great Vision. As Frithjof Schuon explains, the whole tradition of the North American Indians "is contained in the cross inscribed in the circle, from the viewpoint of geometric symbolism: the circle corresponds to the Sky, while the cross marks the Four Directions of space and all other quaternaries of the Universe; it also marks the vertical ternary Earth-Man-Sky, which puts the horizontal quaternary on three levels."[63] He goes on to suggest that Indian cosmology is founded, symbolically, on the numbers four and three, the first being "horizontal," the second "vertical," and on their combination in the number twelve. What Schuon terms "duodecimality" can thus be envisaged as three horizontal quaternaries, one above another, on a central axis. The cross and the circle symbolically combine the static, spatial circle of the earth (the horizon marked by four cardinal points) with the temporal and dynamic circle marked by the daily passage of the sun through morning, day, evening, and night, or by the annual cycle of the seasons. Crucial to this cosmological vocabulary is the notion of Man as Center—from both the horizontal and vertical perspective: man himself is identified with the cosmic tree, the *axis mundi*, and as such he unites the Sky above him and the Earth under his feet.[64]

This cosmology is brought vividly to life in Black Elk's vision. We need hardly labor the pervasive symbolism of the numbers three, four, and twelve, the seven directions, nor of the hoop, the cross of the red and black roads, and the flowering tree at its center. It might be said that just as medieval Christianity finds one of its fullest manifestations in Dante's *Comedia* so too Lakota cosmology is given one of its most sublime expressions in Black Elk's Great Vision. As Raymond DeMallie has observed,

The greatness of Black Elk's vision lies not in its uniqueness, but in its very representativeness. It synthesizes religious themes in Lakota culture and balances all aspects of the Lakota world: destruction and renewal, the powers of the earth and sky and of land and water, the four directions, the living and the nonliving (both dead and unborn). Perhaps its most striking feature is the representation of the circle of life as enclosing a central tree, symbolizing regeneration, with crossed roads from south to north and west to east, the former symbolizing life and harmony and colored red, the latter symbolizing warfare and destruction and colored black. . . . That the circle and the central tree, the axis mundi, are pancultural archetypes leads to many parallels with other religious traditions. But there is nothing in Black Elk's great vision that is foreign to Lakota culture.[65]

The great saints, sages, and mystics in any tradition manifest the quintessence, the peculiar genius of the dispensation in question, its unique spiritual aroma one might say, and they do so even when that genius is inflected in a distinctive or even idiosyncratic fashion. The various facets of a particular religious sensibility are revealed through a range of exemplary spiritual types. In the Christian tradition one need only consider the diversity of, let us say, Paul, Aquinas, Eckhart, Francis of Assisi, and Thérèse of Lisieux. Or to turn eastwards, Paramahamsa Ramakrishna is no less an embodiment of the Hindu tradition than Shankaracharaya or Ramana Maharshi. In Ramana, as Frithjof Schuon observes, "one meets ancient and eternal India again . . . the reincarnation of what is primordial and incorruptible," whilst Ramakrishna, a much more volatile personality and a more plastic spiritual type, was called at a particular moment in history to verify apparently discordant religious forms and to affirm their inner unity. Each of these great sages was not only an archetypal personification—if one be permitted a somewhat contradictory expression—of the Hindu tradition but each providentially fulfilled a spiritual need of the times in which they lived. So it was, and is, with Black Elk. Without surrendering anything of his human personality he became a medium of Lakota spirituality in its highest and most noble register, one in whom, in Neihardt's words, "the highest spiritual conceptions of his race have flowered in beauty and wisdom."[66] If the enigmatic Crazy Horse was the Lakota exemplar *par excellence* of the warrior-mystic ethos, Black Elk was the visionary holy man whose vocation was to preserve the ancestral wisdom of his people. Whatever his personal foibles and imperfections—and they don't seem to have added up to much—and whatever else might be said about the rest of his life, there can be no doubting that, as he himself so clearly and sometimes painfully understood, the Great Vision was the decisive event of his life, one with an abiding significance far beyond the mortal life of a single individual who, like all others, became "grass upon the hills."

5

Preserving Black Elk's Legacy:
John G. Neihardt, Joseph Epes Brown, and Their Critics

No author, either white or Indian, has yet written about
the Lakota people in terms that bring their traditional religion and
culture to life more convincingly than John G. Neihardt.
Raymond DeMallie[1]

America has not produced another scholar of the Native
American traditions who combined in himself, as did Joseph
Brown, profound spiritual and intellectual insight and traditional
understanding, the deepest empathy for those traditions,
nobility of character and generosity.
Seyyed Hossein Nasr[2]

The sketch of Black Elk's life earlier in this study flagged the pivotal
role John Neihardt and Joseph Brown played in the preservation of
the medicine man's occult knowledge of the Lakota tradition and his
account of his own visionary experiences. We turn now to a more
extended consideration of their respective contributions and to some
of the fervid controversies which have accumulated around these two
figures and their books.

John G. Neihardt

In recent decades Neihardt's role in the creation of *Black Elk Speaks*
has come under trenchant scrutiny. Discussing the reception of *Black
Elk Speaks*, Clyde Holler claimed that "it has become painfully clear
that some people greatly prefer the nineteenth century traditionalist
who was *constructed* by Neihardt and Brown to the *real* Black Elk,
the twentieth-century religious leader in dialogue with Christianity."[3]
In modern discourse the term "romantic" has a penumbra of pejorative associations with sentimentality, nostalgia, an idealization of the
"primitive," a rose-tinted view of the past. And these are the charges
brought against Neihardt by McCluskey, Holler, Rice, Powers, Stover,
and others. Some of the criticisms leveled at Neihardt are cogent,
others, to say the least, are misdirected. Rather than surveying the burgeoning field of writings about Neihardt and Black Elk we shall con-

sider only a representative sample of viewpoints. Sustained critiques of Neihardt, as well as more sporadic volleys, can, at the risk of some over-simplification, be briefly summarized as follows:

✧ *Neihardt adhered to a triumphalist and progressivist racism:* Neihardt's outlook, for all his sympathy for and understanding of the Indians, was at least tinged by racism, evident in his ideas about the superiority and inevitable triumph of the "Aryans," celebrated in *The Song of the Indian Wars* as "the driving breed/the takers of the world/The makers and bringers of the law."[4] Blair Whitney accents Neihardt's affirmation of "the poetic, imaginative, and forceful [Aryan] spirit which he sees as the creative source behind the works of Western civilization from the *Iliad* to the Conestoga wagon."[5] Neihardt was also an apostle of the nineteenth-century pseudo-mythology of "Progress." The Italian scholar Elémire Zolla presses this kind of charge, claiming that Neihardt subscribed to "the progressivist frigidity of an Andrew Jackson or a Theodore Roosevelt." Zolla adduces an illustrative passage from an interview Neihardt gave to a Phoenix newspaper in 1966:

> It was [said Neihardt] an old culture being destroyed by a new culture . . . what we did to the Indians was not peculiar in history. You always find when a great mass of human beings are moving they are utterly without morals or pity. They are to be compared to flood, fire, and wind. You can't sentimentalize about it because you are dealing with an unhuman power— the stream of history. It's a pity when somebody falls by the wayside, but if we were God and could see everything, we might feel differently about it.[6]

✧ *Neihardt perpetuated the romantic motif of "the vanishing Indian":* Overlapping the first general criticism is the view that Neihardt was a romantic poet who gave us an idealized, sanitized, and naïve portrait of Black Elk and the old ways, reinforcing the "vanishing Indian" trope popularized by writers like Zane Grey.[7] In a 1972 article entitled *"Black Elk Speaks:* and So Does John Neihardt," Sally McCluskey exposed some of the ways in which Neihardt's biases motivated his editorial interventions in the treatment of the original transcript (this itself already being twice-mediated, by Ben Black Elk as translator and by Enid Neihardt as note-taker). Following McCluskey, in a dense and closely argued article published in 1984, Clyde Holler did some intensive comparative analysis of *Black Elk Speaks* and the original transcript, particularly those segments dealing with the ritual context of Black Elk's narrative and with the Ghost Dance. Holler demonstrated how Neihardt thereby compromised Black Elk's purpose—the preservation and continuance of the religion of the Pipe (including the Ghost Dance)—and distorted his theology (his unwavering faith in the old rituals and in the sacred mission vouchsafed by his Great Vision). "The literary strategy of *Black Elks Speaks*," wrote Holler, "becomes clear when considered in the light of Neihardt's belief [not shared by Black Elk], that the militant perversion of the Ghost Dance was the tragic mistake of the Sioux people."[8] Black Elk's purpose in the ritualized giving of his vision to Neihardt was to preserve the ancestral ways, to "make the tree flower": in stark contrast, the final message of Neihardt's literary text was that "the tree was dead."[9] Neihardt's agenda is conspicuously evident in the narrative's profoundly melancholic ending which has a broken and despairing Black Elk apparently accepting the defeat of his people and the failure of his own sacred mission:

> And I, to whom so great a vision was given in my youth,—you see me now a pitiful old man who has done nothing, for the nation's hoop is broken and scattered. There is no center any longer, and the sacred tree is dead.[10]

This touching epitaph, so frequently quoted, was not only invented by Neihardt but it conveyed a false impression derived from the old man's ritualized attitude misunderstood by the poet. Raymond DeMallie:

> The sense of irreversible tragedy that pervades *Black Elk Speaks* reflects Neihardt's interpretation. . . . With its unrelenting sense of defeat, *Black Elk Speaks* became an eloquent literary restatement of the theme of the vanishing American. . . . Sorrow and despair were outward expressions of traditional Lakota prayer, for the efficacy of prayer depended upon making oneself humble and pitiable before the powers of the universe. But this was a ritual attitude, not an expression of hopelessness.[11]

While scholars like McCluskey, Holler, and DeMallie were intent on laying bare the intent and effect of Neihardt's intrusions, they affirmed the beauty, power, and deeper truth of *Black Elk Speaks* and acknowledged Neihardt's considerable literary skills even while regretting his lack of ethnographic rigor and objectivity. Several more recent critics have been more censorious in their indictment of Neihardt. Thus Thomas Couser:

> To end the narrative *conclusively* with the Battle of Wounded Knee is the literary equivalent of killing off the survivors; it is a subtle but insidious form of cultural genocide. The effect is to encourage white readers to indulge in an uncomplicated pathos at the demise of a noble way of life rather than compel them to contemplate its survival in assimilated forms.[12]

William K. Powers sees *Black Elk Speaks* as one of the "fabrications of white men" about the Indians.[13] Rice suggests that it "may perhaps be relegated to the ranks of nineteenth century curios, reflecting white misconceptions of Indians."[14] Another critic of Neihardt is a recent biographer of Black Elk. After dedicating his book, in a back-handed compliment, to "that glorious amateur John G. Neihardt," Sam Wellman disparages his recording method as "amateurish, decades behind current scholarship," refers to Neihardt's "many errors because Black Elk was too deep a subject for his comprehension," claims that Mari Sandoz was much more knowledgeable about the Lakota than Neihardt, and dismisses the ending of *Black Elk Speaks* as "drivel."[15]

✧ *Neihardt's own Platonic-Christian perspective colored and distorted his understanding of Black Elk and of Lakota tradition:* Julian Rice is the leading proponent of this view:

> Neihardt was a Christian poet in the typological tradition with a strong, consistent view of history as providential progress. His relatively conventional vision foregrounds Platonic dualism and Christian universalism in his epic poetry, and from that standpoint he edited the Black Elk interviews for *Black Elk Speaks.*[16]

Neihardt's Christian background, it is said, underpinned the motif of the white man's "Manifest Destiny" (a pervasive theme in European writings about the West during the span of Neihardt's life, often buttressed by a repellent Social Darwinism).[17] In similar vein William K. Powers: "I believe that *Black Elk Speaks* and the Black Elk myth, as opposed to the Black Elk truth, are so successful because Neihardt and others have consciously molded a character that conforms to the Judeo-Christian model of worldliness, suffering, salvation."[18] Powers, one of Neihardt's more captious critics, goes so far as to claim that *Black Elk Speaks* is "a form of literary imperialism" which obscures rather than clarifies Lakota religion.[19]

✧ *Neihardt was discomforted by Black Elk's conversion to Catholicism and erased its significance in the narrative:* This reproof, from Michael Steltenkamp and others, stands at an odd angle to the claim that Neihardt's Christian/Platonic framework unduly shaped his treatment of *Black Elk Speaks.* Steltenkamp suggests that Neihardt's nostalgic and poetic story privileged "the vanishing American" and the romance of the "old ways" at the expense of a more balanced treatment of Black Elk's testimony and ignored the last fifty years of the medicine man's life. According to Steltenkamp, Black Elk himself was aggrieved that Neihardt had "perpetrated an injustice against him for not mentioning his many years as a catechist."[20]

✧ *Neihardt's project in* Black Elk Speaks *violated the oral tradition to which the holy man belonged:* Neihardt, say these critics, was unable to overcome the more or less insuperable barriers of his own whiteness, his own language, and the literate modes of the Western tradition: "between the mythic world that Black Elk inhabited and recreated and the world we inhabit there remains a gulf created not just by language but by written texts."[21] Writing itself profanes the oral tradition. *Black Elk Speaks* is essentially an attempt to preserve in written form the oral testimony of a non-literate Indian elder. Some Native American commentators have repudiated this kind of project in principle, regardless of the particularities of the case. Thus the well-known Indian activist, Russell Means: "[Writing] itself epitomizes the European concept of 'legitimate' thinking; what is written has an importance that is denied the spoken. My culture, the Lakota, has an oral tradition, so I ordinarily reject writing. It is one of the white world's ways of destroying the cultures of non-European people, the imposing of an abstraction over the spoken relationship of people."[22] In similar vein Dale Stover, writing from a postcolonial perspective, observes that the retelling of Black Elk's narrative "involved relocating Lakota oral discourse within the domain of European written discourse in which the editorial shaping by Neihardt and Brown necessarily reflected their cultural understanding of what Black Elk meant."[23]

More succinctly, Thomas Couser: "in the end, we see Black Elk not face to face but through a gloss, whitely."[24]

As well as these general and far-reaching criticisms of Neihardt there are more specific reproaches about Neihardt's treatment of Black Elk's narrative, especially those likely to alienate Euro-American readers. These charges have been pleaded most tellingly by Holler, who alerts us to the following editorial infringements: the omission of the stories about an old woman being birthed by a buffalo, and a priest who died after interfering in a Lakotan rite; the obscuration of the visionary refrain of Indian conquest of the *wasichus*, as can be seen, for instance, in the elided passages about the "soldier weed";[25] the disappearance of most of Black Elk's allusions and references to Catholicism.[26] Whilst acknowledging that the "beauty and power" of the narrative derive, in part, from Neihardt's literary art, Holler concludes that "the ultimate message and theology of *Black Elk Speaks*— and not merely the chronology and diction—are Neihardt's, not Black Elk's."[27] Frithjof Schuon was also critical of Neihardt's liberties with Black Elk's narrative: "Black Elk's dictation was a real message—it would have been better, after all, [for Neihardt] to have renounced all attempts at stylization and amplification; he should have presented his notes as they were."[28]

*   *   *

We owe a debt of gratitude to the various scholars who have identified the ways in which Neihardt might have modified Black Elk's testimony by comparing Neihardt's finished text to his daughter's stenographic notes and transcripts, thus helping us to ponder anew various aspects of Black Elk's life and message. Sally McCluskey's article of 1972, Clyde Holler's 1984 JAAR article, and the publication of Raymond DeMallie's *The Sixth Grandfather*, marked a breakthrough in our understanding of the ways in which Neihardt's beliefs and attitudes sometimes ran counter to Black Elk's own convictions and purposes. Brian Holloway's 2003 comparative study, *Interpreting the Legacy: John Neihardt and "Black Elk Speaks,"* also provides new insights. The emergent scholarly skepticism about Neihardt's editorial influence has been a healthy antidote to more naïve and romantic understandings which simply took Neihardt's assurances at face value. These comparative studies allow us to identify at least four categories of editorial interference. The first is when Neihardt's editorial changes run counter to Black Elk's own convictions and purposes; the omissions and distortions about the Ghost Dance provide a salient example.

The second is when the author eliminates or simplifies certain sections of Black Elk's story. As Frithjof Schuon notes, "Neihardt felt obliged to simplify the 'great vision'—he was always worried about overlong passages and complications—and in that respect future commentators will have no choice but to resort to the original version given in *The Sixth Grandfather*."[29] Neihardt should, at the least, have noted these editorial changes in his preface. However, to the poet's credit, he meticulously preserved all the stenographic field notes and transcripts so these distortions, simplifications, and eliminations are, for the most part, transparent for readers sufficiently interested to compare these documents.

The third line of criticism is that Neihardt stylized and poeticized Black Elk's language to suit his own tastes and purposes. Brian Holloway reminds us that McCluskey's earlier study finds that Brown's diction and cadence in *The Sacred Pipe* are prosaic while Neihardt's are poetic. "The assumption is that since Brown views himself as a transcriber and that since Neihardt is a poet, we will see a more actively poetic diction in *Black Elk Speaks*." However, Holloway adds a caution, "Yet recall that profound statements tend to sound poetic." Holloway then provides several examples "to help us notice just how 'poetic' Brown's text becomes." He then asks, "Is the truth perhaps that religious expression tends to be formal and incantatory in tone?"[30]

The fourth category of editorial intervention has generated the most heated debate; it concerns Neihardt's addition of material that is not found in the stenographic notes or transcription. In Neihardt's defense, many observers conclude that the poet's augmentations were motivated by his deep understanding of Black's Elk thoughts and feelings which were not necessarily articulated verbally. It has also been pointed out that Neihardt and the holy man had other encounters and conversations which were not recorded in Enid's transcript. Perhaps the most conspicuous editorial addition is the often-quoted end of *Black Elk Speaks* when Neihardt portrays Black Elk as saying, "the nation's hoop is broken and scattered. There is no center any longer, and the sacred tree is dead."[31] Is this a conscious distortion by Neihardt or did he believe this represented Black Elk's thinking? Critics of this elegiac ending tend to forget that Neihardt presents a more hopeful and undoubtedly more accurate picture of Black Elk's thought in his prayer at Harney Peak when, after saying that "the tree is withered," he petitions the Great Spirit, "O make my people live."[32] In any event, there is ample evidence that these closing lines of *Black Elk Speaks* were based on the poet's honestly-held beliefs, shared at the time by many independent observers. For example, in late 1945 Neihardt reported to the U.S. Indian Office that the conditions on Pine Ridge had deteriorated such that "the Oglalas simply are not any longer a tribe in the social sense. . . . Their old culture is dead. They recognize no leader. They are mostly just poor people living together in a land that cannot support them all, and laboring under psychological, social, and economic handicaps."[33]

In the light of the foregoing criticisms of Neihardt it has become commonplace for scholars to insist that *The Sixth Grandfather* provides us with a more reliable narration than *Black Elk Speaks*. Such commentators would do well to heed Brian Holloway's caveat: "Critics who rely on the transcripts of the interviews as though they were the entire teaching Black Elk communicated to Neihardt must recall several points":[34]

First, the typed transcripts Enid Neihardt made convert her shorthand, taken in the field, into regular orthography. This shorthand often employs "short forms" and contains explanatory annotations in the normal handwriting. This is not necessarily clear from reading DeMallie's edited collation. Second, the transcripts do not reflect other situations intended or created by Black Elk to teach John Neihardt: elaborate Lakota ceremonials and candid discussion not set down in writing, such as Black Elk's first encounter with Neihardt, his commentary as they walked at the Wounded Knee site, or his actions and statement on the final hike up Harney Peak; changes in tone or voice; and conversations at home (see H. Neihardt, *Black Elk* throughout for example). Third, John Neihardt possessed a phenomenal recall, as displayed late in life when he recited hundreds of lines of poetry from memory. Fourth, Neihardt relied on the entire experience—not just the transcripts prepared by Enid, which he carefully employed—in writing BES and in determining how the presentation could fulfill Black Elk's wishes. Certainly, in so doing John Neihardt repoeticized the often tangled transcripts and reinforced chronological order to ensure the visionary experience appeared as the book's core. And naturally, sections of BES receive emphasis or the reverse with respect to the transcripts but with a poet's regard for the holy man's fccling. The final result is a book that, like a medicine bundle or a hologram, is a bit of the whole it represents.[35]

What else is to be said of these criticisms of Neihardt? Well, a great deal *could* be said but here, rather than give an exhaustive account of the on-going scholarly altercations, we will restrict ourselves to a few general observations. There can be no doubt that Neihardt left a subjective imprint on Black Elk's testimony. How could he not? He brought to his task his own motives, assumptions, values and, no doubt, some of the prejudices of the age; he was existentially involved in this project. But the question remains: how much weight should be assigned to the various censures made of Neihardt, who has been so central to the preservation of Black Elk's legacy? My own view, stated briefly, is that the controversies of the last twenty-five years of Black Elk-Neihardt scholarship, while often instructive, have obscured one central and abiding truth: Black Elk was heir to a primordial wisdom which we are in a much better position to understand because of the profoundly important work of Neihardt; this remains the case in spite of the inevitable limitations and imperfections in the work he carried out. Thanks to his intelligence, empathy, and dedication we have in *Black Elk Speaks* a monument of the Lakota tradition which will still be standing when the scholarly feuds have been long forgotten. As Brian Holloway has tartly remarked, "Neither the arcana of neoscholastic deconstruction nor the colonialist desire to appropriate *Black Elk Speaks* for sectarian causes has produced much more than sets of opposites annihilating each other."[36] In any case, the main quarry should not be Neihardt but the ancestral wisdom vouchsafed to Black Elk. Moreover, one can only concur with the wise words of Vine Deloria Jr.:

> The very nature of great religious teachings is that they encompass everyone who understands them and personalities become indistinguishable from the transcendent truth that is expressed. So let it be with *Black Elk Speaks*. . . . That [it] speaks to us with simple and compelling language about an aspect of human experience and encourages us to emphasize the best that dwells within is sufficient.[37]

It might also be said that *Black Elk Speaks* and the *wicasa wakan* himself transcend and overwhelm the critical categories of recent scholarship.

Much commentary over the last half-century is littered with an altogether dismissive attitude to the idea of the "noble savage," often seen as a sentimental and fanciful idea associated with a "romantic" outlook—a kind of childishness attributed to both Neihardt and Joseph Brown which, it is supposed, we have now outgrown. One might almost say that this has become the very calling-card of Black Elk scholars. Frithjof Schuon offers this corrective:

> It is a curious fact that many people love the Indians, but that hardly anyone dares admit it; unless they admit it with certain reservations, which all too ostentatiously allow them to disidentify themselves from Rousseau's "good savage" as well as from Cooper's "noble savage"; no one wishes to be taken for a child. Doubtless there is nothing worth retaining in the unrealistic sentimentalities of a Rousseau, and the least that can be said is that the Indians have no need of them; but as for the "noble savage," this idea is not drawn entirely "out of thin air," if only for the simple reason that warlike peoples, by the very fact that they regularly and vocationally court suffering and death and have a cult of self-mastery, possess nobility and grandeur by the nature of things.[38]

One of the more interesting commentators on *Black Elk Speaks* is the Italian philosopher and historian of religions, Elémire Zolla. In *The Writer and the Shaman* (1969), Zolla evinces little enthusiasm for Neihardt's work as a whole, poetic and otherwise, finding him an "undistinguished" writer, the aspiring "romantic bard" of the "Aryan" subjugation of the West, a versifier of "pantingly fierce tone" and "clumsy magniloquence." Despite his deep knowledge of Indian ways and his generous sympathy for their culture, Neihardt's work, both before and after his encounter with Black Elk, is, in Zolla's view, fatally marred by a fault shared by so many commentators, today as then:

> What is missing is the one thing that would transcend the limitations of entertainment literature with all that is catchily superficial patchwork in it: *the abandonment of the point of view of "civilization."* Neihardt could not reach it by himself. In middle age, however, he was singularly fortunate. He encountered a sublime religious figure, Black Elk.[39]

Otherwise, says Zolla, Neihardt might well have remained "the regional storyteller of Nebraska and one of the last provincial versifiers,"[40] or in the dismissive words of Mick McAllister, "a minor anachronism of a poet."[41] (It should be noted that Zolla's assessment of Neihardt's literary standing is not shared by a good many distinguished writers and scholars—N. Scott Momaday, Frank Waters, Alvin M. Josephy Jr., Dee Brown, and Vine Deloria Jr. among them—who have found much to admire and several of whom have argued that Neihardt's modest literary reputation is not commensurate with his achievement.)

On Zolla's view, *Black Elk Speaks* is a somewhat aberrant work in Neihardt's literary trajectory. Neihardt brought to *Black Elk Speaks* his rich experience of Indian cultures and his considerable if hitherto somewhat misdirected poetic gifts. But his role, as Zolla sees it, might be described as *mediumistic*: he became the conduit between the Lakota sage and the white world. Neihardt himself described his role in this way: "I think [Black Elk] knew I was the tool—no, the medium—he needed for what he wanted to get said. And my attitude toward what he has said is one of religious obligation."[42] In a strange way the nature of Neihardt's role is confirmed by the fact that despite the noble service he performed in recording Black Elk's reminiscences and in rendering them into a coherent, poetic, and evocative narrative pervaded by a kind of spiritual lyricism, if one may so put it, Neihardt was not personally transformed by this encounter. As Zolla observes, "he was merely a means, similar to a medium who, after having served alien powers, returns to his narrow, cramped world, a world whose ideology is precisely that of a Carl Sandburg."[43] Sally McCluskey, while praising Neihardt's poetic accomplishments in *Black Elk Speaks*, also affirms that the poet was "for Black Elk, a portal through which his vision could pass to the world."[44]

Zolla's reading of Neihardt accounts for many tensions and paradoxes in Neihardt's life and work which have puzzled writers in this field. It also disarms those critiques which rest on biographical and textual evidence from the rest of Neihardt's output. We can concede that much of Neihardt's work is marred by his own predilections and by the contemporary prejudices to which he was not altogether immune—although it must also be said that many scholars have imprisoned an imaginary Neihardt in an ideological/theological straitjacket of their own making. At various points Neihardt has been seen as triumphalist racist, Christian providentialist, socialist firebrand, a romantic reactionary, a rabid progressivist, literary fraudster, neo-Platonist, a crypto-Marxist, an evangelical Puritan, a colonialist oppressor, and as a proto-New Ager! In fact Neihardt was a complex personality with a supple sensibility, certainly not a rigid ideologue or crusader to be so easily pigeon-holed. But leaving aside the questions raised by these simplistic and contradictory characterizations, *Black Elk Speaks* is a *singular* work: it is *only* in this work that Neihardt meets Zolla's fundamental criterion for any adequate understanding of Lakota tradition, precisely "the abandonment of the point of view of civilization." Neihardt's writing in this particular text was *inspired*— "in-the-spirit"—in a way which is clearly not the case elsewhere in his uneven *oeuvre*. And the key surely is Black Elk himself, his spiritual radiance and the almost telepathic communication which he developed with the poet who, for his part, showed what we might call a mystical receptivity to the holy man's message. Consider the following words from Neihardt:

> A strange thing happened often while I was talking with Black Elk. Over and over he seemed to be quoting from my poems. Sometimes I quoted my stuff to him, which when translated into Sioux could not retain much of its literary character, but the old man immediately recognized the ideas as his own. There was very often an uncanny *merging of consciousness* between the old fellow and myself, and I felt it and remembered it.[45]

Neihardt claimed that *Black Elk Speaks* would be "the first absolutely Indian book thus far written. It is all out of the Indian consciousness."[46] If we take his words about a "merging of consciousness" seriously—and why should we not?—this contention is not to be so easily scoffed at by clever fellows in academia. As Raymond DeMallie has noted, often "critics [have] missed the real dynamic of the book, the electric energy of the meeting of two like minds from two different cultures."[47] Nor should we be too hasty in dismissing Neihardt's claim about the familiar passages at the beginning and end of the book which were his own poetic creations but which were, he said, "what [Black Elk] would have said if he had been able."[48] As Sally McCluskey has so aptly remarked, "Neihardt listened to Black Elk's story with a poet's ear, and he retold it with a poet's gifts. *Black Elk Speaks*, and Neihardt, under 'religious obligation,' gave that speech to the white world; but his own voice, giving form and beauty to that utterance, is softly audible behind every word."[49] Similarly Ruth Heflin: "*Black*

Elk Speaks is a collage . . . not only of a polyphony of Indian voices telling their stories with a sometimes indirect, sometimes overt Euro-American voice chiming in, but also of (at least) two individual souls interpreting the symbols of two seemingly different perceptions of the world that are often remarkably similar."[50] These observations from McCluskey and Heflin strike a judicious balance between the early reception of the book in which Neihardt's contribution was more or less invisible and the more recent deconstructive fixation with Neihardt's distortions (both real and putative).

Zolla also helps to explain not only the (temporary) transmutation of Neihardt's sensibility but the alchemical transformation of his literary style. As N. Scott Momaday, himself an Indian writer of some distinction, has noted:

> Even though he could not understand the language that Black Elk spoke, we cannot doubt, I think, that [Neihardt] discerned quite readily the rhythms, the inflections, and alliterations of the holy man's speech. . . . With the rhythms and pacing well produced, we have a masterpiece of transformation of the oral tradition from one language and culture into another without loss of the essential spirit of the original narrative. . . . He brought extraordinary care, sympathy, and dedication to the task of faithfully reproducing the essence of the speech.[51]

After comparing *Black Elk Speaks* with Enid Neihardt's full transcript, carefully examining John Neihardt's editorial interventions, Michael Castro concluded that

> Unlike most other poets who took liberties in translating Indian materials, Neihardt's changes tend to read like extensions of the informant's consciousness, reflecting less the white writer's independent and impressionistic judgment than a hard-earned mutual understanding and trust. Often, Neihardt relates, reaching this understanding proved 'a grueling and difficult task requiring much patient effort and careful questioning of the interpreter.' The degree of mutual commitment to the project and the spiritual affinity that quickly developed between the two men appear to be the main sources of the unique personal rapport that determined the ultimate success of the translation.[52]

Before leaving this discussion of Neihardt it is also worth noting that though much of his work is indeed tinged with nostalgic romanticism, it is far from the case that this was always the dominant note. Consider this excerpt from a letter Neihardt wrote to the Secretary of the Interior soon after his encounter with Black Elk:

> The simple fact about [the Oglala] is that they cannot be turned into white men and as a people cannot be supervised successfully after our fashion. They are visionary, lively, and improvident for very good reasons. One feels that they as a people have lost their self-respect and that *the only way they could be made really happy and prosperous would be through some revival of their own courageousness and their own religion.* . . . What a pity it seems that these people, who are living now in what amounts to a social vacuum, could not be *encouraged to revive and cherish their ancient culture to the end that they might develop a proud self-consciousness.* . . . I know this is a dream for the reason that the modern world would not allow it but it is not so foolish as it may sound.[53]

Ponder, too, Neihardt's observation in an address at Wayne State College in 1954, that the real victors at Wounded Knee "were the defeated," for "they had seen the great vision of the unity and holiness of all life and the brotherhood of man."[54] Whatever Neihardt's shortcomings, we cannot doubt that his role in creating *Black Elk Speaks* was providentially appointed. Nor can it be denied that this book has played an exigent role in the preservation and dissemination of an imperiled Lakota esoterism from which the modern world may yet learn much. Raymond DeMallie reminds us that

> If Neihardt had never been interested in the Lakotas, and, particularly, if he had never talked with Black Elk . . . our knowledge of the old Lakota way of life would be much poorer. We would know far less about the Lakota concept of the sacred, of visions and of the powers that rule their universe. Through his work we have an invaluable perspective, an empathetic one, based on his particular life experiences and his readiness and ability to explore the domain of the "other world". . . . We honor him as he honored his aged Lakota teachers; together,

the wisdom and beauty of their words have left our world greener and more fruitful.[55]

This is well said. But it doesn't go far enough: without John Neihardt we would not have had intimate access to one of the most extraordinary visionaries and mystics of our era and would be without one of the most luminous spiritual documents of the twentieth century.

Joseph Epes Brown

What, it might be asked, are the ideal credentials for a non-native writing about the spiritual legacy of the American Indians? Well, here at least are some of them: intellectual discernment in doctrinal and spiritual matters, nourished by an understanding of the *sophia perennis* which underlies all integral traditions; fluency in the symbolic vocabulary at hand; a direct personal immersion in the traditional religious life of the peoples in question, guided by a qualified master or adept able to explain authoritatively the meaning of the phenomena encountered; a detachment from such sentimentalities and delusions of modernism as cultural evolutionism, progressivism, and historicism, to name three closely related follies; a moral integrity and probity of character which ensures that the inquiry is not unduly contaminated by subjective prejudices and ambitions. The last criterion might puzzle some but it is of critical import: the Plains Indians themselves and the various forms in which they expressed their spiritual genius exhibited an aquiline nobility and a grandeur which can only be fully appreciated by those with something of these same qualities in their own souls. If it further be asked how many writers on American Indian religions satisfy these criteria, then one can only answer, precious few! But one such was Joseph Epes Brown.

Brown's most enduring contribution was the compiling and editing of *The Sacred Pipe*. This alone would have assured him an honorable place amongst those who have strived to keep alive the ancient wisdom of the Plains Indians. But to that signal contribution must be added two others: the rest of Brown's writings on the Indians, most notably the collection of essays, *The Spiritual Legacy of the American Indian* (1982); and his pioneering role in unshackling the study of Native American religion from anthropology and establishing it as an independent field within the wider discipline of the history of religions. *Teaching Spirits: Understanding Native American Religious Traditions* (2001) is a compilation of Brown's lecture notes and other writings, edited by Emily Cousins with help from Brown's wife and daughter; it charts a thematic approach to the subject and sheds some light on Brown's own teaching practice. Some account of Brown's academic contribution can also be found in Åke Hultkrantz's Introduction to the 2007 edition of *The Spiritual Legacy of the American Indian.* Given that Joseph Brown's work beyond *The Sacred Pipe* is still too little known, it is worth quoting at length the words of Peter Nabokov, written to mark the appearance of *Teaching Spirits*:

> In this medicine bag of empathetic and insightful essay-lectures, the legacy of a preeminent scholar of American Indian traditions is opened. . . . The late Joseph Brown was a legendary mentor whose gentility and grace in person and on the page lent dignity and depth to the indigenous ways of knowledge and ceremony he passed on to others. Here we have Brown's thoughts on themes that preoccupied his scholarly and lecturing life: Indian concepts of time and space, language and song, animals and hunting and nature, and varieties of ritual practice. But Brown is always probing beneath these topics to a deeper almost wordless realm, where he provokes us to ask how these American Indian ways of knowledge might, in turn, teach us to become fully human.[56]

Whether starting from a concern with the preservation of Lakota tradition or from a scholarly vantage point, it is widely recognized that *The Sacred Pipe* is a seminal work whose significance can hardly be overstated. Nevertheless, it has received far less attention than *Black Elk Speaks* and has certainly not had anything like the impact on the popular consciousness. There are two readily apparent reasons: unlike its predecessor, and despite Black Elk's palpable presence in the book, it has neither a captivating narrator nor a spellbinding narrative; secondly, it encompasses a detailed exposition of matters—metaphysical, cosmological, and ceremonial—which are beyond the reach of many readers. It is, in the proper sense of the word, an *esoteric* work, which is not to say that its outer layers are not accessible to almost anyone.

Some of the criticisms of Neihardt were also made against Brown. Amidst the many acclamations of *The Sacred Pipe* three inter-related criticisms demand attention here. To state them as briefly as possible: Brown was not an objective observer/commentator but, like Neihardt, one encumbered by a "romantic" agenda; more particularly, the account of Lakota rites is jaundiced by the Christian affiliations of both Black Elk himself and Brown; *The Sacred Pipe* is not and could not be a "canonical" text and should not be treated as such.

Before turning to these specific criticisms it will be helpful to outline Brown's methodology in recording Black Elk's testimony for *The Sacred Pipe*. In an illuminating letter to Marina Brown Weatherly, Michael Fitzgerald recalls Joseph Brown's own account of his working method. It is worth quoting at some length as it disarms some of the more reckless reproaches in circulation in the last few decades.

> Your father personally explained to me his recording and editing process with Black Elk. Your father stayed with . . . me twice, once in about '81 and then again in about '84. I was in the midst of the recordings with Grandpa Yellowtail during your father's visits.[57] I asked your father about his experience editing *The Sacred Pipe* so that I could understand the best way to proceed on the Yellowtail book. He explained that Black Elk spoke and then Ben [Black Elk] translated while your father wrote transcriptions that focused on key words and concepts. If the meaning was vague, then your father asked an immediate question. In addition, your father read his notes back to the Black Elks during pauses in the narrative in order to be certain that his notes and understanding were accurate. In effect, he read back a rough draft manuscript for approval as part of the recording process. There were often discussions about the concepts and the right words to use, some of which were long. Your father kept adding margin comments to his field notes and restating his understanding of what the elder Black Elk had said. This back and forth refined his understanding and continued until Ben confirmed that Joseph's restatement was correct.
>
> Your father wrote out some of his transcriptions into prose while he was still living in the West. Whenever he had questions he read the draft edits to Ben and the Lakota sage.
>
> I believe the process was similar for Neihardt and Black Elk, so the basic process itself is not in question. The problem is that skeptics were emboldened when it was disclosed in *The Sixth Grandfather* that Neihardt took liberties in his final editing of his daughter's transcriptions. The skeptics, particularly those with their own agenda, wonder if your father might have added or subtracted anything when he did the final editing of his field notes.

Your father stressed to me the importance of word for word transcriptions without the editor adding anything to the narrative. I remember specifically asking him about whether an editor should correct grammar. Your father told me he did correct some of Ben Black Elk's grammar during the transcription and final editing processes, but he never made any substantive alterations.

. . . Others who knew your father also attest to his fidelity to Black Elk's words. As you know, your father lived in Lausanne while he was reading through his notes and editing the book. Mr. Schuon was one of the early readers of the book . . . [and] wrote the Introduction to the French edition. As a result, Schuon was familiar with your father's editing process. In 1984 Schuon wrote a letter to William Stoddart that criticized Neihardt for taking liberties with *Black Elk Speaks.* Schuon closes his letter with this statement, ". . . for the doctrine one has to refer to *The Sacred Pipe,* all the more as this book is strictly faithful, word for word, to the account given by the Indian author."[58]

Joseph Brown's letters provide further insights into his editing process and its timeline. In March 1948 he wrote from Aiken, South Carolina, "I have a quiet place, and am starting to work immediately on the book. I hope in two months to have it in decent enough shape to show to a publisher, and get all that arranged—and then the finishing touches, additions, illustrations, etc. can be finished up in Switzerland."[59] A June 1948 letter to Fr. Gall indicates the progress to that point and corroborates Brown's comment to Fitzgerald that the text closely follows his field notes: "Several weeks ago I sent you a rough draft of two of the most important chapters of the book—on the rites of the *Inipi* and the lamenting. This is still rough, and is really just as I copied it from my notes, but I thought you would like to have them even in this shape."[60] Five months later Brown sent his first draft of the entire book to Fr. Gall: "The first draft of the book is now completed, and there remains only a few notes, corrections, precisions to make. I am preparing a list of Lakota words which I will send to you soon & trust you will have time to correct them according to ethnological standards, about which I know nothing. Also you may be able to give me more precise translations."[61] Joseph Brown's December 1948 letter verifies his comment to Fitzgerald that he spent time reviewing his field notes with the venerable holy man's son while he was living with Black

Elk: "*Hokshichankia* is a difficult word—Ben and I spent several days struggling over it so do not worry if you cannot locate it!"[62] The same letter demonstrates the care Brown took over various Lakota terms: "I am indeed grateful to you for your fine work on the Lakota words. . . . I think *Inikage* satisfactory—have written Ben to check on it, along with several other odds and ends."[63] This letter also confirms Brown's request that Ben Black Elk review parts of the book for accuracy. The editing process was completed sometime in the spring of 1949 and the manuscript for *The Sacred Pipe* was sent to the University of Oklahoma Press prior to Brown's return to visit Black Elk that summer.[64]

It is not surprising that some of the earlier reviews of the book by anthropologists should disparage the lack of "ethnological rigor" and speculate about the extent to which Brown's own beliefs mingled with those of Black Elk. They also suggest, often by implication, some distaste for Brown's evident "sincerity" (this betraying a regrettable emotional investment), his personal engagement with his material, and his relationship with Black Elk, as if, in the words of Zolla, "to comprehend and to love would constitute an obstacle to objectivity."[65]

Later critics were more explicit in the charges leveled at the book: the account of the rites is vitiated by Black Elk's conversion to Christianity, by Brown's own Christian background, and by his hermeneutical notes paralleling Lakota and Christian rituals and other observances taken from the great religious traditions of the East. Thus Julian Rice writes that Black Elk's "detailed descriptions of Lakota ceremonies . . . is often overtly Catholic, as if he were trying to make the Lakota religion more acceptable to Christians."[66] Likewise: "*Although it has many Christian elements . . . The Sacred Pipe* remains one of the best-written descriptions of Lakota ceremonies";[67] the "although" here clearly means "in spite of the fact that." Considering the allegations about the undue influence of Catholicism on *The Sacred Pipe*, Clyde Holler wrote: "We may never know the precise role Joseph Epes Brown played in shaping *The Sacred Pipe*. At this point, however, I certainly do not share the extreme skepticism expressed by one of my prepublication reviewers that the dialogue with Catholicism in the book was 'simply and wholly Brown's creation.'" He goes on to say that Black Elk/Brown "creatively adapts traditional religion in the light of Catholicism" and that "Brown's angle, like Neihardt's, is to portray Black Elk as a traditionalist. The Christian perspective hardly facilitates this portrait, and the fact that the book was taken for so many years as an unvarnished ethnographic account hardly suggest that Brown was at pains to portray Black Elk as a syncretist."[68]

One of the tropes in Black Elk scholarship is the claim that the medicine man and Brown deliberately structured *The Sacred Pipe* so as to parallel the seven Lakota rites with the seven sacraments of the Catholic tradition.[69] This claim seems to be based on little more than the coincidence of the number seven. It is true that there are some references to Christian sacraments—but then too there are comparisons drawn with doctrines and rites from other traditions. In any case, some of the similarities of Lakota rituals and Christian sacraments—say, those between the smoking of the Pipe and the Eucharist—would strike any religiously literate observer. Joe Jackson claims, as have many before him, that Black Elk not only "structures Lakota ritual in parallel to the holy sacraments of Catholicism" but that he omitted the *heyoka* ceremony "since its strange clownishness probably put it beyond the understanding of Christians, as he knew them. Likewise he omitted animal mysteries such as bear ceremonies, since he'd seen these derided as 'savage' polytheism. His choices tried to bridge the two religions."[70] Jackson misses the more obvious reason for Black Elk's choices: both the *heyoka* and animal ceremonies were *not* associated with the original Sacred Pipe and were only available to a very few who were specially qualified by their exceptional visions. Thus, unlike the seven rites which Black Elk explicates, they were *not* part of the everyday religious life of the Sioux people as a whole.[71] Not one of the scholars who find something factitious in Black Elk's exposition of *seven* Lakota rites has made any cogent suggestion as to what Black Elk/Brown improperly included, nor what should have been added.

The critics' assumption of the book's "Christian elements" seems to be that the Lakota oral tradition was hermetically sealed, impervious to outside influences until the recent and corrosive interventions of reservation missionaries. Further, Black Elk's Catholicism and Brown's interpretive lens, it is suggested, inevitably contaminated their respective understandings of Lakota wisdom. In response to this kind of criticism it must firstly be said that the Sioux tradition was never static, nor, for several centuries hitherto, impervious to European/Christian influences; as Brian Holloway has observed, "Christianity's influence on the Lakota is part of a centuries-long process of filtration, absorption, and contact rather than an instantaneous appearance and construction within a newly instituted reservation system, as missionaries and traders had long been in contact with the Lakota and their allies";[72] secondly, a familiarity with and a well-founded understanding of a religious tradition other than one's own may enrich understanding in ways not available to those whose view remains circumscribed by a single perspective; thirdly, there *are* manifest parallels between the two traditions such as may be found when *any* two traditions are juxtaposed—providing, of course, that one has eyes to see. (One such obvious parallel between the Lakota and Christian traditions is the privileged ideal of sacrificial heroism.) Black Elk's Catholicism and Brown's knowledge of non-Indian traditions, far from being an impediment to their collaborative project, become invaluable assets. Furthermore, it cannot be assumed that Black Elk's conversion *necessarily* precluded either his *allegiance* to or *understanding* of the old ways, a subject to which we return in the next chapter.

Standing at right angles to the claim that both Black Elk and Brown gave an undue Christian coloring to their account of traditional Lakota rites is Michael Steltenkamp's counter-argument that Brown, in his intent to preserve the ancestral ways, deliberately obscured Black Elk's conversion to Catholicism, as Neihardt had done before him. Steltenkamp lamented the fact that both Neihardt and Brown more or less ignored the last sixty years of Black Elk's life. Steltenkamp also spurned the misleading impression left by the ending of *Black Elk Speaks*:

> In sum, the two books [*Black Elk Speaks* and *The Sacred Pipe*] portray Black Elk and the social institutions he so cherished as paralyzed victims of Western subjugation. Doomed to live out his years as a relic of the past and a prisoner of irreconcilably foreign ways, the holy man (and his people) becomes an object of pity. Readers are left to conclude that Black Elk lived his first thirty years productively and his last sixty tearfully.[73]

Then, too, we have what is more a cautionary note than a criticism *per se* from Gregory P. Fields:

> [Black Elk's] account [mediated by Brown] of the rites is, however, one man's expression of a profound religious cosmology and path that can be understood only in lived experience. Readers operating under the presumptions of the text-based Anglo-European intellectual tradition and scripture-based Western religious traditions could mistakenly regard the book *The Sacred Pipe* as canon, a complete and correct expression of the teachings of the Lakota sacred rites.[74]

This is salutary. However, Black Elk was not just "one man" but an extraordinary knowledge-keeper exceptionally well-placed to transmit Lakota esoterism; furthermore, whilst *The Sacred Pipe* cannot and should not be regarded as a canonical text in the manner of a scripture, it remains the most detailed, coherent, and authoritative native account of the ensemble of Lakota traditional rites.[75] If we are to have a written account at all then it is hard to see how *The Sacred Pipe* could be bettered. Huston Smith identified the pre-eminent achievement of the book in writing, "Brown stands alone in detailing, in his important study . . . the way in which the Native American religion embodies the *Sophia Perennis* in its own distinctive idiom."[76]

At this point it is also worth mentioning Brown's relationship with the holy man's son, Ben Black Elk, the interlocutor and interpreter of his father's words for both *Black Elk Speaks* and *The Sacred Pipe*, and thus uniquely qualified to verify their authenticity. Ben became a widely-recognized representative of his people.[77] As Joe Jackson remarks, "It could be said that Ben was the public face of the Oglala in the 1960s."[78] The younger Black Elk would surely have objected if there were any serious distortions in *The Sacred Pipe*. Moreover, he would not have maintained a cordial relationship with the authors if he did not agree with their finished works. Michael Fitzgerald provides this insight into Ben Black Elk's enduring relationship with Joseph Brown:

> In 1971 Ben Black Elk visited Bloomington to give a series of lectures for Joseph Brown's class, "Spiritual Traditions of the North American Indians." I helped escort Black Elk during his visit. At a family dinner at the Brown home there were long reminiscences of the olden days. The deep and abiding affection between the two old friends was tangible and would have been impossible if Ben Black Elk thought that Joseph Brown had not faithfully recorded his father's words.[79]

The Spiritual Legacy of the American Indian first appeared in 1982. In 2007 a commemorative edition was published, encompassing new material which illuminated previously unknown aspects of the lives of Brown himself and of Black Elk. All of the essays found in the first edition are reproduced in the commemorative edition. Several of these—"The Spiritual Legacy," "The Roots of Renewal," "Sun Dance: Sacrifice, Renewal, Identity"—have become classics and have reappeared in various anthologies and compilations. These pieces comprise an invaluable introduction to the spiritual economy of the American Plains Indians in general. Brown works on a large canvas and is particularly adept at sketching out for the general reader the *principles* which must inform any real understanding, something altogether different from the accumulation of data and the tedious and often sterile typologies, classifications, and iterations of anthropologists who remain intent on a "scientific" and "empirical" study of the phenomena in question. In this book Brown's explication of myths, rites, and symbols is profound without ever becoming too burdened with detail or retreating into abstract metaphysical realms where many readers would be unable to follow. He also throws into sharp relief the sacramental value which, for the Indians, saturated the natural order, and thereby signals the ways in which the modern world might yet find a way out of the ecological catastrophes which we have brought upon ourselves, upon "all our relatives," and indeed, on Mother Earth herself on whose bounty depends our very existence.

It is worth noting several interesting additions to the first edition of *The Spiritual Legacy*: an informative preface by the three editors (Brown's wife, daughter, and former student and friend, Michael Fitzgerald); an Introduction by the late Åke Hultkrantz giving a conspectus of Brown's work and situating it in the framework of the *philosophia perennis*; a biography of the author and a comprehensive bibliography; and a series of previously unpublished photographs of some of the most imposing of the spiritual leaders amongst the Indians. The commemorative volume of *The Spiritual Legacy* stands next to *The Sacred Pipe* as a beautiful tribute—to the primordial tradition which is its subject, to Black Elk whose testimony and example was a lodestar for the author, and to Joseph Brown himself, in whom the Indians found a true friend and a scholar adequately equipped to expound that spiritual wisdom which is indeed the Indians' most precious legacy.

The 2007 edition of *The Spiritual Legacy* also contains a substantial selection letters written by Joseph Brown, some from his sojourn with Black Elk in the late 1940s, some describing his fertile encounters with other spiritual leaders, and recounting time spent with the Hopi, Navaho, and Pueblo peoples. These excerpts from Brown's letters, published for the first time, provide a rich deposit which no one engaged in the debate about Black Elk should henceforth ignore. The recent discovery of yet more letters written by Brown in this period shed light on his relationships with Black Elk, Frithjof Schuon, and Fr. Gall, a Trappist monk of the Abbaye Notre Dame de Scourmont in Belgium, and the elder brother of Frithjof Schuon. During Joseph Brown's visit to Europe in July 1948, after his first sojourn with Black Elk, he became close friends with Fr. Gall and subsequently carried out an extensive correspondence with him.[80] It was also on this trip that Brown first met Frithjof Schuon face to face, later writing to Fr. Gall, "The long anticipated meeting with your brother is for me a very great event, for he is, and I have long considered him to be, my spiritual master—on a plane even above that of our father Black Elk."[81] Of special interest in Brown's letters are the tantalizing references to Black Elk's spiritual kinship with both Fr. Gall and Frithjof Schuon. Like his brother, Erich Schuon (who was to become Fr. Gall) was amazed by the Indians he witnessed in the Alsace Western circus in 1923, and subsequently dreamed of himself *being* an Indian. So keen was his interest that he learnt the Lakota language, later collaborating, as we have seen, in Brown's translation of some difficult terms in *The Sacred Pipe*. When Brown told Black Elk of his encounter with Erich, now known as Fr. Gall, the old man was intrigued and himself had a dream of visiting Belgium and meeting the Trappist monk whom he named Lakota Ishnala or "Lone Sioux," adopting him as his son.[82] Brown later wrote to Fr. Gall that "[Black Elk] said that he had told you that you shall always be a Lakota, for when you die your body, which is of earth, shall remain with the white man, but your soul shall return to us."[83] The story of Black Elk's relationship with Frithjof Schuon is taken up in Chapter 7 and new excerpts from Brown's letters to Fr. Gall are provided in Appendix I.

Black Elk

John G. Neihardt

Joseph Epes Brown

Frithjof Schuon

Hilda Neihardt, Black Elk, Chase-in-the-Morning, and John G. Neihardt, with hoops and spears for the hoop and spear game

Black Elk and Ben Black Elk gesture to make a point during a typical interview scene for the recording of *Black Elk Speaks*, Manderson, South Dakota, 1931. *From left*: Enid Neihardt, Black Elk, Ben Black Elk, Standing Bear, and John G. Neihardt.

Black Elk and John G. Neihardt at the Lakota Victory Celebration, 1945

Black Elk and Joseph Epes Brown, Manderson, South Dakota, 1947

Joseph Epes Brown, Manderson, South Dakota, 1948

Ben Black Elk and Frithjof Schuon, Pine Ridge
Reservation, South Dakota, 1963

The White Buffalo Calf Woman bringing the Sacred Pipe,
by Frithjof Schuon, 1959

Top: Father Gall during Mass, Abbaye Notre Dame de Scourmont, Belgium; *Bottom*: Black Elk, Manderson, South Dakota, 1948

6

Lakota Traditionalist and/or Catholic Catechist?

I shake hands with my white friends. Listen! I will speak
words of truth. I told about the people's ways of long ago and
some of this a white man put in a book but he did not tell about
current ways. Therefore I will speak again, a final speech. . . .
Now I have converted and live in the true faith of
God the Father, the Son, and the Holy Spirit.
Black Elk[1]

The only thing I really believe in is the pipe religion.
Black Elk[2]

The Debate about Black Elk's Conversion

In 1993 Michael Steltenkamp, anthropologist and one-time student
of Joseph Brown, published *Black Elk: Holy Man of the Oglala*.
Drawing heavily on interviews with Black Elk's daughter Lucy Looks
Twice and granddaughter Olivia, on the testimonies of other Lakota
converts (Ben Marrowbone, John Lone Goose, and others), and on
written sources from Jesuit fathers (Eugene Buchel, Florentine Dig-
mann, Joseph Zimmerman), Steltenkamp furnished us with a detailed
picture of Black Elk's life as a Catholic catechist, evangelist, prayer
leader, spiritual mentor, and church organizer. Apart from a few
oblique references and allusions, neither *Black Elk Speaks* nor *The
Sacred Pipe* had provided any account of Black Elk's conversion, his
commitment to the Christian faith, and his energetic involvement in
church activities over the last forty-five years of his life. In ignoring
this, Brown and Neihardt had neglected the evolving ways in which
Black Elk remained a spiritual and religious leader, and sidestepped
many sensitive issues concerning religious and cultural interactions.
In correspondence with Steltenkamp, Joseph Brown himself wrote,
"I have felt it improper that this phase of [Black Elk's] life was never
presented either by Neihardt or indeed by myself. I suppose somehow
it was thought this Christian participation compromised his 'Indianness,' but I do not see it this way and think it time that the record
was set straight."[3]

Steltenkamp's book helped to initiate a new era in Black Elk
studies, one which highlighted issues of conversion, religious syn-

cretism, and cultural adaptation. It was followed a few years later by another landmark work, Clyde Holler's *Black Elk's Religion: The Sun Dance and Lakota Catholicism* (1995) in which the holy man is seen as a creative religious thinker with an allegiance to both Lakota tradition and Catholicism, and as an adaptive bridge-builder between two worlds.[4] Side by side with these inquiries was an emergent skepticism, sometimes impelled by recent postcolonial theorizing, about the Neihardt-Brown representation of Black Elk.[5]

Since the publication of *Black Elk: Holy Man of the Oglala*, one of the exposed nerves in scholarly disputation has been the nature of the medicine man's conversion to Catholicism and his subsequent relationship to the ancestral ways of the Lakota. His most recent biographer suggests that Black Elk's conversion "is probably the greatest mystery of his life."[6] Scott J. Howard identifies three different schools of thought about the holy man's post-conversion religious orientation which variously see him as: (a) a Lakota traditionalist whose engagement with Christianity was more or less nominal; (b) a zealous Catholic catechist and dogmatist who discovers "the presence of the unknown Christ in his Lakota tradition";[7] or (c) a Lakota-Christian syncretist/universalist. The exponents of these somewhat elastic schools of thought include: (a) Julian Rice, William K. Powers, Hilda Neihardt, Thomas Couser; (b) Michael Steltenkamp, Paul Steinmetz; and (c) Clyde Holler, Michael Fitzgerald, Raymond DeMallie, Frithjof Schuon, Ruth Heflin, and Joe Jackson. These groupings are not monolithic: for instance, the ways in which Holler and Fitzgerald understand the matter overlap but do not coincide. Furthermore, the views of some of these scholars have changed over time. Raymond DeMallie believed that Black Elk's conversion to Catholicism was heartfelt but that he reverted to the old ways in his later years: his Catholicism was, so to speak, a parenthetical experience. In more recent reflections DeMallie seems to have moved towards the view that in his later years Black Elk somehow integrated Catholicism and the old ways.[8] Damien Costello subverts these categorizations by reading Black Elk's experience through a postcolonial frame which rejects many of the key premises of earlier scholars. These discordant accounts arise, in part, from Black Elk's own conflicting statements about his religious posture in the years after his conversion. Perhaps none of these characterizations are altogether adequate, but for the moment they can serve as a gateway to our inquiry.

As we have seen, Neihardt and Brown were intent on preserving Black Elk's Great Vision and the esoteric Lakota wisdom which it dramatized. They each more or less ignored Black Elk's conversion to Christianity, apparently regarding it as of little importance. This view remained more or less stable for the fifty years following the first publication of *Black Elk Speaks*. It was reinforced by Julian Rice's *Black Elk's Story: Distinguishing Its Lakota Purpose* (1991), which sought to identify the purely Lakotan message of the holy man's narrative, pruned of the imputed Platonic/Christian influences of Neihardt and Brown. Rice contended that Black Elk's conversion was "more social than spiritual."[9] Similarly Thomas Couser: "Black Elk's conversion to Christianity was probably less a matter of profound and total inner change than of accommodation to the repression of traditional religious practices."[10] At heart, it was thought, he remained a Lakota of the old ways. Hilda Neihardt drew attention to Black Elk's response to a query from her father about why he had joined a white church: "Because my children have to live in this world."[11] *Black Elk Speaks* and *The Sacred Pipe* seemed to be impregnable supports for Black Elk's elevated standing as a Lakota traditionalist, visionary, and holy man. Since the publication of *The Sixth Grandfather* (1984) and Steltenkamp's book, this outlook has come under fire from various quarters.

Equipped with the full transcription of the Black Elk-Neihardt material, Steltenkamp's researches, and more recent work by other scholars, we now understand that Black Elk's conversion was deeper and more durable than had been previously thought. We are also now more finely attuned to some of the veiled Christian imagery in *Black Elk Speaks*, especially in his Great Vision, and in *The Sacred Pipe*. Steltenkamp makes much of the apparent similarities between the symbolic geography of the visionary "cloud world" and the Two Roads Map, a teaching device used by Catholic catechists in evangelizing the Lakota.[12] In his 2009 biography Steltenkamp writes of Black Elk's narrative: "Instead of solely recounting an unaltered vision from a boyhood experience, the holy-man might have provided the poet with a synthesis of religious images that engaged him from boyhood through adulthood—that is, vision images fused with images from the Two Roads Map."[13]

There is some evidence to suggest that Black Elk did indeed, at times, see Catholic Christianity as replacing the old beliefs and practices—which is to say that he apparently shared the religious exclusivism of his Jesuit mentors. For instance, in a letter to the *Catholic Herald*, November 2, 1911, Black Elk stated, "Perhaps you cannot live lives split in two, which does not please God. Only one church, one God, one Son, and only one Holy Spirit—that way you have only one faith, you have only one body, and you have only one life and one spirit."[14] Then, too, we have the declaration made soon after his near-fatal wagon accident in 1933, and not so long after the meetings with Neihardt:

> I am a believer. The Catholic priest Short Father baptized me thirty years ago. . . . Now I have converted and live in the true faith of God the Father, the Son, and the Holy Spirit. . . . I believe in the seven sacraments of the Catholic Church. . . . For many years I went with several priests to fight for Christ among my people. For about twenty years I helped the priests and was a catechist in several communities. So I think I know more about the Catholic religion than many white men. . . . All my family is baptized. All my children and grandchildren belong to the Catholic Church and I am glad of that and I wish very much that they will always follow the holy road. . . . I know that the Catholic religion is good, better than the Sun dance or the Ghost dance.[15]

Black Elk's avowal, made in Lakota, was translated into English and typed up in a document dated January 26, 1934, signed by Black Elk himself, by his daughter Lucy, and by Father Joseph Zimmerman. DeMallie believes, as I do, that the statement "has all the indications of sincerity."[16] However, without doubting Black Elk's probity, we should also take into account the fact that the statement was made against the backdrop of contemporary Jesuit disapproval of *Black Elk Speaks*. DeMallie supplies the context in which this "final speech" needs to be situated:

> [The publication of *Black Elk Speaks*] put Black Elk in an awkward position in relation to the Catholic Church. His reputation on the reservation was built as a Catholic catechist, not as a native religious leader. The Jesuit priests at Holy Rosary Mission were shocked and horrified at the suggestion that one of their most valued catechists still harbored beliefs in the old Indian religion. For them to accept *Black Elk Speaks* at face value necessarily called into question the genuineness of their success in converting the Lakotas to Catholicism. Rather than accepting the book as a true representation of Black Elk, they blamed Neihardt for telling only part of Black Elk's story.

The priests objected most strongly to the epilogue portraying Black Elk as a believing, practicing "pagan" praying to the six grandfathers when he knew well that the Christian God was the only source of salvation. Ben Black Elk told the missionaries, no doubt truthfully, that he and his father had not realized that Neihardt intended to include the final prayer on Harney Peak in the book. Although the old man was embarrassed in front of the priests . . . he never denied the sincerity of his final appeal to the six grandfathers.[17]

Further support for the view of Black Elk as an ardent Catholic was provided in a letter that Black Elk purportedly dictated to his daughter Lucy in September 1934. In it he states that he had requested Neihardt to include in *Black Elk Speaks* an account of his conversion and work for the Church. However, this document is somewhat problematic: it too was possibly the result of pressure from the Jesuits who had been alarmed by Neihardt's visit to Black Elk in the summer of 1934; it is unsigned and, DeMallie suggests, may have been composed by Lucy, herself a committed Catholic with little understanding, at that time, of the old ways.[18] Recently Joe Jackson has suggested, persuasively, that this letter was actually a fraudulent document, imitating what the perpetrator imagined to be Black Elk's manner of expression, and composed by Fr. Placidus Sialm. Sialm was a rigidly exclusivist priest, hostile to Lakota "paganism" in all its forms, and more outraged by the publication of *Black Elk Speaks* than the other Jesuits at Pine Ridge.[19]

Black Elk's various professions of his Catholic faith sometimes triggered exclusivist and triumphalist claims from Catholic missionaries such as Sr. M. Claudia Duratschek, author of *Crusading Along Sioux Trails* (1947): "A fervent and outstanding catechist who, however, has been cast [in *Black Elk Speaks*] incorrectly as a pagan medicine man, was Black Elk. This quondam Ghost Dancer and chief of medicine men, after his conversion, like a second St. Paul, went around trying to convert his tribesmen whom, before his conversion, he had helped to *shackle in the fetters of paganism.*"[20] However, the picture is complicated by other testimony from Black Elk himself, and from those close to him, which sometimes suggests, at the least, that he did *not* see the old ways and Christianity as incompatible or, at other times, indicates some ambivalence. Frank Fools Crow says that his uncle "had decided that the Sioux religious way of life was pretty much the same as that of the Christian churches, and there was no reason to change what the Sioux were doing. We could pick up some of the Christian ways and teachings, and just work them in with our own, so in the end both would be better."[21] Ben Black Elk reported that in his father's last years their conversations were about the ancestral ways and that Black Elk felt he may have made a mistake in converting, that traditional Lakota religion might have been better for the people.[22] Lucy recalled that in his last days the old man had said, "The only thing I really believe in is the pipe religion."[23] Others have pointed out that some of Black Elk's statements were made under duress, that he may have been motivated by extra-religious pressures, that certain material and social benefits issued from his self-identification as Catholic, and that in any event, at different times, he made contradictory statements about his religious commitments.[24]

Steltenkamp's book has attracted a range of critics, including Scott J. Howard, who argues that, "There are three major problems with Steltenkamp's argument: the many variables involved in a direct comparison between Black Elk's vision and the Two Roads Map; the author's disregard of the full context of the symbols in Black Elk's vision and their relationship to other views that Black Elk expresses elsewhere in *The Sixth Grandfather,* and the author's one-eyed approach of interpreting everything from a Christian perspective."[25] In the years that have elapsed since Steltenkamp's first book on Black Elk there has been a significant (but by no means unanimous) reaction against the view that Black Elk's conversion to Catholicism constituted a repudiation of Lakota tradition. In his recent biography, *Nicholas Black Elk* (2009), Steltenkamp himself takes a more nuanced position, believing that Black Elk's position was "fully Catholic and fully Lakota."[26] This school of thought, headed by Clyde Holler, rejects both the "romantic" picture of Black Elk with its attendant motifs of "the noble savage" and "the vanishing Indian," and the somewhat one-dimensional view of him as Catholic evangelist. Holler, Heflin, Fitzgerald, Schuon, and others disavow the notion that Black Elk in his later years must *really* have been *either* a committed Catholic *or* a Lakota traditionalist, arguing that in some sense he was *both*, a "dual participant." Schuon, who was close to both Joseph Brown and Ben Black Elk, speaks to this question at length in a letter in Appendix III.[27] Some scholars have also foregrounded both "syncretic" and "universalist" strains in Black Elk's later understanding.

Cultural Adaptation and "Dual Participation"
In the late 1980s William K. Powers noted that anthropologists had long been puzzled by the "dual religious participation" of Native Americans in both their own indigenous tradition and Christianity. He argued that this conundrum only persisted because these traditions were understood primarily as belief systems: as traditional and Christian beliefs clearly contradicted each other, Powers maintained, one could not believe both simultaneously. He then suggested that "Christianity and Oglala religion coexist because they serve quite disparate functions. . . . I regard the participation by Oglala in Christian sects as social, political, economic, and religious *strategies.*"[28] Conversion to Christianity was seen as a *creative adaptive move* by which Lakota values and practices were protected by a Christian overlay. "Thus the Oglala were not so much to become Christianized as Christianity was to become nativized. . . . The Oglala in fact used Christianity consciously and positively in order to survive."[29] For instance, church membership provided access to literacy skills, food and clothing, and provided a means of preserving traditional forms of social organization. Catherine Schuon recalls that Elva One Feather once remarked, "Indians liked to go to church on Sundays because it was for them the only way to come together and meet old friends since their homes were built by the government on purpose miles apart from each other to prevent possible uprisings."[30] This supports Powers' claim that, "As a means of survival and adaptation to the unalterability of the white man's dominance, Christianity has been used in such a way that old cultural institutions and their associated values may persist under new labels."[31] On the other hand, Powers contended, Lakota beliefs and practices continued (sometimes covertly) to serve their religious and spiritual needs.

Powers has been one of the more vocal critics attempting to puncture what he calls "the Black Elk myth," believing that there is no reason for distinguishing Black Elk from other Lakota medicine men. Powers is clearly hostile to Neihardt, Brown, and to Black Elk himself because of his "Christianizing" of the Ghost Dance and his supposedly opportunistic conversion to Catholicism.[32] Not surprisingly Powers' anti-Christian animus and his structural-functional model have not found much favor amongst those who see Black Elk's conversion to Catholicism in positive religious terms. It must also be said that while Powers' model yields some insights its overall effect is reductive: it takes neither Lakota tradition nor Christianity seriously in their own terms, which is to say that Powers, like many anthropologists, etiolates religion by treating it as no more than a cultural production, a socio-logical phenomenon, thereby exemplifying what Eliade called "the religious illiteracy" of much modern scholarship.

A more sophisticated and supple version of the "dual participa-tion" interpretation of Black Elk's religious affiliations is provided by Clyde Holler, who is more sensitive to the religious and spiritual dimensions of Lakota-Christian interactions. Holler is surely right in pointing out that Black Elk did not see the two traditions primarily in terms of theological propositions or doctrines which were logically incompatible: rather, Black Elk came to see both the ancestral ways and Christianity as *manifestations of the sacred.*

> It is simply ethnocentric to assume without further ado that Black Elk must have experienced Christianity and traditional religion primarily as conflicting belief systems. It seems much more likely that Black Elk was predisposed to see religious statements as symbolic expressions of truths that could not be fully captured outside the context of religious ecstasy. . . . If Black Elk did not share our culture-bound concept of religion as propositional truth, what reason is there to believe that he even felt the conflict? If they were to him two alternate ways of envisioning the sacred—or two stories about the sacred—not two mutually exclusive and absolute truth claims, it becomes easier to see how he could accept Christianity as a further unfolding of his vision, weaving Christian elements back into his account of his original power vision.[33]

Similarly,

> If his vision and his relationship with sacred power was truly paramount in his religious understanding, Black Elk may have seen one thing—the sacred—where others see two things—traditional religion and Christianity. . . . If Black Elk regarded these two traditions as two expressions of the same sacred reality, much of the tension that commentators have per-ceived in his dual participation is dissipated.[34]

All the available evidence suggests that Black Elk's commitment to his Great Vision was deep, sincere, and enduring: there is no evidence that he ever abandoned the belief that this was the defining moment of his life which left him with a peculiar and inescapable destiny. As

Holler observes, the "essential touchstone of religion for Black Elk was his vision."[35] This fact is buttressed by the immense trouble he took to ensure that his recollections of the Great Vision in particular were accurately and fully recorded. In Neihardt's words, Black Elk remained a man "sure of what he knows and that what he knows is worth knowing."[36] These are not the actions and attitudes of a man who has abandoned the traditional ways and disowned the spiritual ideals they embodied. Similarly, the meticulous account of the Lakota rituals he gave to Brown in no way suggests a man who believes the old ways are "obsolete" or "outmoded"—quite the contrary! Furthermore, as Holler pointed out in 1995, Black Elk became "the key figure in the contemporary revival of traditional religion."[37] Holler is surely right in arguing that Black Elk pioneered "an authentic Lakota Christianity" *and* played a crucial role in the preservation of the Lakota tradition, and that he did this partly by his "creative and courageous confrontation with Christianity and with the challenges of modernity. His legacy to all contending factions is his lifetime of thoughtful and authentic engagement with the problems of his people, justifying his place in his people's hearts as their greatest *wicasa wakan*."[38]

In 2005 Damien Costello's *Black Elk: Colonialism and Lakota Catholicism* challenged several tropes and assumptions which circulated through much of the literature on Black Elk, particularly concerning the Lakota/Catholic issue. Drawing on postcolonial theory[39] Costello identified several currents of thought which might help to situate the debate in a different context: the rejection of the various prejudices which had informed the "noble savage" theme; the repudiation of a "binary cultural system" and the "Western colonial paradigm" in which "all members of a particular culture share similar traits by nature" (for example, missionaries, as members of the colonizing culture, must be oppressive and unjust); the affirmation of native agency; a recognition of the anti-colonial uses of Christianity; and the formation of indigenous forms of Christianity.[40] Costello wanted to fix attention on the creative intercourse between Lakota tradition and Catholicism, and to underscore their mutual transformation. In this way the apparent dissonance between Black Elk's loyalty to Lakota tradition and his Catholic commitment was, to some extent, neutralized.

A few general observations about "dual participation" and so-called "syncretism" can bring this part of our inquiry to a conclusion. Properly speaking syncretism is the attempt to mix together heterogeneous elements from different religious traditions to create something new, a practice which violates the principle, accepted by both Lakota and Christians, that the formal elements of an integral religious tradition derive from a supra-human Revelation and are thus inviolate. In the case of the Lakota this conception of revelation encompasses visions of which individuals are not the authors but recipients and conduits. In the Indian milieu, every man might be a prophet. However, anthropologists and other scholars often use the term syncretism in a much looser sense, signifying what is more precisely termed "dual participation," a notion unpalatable to many Christians who have been taught to believe that the Christian Revelation is the *only* path to salvation. Such exclusivism is quite alien to the Lakota tradition, where the idea of differing but equally valid revelations is taken for granted: "multiple forms of revelation and inspiration are accepted as a self-evident reality."[41]

It is worth noting that dual religious affiliations—Muslim-Hindu, Hindu-Buddhist, Christian-Confucian—are not uncommon in the more universalist milieu of the East. One finds recent instances of Christian-Hindu dual participation in the theologian Raimond Panikkar and the Benedictine monk, Henri le Saux who became Swami Abhishiktananda. In such cases it is not a matter of being "half" one thing and "half" another, nor of veering from one to the other, but of belonging fully to both by virtue of "the esoteric ability to situate a plurality of . . . perspectives within an essential and objective vision." This is not syncretism, which is an "exterior accretion of disparate elements," but an esoterism which "proceeds from within and envisages the plurality of forms from the standpoint of their synthetic or essential unity."[42] This is not always an easy position to occupy. Abhishiktananda wrote of his own struggle to remain faithful to the truth of both the Gospels and the *Upanishads*: "It is precisely the fact of being a bridge that makes this uncomfortable situation worthwhile. The danger of this life as a 'bridge' is that we run the risk of not belonging to either side; whereas, however harrowing it may be, *our duty is to belong wholly to both sides*. This is only possible in the mystery of God."[43]

Black Elk's allegiance to both Christianity and the ancestral ways of the Lakota is by no means an unusual phenomenon. Michael Fitzgerald identifies a number of spiritual leaders amongst the Plains Indians who followed the same path: Thomas Yellowtail and Leonard Bends (Crow), Chief Washakie, John Trehero, James Trosper (Shoshone), Spotted Tail, Charles Ohiyesa Eastman (Santee), Fools Crow (Lakota), as well as other prominent Indians such as John Stands in Timber (Cheyenne) and Joe Medicine Crow (Crow). We may add

Benjamin Black Elk[44] to the list, and no doubt there are many others. As Joe Medicine Crow explained of the Crow experience,

> Over time almost every Christian denomination opened churches and schools on the reservation; each family was assigned to become a member of one or another of the churches. The government encouraged this process to help assimilate the Indians because the churches actively tried to convert the Indians away from their traditional ceremonies. Children who went to church schools were not mistreated, so families preferred to send their children to the church schools instead of the government boarding school. . . . Of course, some Indians did turn away from their traditions; but *most Indians embraced Christianity without abandoning their own cultural traditions.* There was no problem in the Indian way; everyone had a little different way to pray but everyone was praying to the same, one God, so there was no problem.[45]

In most of these cases, as in Black Elk's, it was not a case of "blending" or "fusing" Christian and Lakota practices; as Fitzgerald notes, "it is generally considered 'bad medicine' to mix a practice from one religion into the rites of a different tradition." It is therefore usually a matter of *successive* rather than *simultaneous* practices: many Native Americans "will fervently participate in their ancestral rites in a completely traditional manner; then later they will go to Church and pray in a Christian manner."[46] Often they are able to do so because, in Schuon's words, "the person of Christ appears to them as an irresistible spiritual reality, and they see no reason not to integrate Him into their religious life; they see no contradiction in this."[47] It is also true that many Indians have long pondered the flagrant contradictions arising out of white professions of Christian faith juxtaposed with the most un-Christian behavior. As Ohiyesa remarked, "I confess I have wondered much that Christianity is not practiced by the very people who vouch for that wonderful conception of exemplary living. It appears that they are anxious to pass on their religion to all races of men, but keep very little of it themselves."[48] But even with this galling irony in front of them, many Indians understand the simple but profound truth also plainly expressed by Ohiyesa: "We know that all religious aspiration, all sincere worship, can have but one source and one goal. We know that the God of the lettered and the unlettered, of the Greek and the barbarian, is after all the same God."[49] How many troubles and perplexities vanish in this light!

Drawing on some key ideas in the writings of Frithjof Schuon, Joseph Brown has provided us with a cogent explanation of the whole "conversion" phenomenon.

> Throughout virtually all indigenous American Indian traditions, a pervasive theme has been that all forms and forces of all orders of the immediately experienced natural environment may communicate to human beings the totality of that which is to be known of the sacred mysteries of creation, and thus of the sacred essence of being and beings. . . . Such conditioning to openness of mind and being towards manifestations of the sacred makes it understandable that for these peoples religious matters of whatever origin are not open to either question or argument. When, therefore, the Christian message came to the peoples through dedicated missionaries who led exemplary and sacrificial lives, the people easily understood the truths of message and example due to the profundity of their own beliefs; it was not difficult for them to adapt new expressions of values into the sacred fabric of their own culture. The historical phenomenon is thus not conversion as understood in an exclusivistic manner by the bearers of Christianity, but rather a continuation of the people's ancient and traditional facility for what may be termed non-exclusive cumulative adhesion. If this process of polysynthesis can be accomplished with neither confusion nor dissonance, it is ultimately due to the ability of American Indian peoples to penetrate and comprehend the central and most profound nature of all experience and reality.[50]

Brown's account has been available since 1982; many subsequent commentators on the religious life of Black Elk and other Indian leaders might profitably have paid it more attention!

Black Elk and the Revival of Traditional Rites

During the last decade a further body of highly significant material has come to light, one still not fully assimilated by contemporary scholarship: a selection of Joseph Brown's letters, written in the period covering the last three years of Black Elk's life but only published in the 2007 edition of *The Spiritual Legacy of the American Indian*. Even more recently further correspondence from Brown in this period has surfaced.[51] Several facts emerge from this correspondence, highly germane to the debate about Black Elk's later religious orientation.

It has been asserted that after 1904 Black Elk no longer practiced any of the traditional rites and observances. This claim ignores plentiful evidence to the contrary in both *Black Elk Speaks* and *The Sacred Pipe*—for instance, the prayers that Black Elk addresses to *Wakan-Tanka* and the six Grandfathers. Brown's letters provide further evidence that during the last years of his life Black Elk participated in the sweat-lodge ceremony, *yuwipi*, and praying with the pipe.[52] He was also actively involved in reviving what he referred to as the "religion of the Pipe" amongst the Lakota.[53] In a letter written soon after his first encounter with Black Elk, Brown states that

> Black Elk is carrying out something which he has felt he must do for some time, but has lacked the necessary encouragement and assistance. This work is to restore the religion of the Pipe—to reconstitute a new order—and thus ensure that the Spiritual Transmission shall not be broken. We are contacting the elderly men of prayer not only in this area, but in the other Sioux reservations, and it is most encouraging to note the manner in which they have responded—and how anxious they are to assist. Just today we have spoken with Spotted Cow, Dull Knife, and Red Cloud—son of the great chief.[54]

Elsewhere Brown describes a major ceremonial gathering in December 1947 when about a hundred old Lakota traveled by horse and wagons from all over the reservation:

> The ceremonials, all different, but all centering around the pipe, went on every night for about five days. Then on the 18th we had the large pipe ceremonial at Manderson. . . . This was of course the great day for Black Elk, for his vision was now being realized, and he was as happy and excited as a child. He and Little Warrior painted their faces red, and put on their best clothes, and what traditional clothing they had. . . . Never have I seen a priest officiate at a rite with more dignity, confidence, and majesty.[55]

Brown went on to observe that at one point, "Many of the old men . . . now arose and one by one gave a short speech, most of them expressing that they had neglected the pipe given to them by *Wakan-*

Tanka, and that it is now a necessity that they use it once again."[56] Shortly after this ceremony Brown wrote, "It was agreed that the Pipe of every old man be handed down to the most worthy of his descendants. This shall be good, for somehow these pipes have a way of getting into the museums, or into the hands of the profane whites."[57]

This angered the Jesuit priests at Manderson who harshly rebuked Black Elk—but the Lakota visionary was not to be deterred and he, in turn, rebuked the priests.[58] Brown recounts that, "Black Elk says he is sorry that his present action towards reviving Lakota spiritual traditions shall anger the priests, but that their anger is proof of their ignorance; and in any case *Wakan-Tanka* is happy; for he knows that it is His Will that Black Elk does this work."[59]

Fitzgerald has observed that Brown's letters

> Provide a final chapter to Black Elk's life because of their sharp contrast to the despair in Black Elk's closing words in *Black Elk Speaks*, "you see me now a pitiful old man who has done nothing, for the nation's hoop is broken and scattered. There is no center any longer, and the sacred tree is dead." These words were spoken at a time when most American Indian traditional ceremonies were still outlawed. . . . Joseph Brown's arrival in 1947 was a catalyst that provided Black Elk the practical support to work toward perpetuating ancestral spiritual traditions, both through the recording of his account of the seven sacred rites of the Lakota and through Black Elk's efforts to reestablish an "Order of the Pipe" for his tribe.[60]

The 1947 ceremonies had the immediate result of stimulating daily prayer with the sacred pipe on Pine Ridge, a practice which had fallen to the wayside during the period of cultural repression. In the years since Black Elk's death we have witnessed a widespread revival of traditional practices amongst the Lakota, and indeed among many other Plains Indians. The Sun Dance was generally not publicly practiced in its traditional form prior to the 1947 ceremonies[61] but there is some disagreement about the extent to which the Lakota Sun Dance was secretly performed during the almost fifty years of its legal prohibition. In her classic study of 1918, *Teton Sioux Music*, Frances Densmore refers to the Sun Dance of 1881 as "the final ceremony held by the Teton in Dakota."[62] The respected historian, Robert Utley, states that the dance on Pine Ridge in 1883 was "the last held anywhere on the Great Sioux Reservation."[63] The story of the Sun Dance since its banning in 1883 is actually more complicated. There is a photograph of a Sun Dance, probably at Rosebud, taken by John Anderson in 1910,[64] while Paul Steinmetz uncovered evidence of Sun Dances at the Pine Ridge village of Kyle in 1917, 1918, and 1919.[65] Thomas Mails states that the Sun Dance was covertly practiced during the period after 1929. On the other hand, he goes on to explain, "In the forties, interest in the Sun Dance lagged. Some returning Sioux World War II veterans had to go to the Cheyenne to find Sun Dances to share in. In the late fifties, enthusiasm for the Sun Dance revived, and the public piercing was begun by the traditionalists."[66] Beginning in 1952, the Sioux Sun Dance was once again openly performed on Pine Ridge Reservation when Fools Crow was granted permission to pierce sun dancers in the traditional manner.[67]

Nowadays the Sun Dance is held many times every summer on each Sioux reservation and the sweat lodge purification, daily prayer with the sacred pipe, and the vision quest are widespread on most Indian reservations across the American Plains.[68] Native Americans continue, in Vine Deloria's words, to "look to [*Black Elk Speaks*] for spiritual guidance, for sociological identity, for political insight, and for affirmation of the continuing substance of tribal life."[69] Lakota traditionalists today largely follow Black Elk's account of the Sun Dance, and indeed all the sacred rites recorded in *The Sacred Pipe*.[70] Many observers will conclude that the authenticity of Black Elk's recollections is verified by *vox populi*.[71] Fools Crow is widely acknowledged as the preeminent Lakota Sun Dance chief of the last half of the twentieth century.[72] It is difficult to dispute his assessment that "Black Elk has earned a place above all of the other Teton holy men. We all hold him the highest."[73]

Neihardt had penned an elegiac epitaph for the old ways in his ending to *Black Elk Speaks*. But as he was later happy to acknowledge, this "book that would not die" was, after decades of neglect, spreading Black Elk's message anew. Neihardt, Brown, and Black Elk had each made immense creative contributions to the spiritual renaissance which has flourished in the last half-century. The hoop, after all, was not broken and the tree still flowered!

7

The Holy Man from the East

I see that the American Indians have been crushed and their
culture has been destroyed. I am a European, so I feel a debt towards
the red race; I want to help revive Indian culture.
Frithjof Schuon[1]

The Indian world signifies first and foremost the reading of the
primordial doctrine in the phenomena of Nature.
Frithjof Schuon[2]

Frithjof Schuon and the Plains Indians
Frithjof Schuon's role in helping to preserve the spiritual heritage
of the Plains Indians has only recently come to light and must be
reckoned among his many outstanding achievements. His writings
comprise the most penetrating non-native account yet written of this
primordial tradition. Schuon himself lived a reclusive life, out of the
public eye. However, since his death in 1998 his friend and biographer, Michael Fitzgerald, has told the extraordinary story of Schuon's
close involvement with the Indians and his relationship with the sage
of the Oglala.[3] Fitzgerald is well-equipped for this task: not only did
he know Schuon intimately, but he was also a student, colleague, and
friend of Joseph Brown. Fitzgerald himself developed a close relationship with several Indian tribes, and is an adopted son of Chief Thomas
Yellowtail whose "autobiography" he recorded in *Yellowtail: Crow*
Medicine Man and Sun Dance Chief (1991).

In a letter written in 1947 to Chief Medicine Robe of the
Assiniboine tribe, Frithjof Schuon recollects that the members of
his family "were educated in the love of the Indian peoples, and this
was a providential disposition in the plan of the Great Spirit."[4] This
family proclivity dated back to his paternal grandmother's encounter
with an Indian chief in Washington D.C. The Plains Indians were to
figure prominently in the last five decades of Schuon's life. However,
there is no point in fully rehearsing the story already told by Michael
Fitzgerald; interested readers are directed towards his biography of
Schuon. Here we will touch on only a few suggestive incidents from
Schuon's lifelong engagement with the Indians.

It was Frithjof Schuon who, early in 1947, suggested to Joseph Brown that he should locate Black Elk to learn more about the Lakota tradition.[5] Catherine Schuon remembers that, "John Murray gave *Black Elk Speaks* to my husband, who was very impressed by the book. He thought that Black Elk surely knew more about his religion than is revealed in that book so my husband asked Murray whether he or someone he knew could try to find Black Elk out west."[6] Murray discussed Schuon's suggestion with his good friend, Joseph Brown, who took up the quest and found Black Elk in September 1947 in South Dakota. Brown spent a good deal of time, over a two-year period, with Black Elk and his family. During this time Schuon corresponded not only with Brown but also wrote two letters to Black Elk himself, each of them, according to the holy man's son Ben, having "a tremendous impact." The *wicasa wakan* confided to Brown that he had been chosen as the one to record the sacred rites because he had been sent by a "holy man from the East."[7] He went on to tell Brown that his own imminent death did not trouble him as he knew that his own work would be continued by this same holy man. Joseph Brown recounted what he was told by Black Elk's daughter, Lucy Looks Twice, about the Lakota visionary's final weeks:

> Every afternoon at about the same time he would go into something of a trance as if he were talking with some unseen person. Once he scolded his daughter-in-law for entering the house at that time, for he said that she had made the man leave. When they asked him who it was who came to talk with him (more precisely this person came to pray for Black Elk, saying that he knew he was soon to die, and he wished to help him in his suffering), he said it was "a holy man from Europe." His relatives were frightened by these experiences, and Mrs. Looks Twice noticing a large wooden rosary which always hung over his bed—a Moroccan one that I had given him because of his fondness for beads, and for the *barakah*—took this away from him, and according to her after this he did not talk anymore with the "strange man." At Black Elk's death, possibly thinking that it had not been right to do this, she saw that this rosary was buried in the coffin with him.[8]

Catherine Schuon explained that "My husband gave a Moroccan rosary to Joseph Brown when he was staying in Lausanne during 1949. Joseph Brown gave that rosary to Black Elk later that same summer."[9]

For the last month of Black Elk's life, Schuon and his wife, informed by Brown of the old man's illness, recited prayers for him every evening in their house in Lausanne. These evening prayers, calling on Divine Mercy, took place at the time of Black Elk's afternoon dream visions of "the holy man from Europe." (Lucy Looks Twice was unaware that the disembodied visitor was undoubtedly Schuon, speculating that it might have been a "Blackrobe priest."[10])

Schuon was a prolific writer but during his long life he only once contributed to a book written by another author: this was his Introduction to the first French edition of *The Sacred Pipe*. Parts of this were read to Black Elk who, Joseph Brown reports, was "extremely pleased."[11] Catherine Schuon and Jacques Chevilliat, one of the Schuons' close friends, translated *Black Elk Speaks* into French and also assisted in translating *The Sacred Pipe*.[12] The French edition was published in the same year as the English edition, a rare case of the simultaneous publication in a foreign language of a book about Native American spirituality. Chevilliat was the intermediary with the French publishers for both books. It seems fair to say that Frithjof Schuon and his circle were responsible for bringing both of Black Elk's books to the attention of the Francophone world.

Another decisive episode in Schuon's encounter with Native Americans was his meeting with Thomas and Susie Yellowtail in Paris in 1954. They became the first house guests in the Schuons' new home in Lausanne. Thus began an enduring friendship of kindred spirits. In the late 50s and early 60s Schuon and his wife spent time in the American West with several Plains Indians tribes, including the Lakota, Crow, Cheyenne, and Blackfeet.[13] From these experiences emerged many of Schuon's resplendent paintings on Indian themes as well as his writings. Thenceforth Schuon maintained close relations with the Yellowtails and with many other Indians, and played no small role in efforts to preserve their imperiled heritage. It was Schuon who introduced Thomas Yellowtail and Joseph Brown, the latter in turn putting Michael Fitzgerald in touch with the Crow Sun Dance Chief. So it was that Schuon played an important role in the germination of two books—*The Sacred Pipe* and *Yellowtail: Crow Medicine Man and Sun Dance Chief*, each seminal in the Native American spiritual renaissance.[14] Schuon was adopted into both the Lakota and Crow tribes, remarking of his encounter with the former, "I believe it was only then that my soul was fully healed of the wounds of my youth; I also received from the Indians a special kind of spiritual blessing."[15]

Late in his life Schuon made special mention of two men he called his "profound spiritual friends": one was his schooldays companion, lifelong friend, and fellow-Perennialist, Titus Burckhardt; the other was Thomas Yellowtail, of whom Schuon wrote:

> With Yellowtail I have a quite special relationship; between him and me there is a kind of unspoken friendship which is rooted in our natures. . . . Yellowtail is a combination of a kind of childlike earth-heaviness and simplicity with an undertone of saintliness. . . . At a deeper level [he has] something contemplative, sacerdotal, serene, profoundly good, and God-centered. . . . Withal he is a rock, not out of hardness, but out of strength and patience, and something recollected and profound permeates his whole being.[16]

Of Schuon, Yellowtail said, "He is my brother. We are in the same boat together in all things," and, "I think that he is a great man. . . . I regard him as a holy man. . . . Considering this and because he is a good friend, my wife and I decided that we'd adopt him. We did something well worth doing by adopting a great man into the family."[17] After Schuon settled in Indiana in 1980, Yellowtail visited him every year until his own passing in 1993.

Writings on the Plains Indians
Most of Schuon's writings are concerned with the world's major historical religions—the Abrahamic monotheisms, Hinduism, Buddhism, the Chinese tradition. However, his writings on primordial shamanic traditions and mythologies, especially those of the Plains Indians, occupy a distinctive place in his *oeuvre*. In one vital respect such traditions constitute the purest expression of the *sophia perennis*: they express a spontaneous and intuitive understanding of the metaphysical transparency of the natural order. One might well illustrate the point through such peoples as the Bushmen of the Kalahari or the Australian Aborigines, to name only two, or to primordial traditions which, like tributaries of a mighty river, were later absorbed into the major historical faiths—Siberian shamanism, Tibetan Bön-po, Japanese Shinto, Chinese ancestorism, Scandinavian paganism, and the like. Such phenomena form a bridge between the orally-transmitted mythologies and the "logocentric" and "axial" religions. Here, however, we turn our attention only to Schuon's writ-

ings on the American Indians, who can, in a sense, stand in for all the indigenous traditions.

Patrick Laude has written of shamanism that,

> this most encompassing perspective emphasizes the participation and integration of mankind into the interdependent totality of the spirits and powers of Nature. The ecological participation in the supernatural vocation of Nature is like the external dimension of the innermost participation in the Self.[18]

Considering the corpus of Schuon's writings on the Indians, Laude goes on to say,

> For Schuon, the spirituality of the North American Indians of the Plains is characterized by the coincidence of the most universal metaphysics and the most integral and primordial way of being. This way of being is expressed first and foremost in a synthesis of moral virtues that comprises domination of self, courage, serenity, and generosity. In addition, the shamanic and primordial perspective cannot be severed from alchemy and white magic, in the sense that the latter constitute a means of integration of the animic substance—including its relatively lower strata—into the perspective of the Spirit.[19]

As Laude intimates, Schuon's sensitivity to the metaphysical dimension of the natural order and the "symbolist outlook" of the Indians were in deepest accord. What another commentator has written of the metaphysician applies no less to the Indians themselves: "For Schuon, virgin nature carries a message of eternal truth and primordial reality, and to plunge oneself therein is to rediscover a dimension of the soul which in modern man has become atrophied."[20] Indeed, virgin nature, for the Indian, is both temple or sanctuary and divine book; it might also be called a speculum of the soul.[21]

Frequent reference has been made to Schuon's work throughout this study, often to tease out the more recondite significance of various phenomena which remain intractable when approached with a rationalistic-empiricist mentality. In what follows we will make no attempt at a systematic account of Plains Indian metaphysics, cosmology, and spiritual life, nor a conspectus of Schuon's Indian writings. Rather, we will spotlight a few aspects of Schuon's matchless work on this unique tradition, taking particular note of his observations concerning the place of the Indians in hyperborean shamanism, their "symbolist mentality," "polysynthetic animism," and the central place of the sacred pipe and sun dance in their cosmology and ritual life; thus Schuon's writings will clarify, extend, and deepen some of the observations made earlier in this study. Readers to whom Schuon's work is unknown will be able to sense, even if only in fragmentary fashion, something of the beauty and depth of his Indian writings.

The American Indians belong in the great arc of hyperborean shamanism which stretches from Mongolia and Siberia into North and South America, the peoples in question embodying "the heroic side of the yellow race, in the broadest sense of the word." Not for nothing is it that the spiritual disposition of the Indians should exhibit striking affinities with certain Far Eastern forms, particularly those of Shinto, Zen, and of Siberian, Mongolian, and Tibetan shamanism.

> For these peoples, it is above all Nature that is the sanctuary.
> . . . The North American tradition knows the cult of the great phenomena of Nature: sun, moon, rain-bearing hurricane, wind, thunder and lightning, fire, animals, rocks, trees, without forgetting the sky and earth which are their containers; above them all . . . [the] "Great Spirit."[22]

The spiritual congruence of Shintoists and Native Americans is evident in their "many mythological, and even vestimentary similarities," in the cult of Nature, and in "their thirst for freedom, their contempt for luxury, their taciturnness, and other similar characteristics."[23]

Despite the variegation of Indian cultures throughout North America,

> There is nevertheless a unity based on the symbolism of the Directions of Space and on the use of the Sacred Pipe, and above all on the idea of a Supreme Being. And this religion too, with its many forms and its many different symbols is firstly discernment and then union—discernment between this vanishing world of dreams and the everlasting Reality which lies behind it, and union with this Reality even on this earth and in this life.[24]

The fact that the metaphysical understandings of the Indians were expressed primarily in myth, symbol, and ritual, and through a reading of the Book of Nature, rather than through abstruse texts and verbal elaborations, should not blind us to their profundity. Metaphysical truths can be expressed in myth, in the visual language of symbolism, in ritual: indeed, there are good reasons to suppose that these are the best means of doing so, remembering that any expression of a timeless principle or truth can be adequate but never exhaustive; as Schuon says, "Doctrine is to Truth as the circle or spiral is to the center."[25] Moreover,

> the criterion of metaphysical truth or of its depth lies not in the complexity or difficulty of its expression, having regard to a particular capacity of understanding or style of thinking. Wisdom does not lie in any complication of words but in the profundity of the intention.[26]

Witness the Buddha's Flower Sermon! We might also recall Seyyed Hossein Nasr's reminder that contemplative intelligence—evinced in high degree by the Indians—"differs from mental virtuosity as the soaring flight of an eagle differs from the play of a monkey."[27]

The Native American perspective is rooted in a metaphysic of Nature. All natural forms and phenomena reflect qualities or aspects of the Great Holy. As Joseph Brown tells us:

> The term *Wakan-Tanka*, Great Mysterious, is an all-inclusive concept that refers both to a Supreme Being and to the totality of all gods or spirits or powers of creation. Such conceptualizations embracing both unity and diversity are typical of the polysynthetic nature of the languages of these peoples, and thus of their modes of conceptualization and cognitive orientations.[28]

Moreover, Schuon adds,

> The Indian like all the yellow race . . . stays in Nature and is never detached from it; psychologically he is like a samurai become hunter or nomad; his contemplativeness, where it is most intimate and exalted, is without doubt not unrelated to that intuitive and inarticulate method which is Zen, or in other respects, to the spiritualized Nature in Shinto.[29]

It is a symptom of modern confusions that it should so often be supposed that the Indians were "pantheists," "nature-worshippers."

It is true that they sensed a numinous presence in all phenomena, particularly animals, but they certainly did not confuse physical entities with their celestial prototypes. Schuon refers to "the symbolist vision of the cosmos [which] is *a priori* a spontaneous perspective that bases itself on the essential nature—or the metaphysical transparency—of phenomena, rather than cutting these off from their prototypes."[30] The Indians did not imagine that *Wakan-Tanka* was simply the sum of all things, nor that God was "in the world," nor that God was the sun (though they shared with Dante the belief that "No object of sense is more worthy to be made a type of God than the sun"[31]); rather, they knew that "the world is mysteriously plunged in God."[32] That *Wanka-Tanka* is, in the terms of monotheistic theology, both transcendent and immanent, is unambiguously affirmed by Black Elk: "We should understand well that all things are the works of the Great Spirit. We should know that He is within all things . . . and *even more important, we should understand that He is also above all these things and peoples.*"[33] Or, in similar vein, this from Luther Standing Bear:

> The Lakota loved the sun and earth, but he worshipped only *Wakan-Tanka,* or Big Holy, who was the Maker of all things of earth, sky, and water. *Wakan-Tanka* breathed life and motion into all things, both visible and invisible. He was over all, through all, and in all, and great as was the sun, and good as was the earth, the greatness and goodness of the Big Holy were not surpassed. The Lakota could look at nothing without at the same time looking at *Wakan-Tanka,* and he could not, if he wished, evade His presence, for it pervaded all things and filled all space. All the mysteries of birth, life, and death; all the wonders of lightning, thunder, wind, and rain were but the evidence of His everlasting and encompassing power.[34]

Far from being credulous nature-worshippers, the Indians see everywhere in Nature "the translucence of the Eternal," to recall Coleridge's marvelous phrase.

> The most important manifestations of the Great Spirit are the West, the North, the East, the South, Heaven and Earth; then come forms like the Sun, the Eagle, the Buffalo, the Rock, the Morning Star. . . . They are prefigured in the Great Spirit Himself: although He is One, He has in Himself all these Qualities

whose outer form we see in the Directions of Space and in certain phenomena of Nature.[35]

As Schuon has also observed,

The Indian is predisposed towards the suprasensible and strives to penetrate the hard wall of the sensible world, seeks openings where he can, and finds them chiefly in phenomena themselves, which indeed, in their contents, are nothing other than signposts to the suprasensible. Things are hard-frozen melodies from the Beyond.[36]

The Indian outlook is shaped by what Schuon has called "poly-synthesism," that is, "a consciousness of the profound homogeneity of the created world and the sense of universal solidarity which results therefrom,"[37] a spiritual sensibility "which sees appearances in their connection with essences."[38] Again, Black Elk beautifully expressed the principle in the inimitable parlance of his people: "Peace . . . comes within the souls of men when they realize their relationship, their oneness, with the universe and all its Powers, and when they realize that at the center of the universe dwells *Wakan-Tanka*, and that this center is really everywhere, it is within each of us."[39]

It is often remarked, by anthropologists and others, that the beliefs and practices of the Indians were "animistic"—but all too often we are left with the impression that this amounts to little more than a superstitious belief in "spirits" inhabiting various natural phenomena, which is only to be expected amongst "primitives" bereft of a properly-constituted science which would disabuse them of these quaint notions. In other words, many modern commentators have not even a glimmer of an understanding of the realities to which they so glibly refer. By contrast, Schuon's relatively slender corpus of writings on the Indians contains more insights than a whole library of anthropological works for the simple reason that here is an intelligence and metaphysical discernment adequate to its subject. As Schuon himself remarks, "to be able to know the wisdom of a people we must first of all possess the keys to such wisdom, and these indispensable keys are to be found, not in any subsidiary branch of learning [such as ethnography] but in intellectuality at its purest and most universal level."[40] Plotinus stated the principle tersely: "knowing demands the organ fitted to the object."[41] Likewise Aquinas: "the thing known is in the knower according to the mode of the knower."[42] In a characteristic passage, Schuon goes directly to the heart of the matter of "animism": "It means, in principle and metaphysically, that, whatever be the object envisaged, there springs from its existential center an ontological ray, made up of 'being,' 'consciousness,' and 'life,' whereby the object in question is attached, through its subtle or animic root, to its luminous and celestial prototype."[43] Elsewhere he writes, "It is through the animal species and the phenomena of Nature that the Indian contemplates the angelic Essences and the Divine Qualities." He goes on to quote the following passage from one of Joseph Brown's letters:

> For these people, as of course for all traditional peoples, every created object is important simply because they know the metaphysical correspondence between this world and the "Real World." No object is for them what it appears to be, but it is simply the pale shadow of a Reality. It is for this reason that every created object is *wakan*, holy, and has a power according to the loftiness of the spiritual reality that it reflects.[44]

Schuon adds the caveat that "We do not say that the symbolist [i.e., the Indian] thinks 'principle' or 'idea' when he sees water, fire, or some other phenomenon of Nature; it is simply a question of our making the reader understand what the symbolist 'sees,' *inasmuch as 'seeing' and 'thinking' are for him synonymous.*"[45]

This "polysynthetic animism" explains a great deal about the spiritual ecology of the Indians—amongst other things, the so-called "magical" techniques which operate "in virtue of the analogies between symbols and their prototypes" and which enable the shaman to access the "subtle and suprasensorial roots of things," thereby to influence natural phenomena in ways which absolutely escape the ken of the modern mind. It also informs the reluctance of the Indians to detach themselves from the natural world and to succumb to a civilization made up of "artifices and servitudes."[46]

Schuon's writings and, indeed, his paintings on Indian themes, illuminate almost every aspect of the Indian tradition: not only their "religion"—metaphysics, cosmology, mythology, values, codes, ritual life, and the symbolic language in which these are expressed—but also the ways in which "religion" pervades their material culture and is inseparable from their modes of subsistence, their hunting, warfare, dress and deportment, habitations, their arts and crafts, and so on.

The sacred pipe, or calumet, is central to the ritual life of the Plains Indians: it constitutes "a doctrinal synthesis, both concise and complex" and to describe its symbolism is "in a certain sense, to expound the sum of Indian wisdom."[47] Schuon demonstrates the ways in which the pipe itself incarnates teachings which are metaphysical (i.e., concerning the Absolute and universal realities of various degrees), cosmological (concerning the manifest worlds, including the heavenly bodies as well as the terrestrial order), and anthropological (concerning the human situation *vis-à-vis* these metacosmic and cosmic realities).

Schuon notes that "When one stands in the midst of a plain, three things strike one's vision: the immense circle of the horizon; the immense vault of the sky; the four cardinal points. It is these elements which primordially determine the spirit and soul of the Indians; it could be said that the whole of their metaphysics or cosmology is based on these initial motifs."[48] The calumet expresses the symbolism of the cross within the circle, the six directions, and the center where they meet. The circle "corresponds to the Sky, while the cross marks the Four Directions of space and all other quaternaries of the Universe; it also marks the vertical ternary Earth-Man-Sky, which situates the horizontal quaternary on three levels."[49] The Four Directions provide the frame for an exceptionally eloquent symbolism. Man stands at the center of the four horizontal directions of space; as well, he is the axis of the vertical ternary, thus becoming mediator between Earth and Sky. Man is thus a totality, bearing the whole universe within himself, just as does the microcosmic calumet, as is apparent in this passage from Black Elk:

> I fill this sacred Pipe with the bark of the red willow; but before we smoke it, you must see how it is made and what it means. These four ribbons hanging here on the stem are the four quarters of the universe. The black one is for the west where the thunder beings live to send us rain; the white one for the north, whence comes the great white cleansing wind; the red one for the east, whence springs the light and where the morning star lives to give men wisdom; the yellow for the south, whence come the summer and the power to grow. But these four spirits are only one Spirit after all, and this eagle feather here is for that One, which is like a father, and also it is for the thoughts of men that should rise high as eagles do. Is not the sky a father and the earth a mother, and are not all

living things with feet or wings or roots their children? And this hide upon the mouthpiece here, which should be bison hide, is for the earth, from whence we came and at whose breast we suck as babies all our lives, along with all the animals and birds and trees and grasses. And because it means all this, and more than any man can understand, the Pipe is holy.[50]

"The Sacred Pipe means prayer. With it, man prays not only for himself, but also for the whole Universe. The whole Universe prays with him."[51]

The Four Directions, which played so significant a part in Black Elk's Great Vision, also correspond to the cardinal virtues, which together reveal much of the Indian "character," if one may so put it: courage, which manifests itself in stoic heroism in combat or adversity; patience, displayed during the hunt or in the various trials and austerities in the solitude of virgin Nature; generosity, expressed in the love of gift-giving;[52] and fidelity, which shows itself in the lofty sense of honor and duty most evident in the Indian's dealings with his fellow tribespeople.[53] Thus, "A fascinating combination of combative and stoical heroism with a priestly bearing conferred on the Indian of the Plains and Forest a sort of majesty at once aquiline and solar, hence the powerfully original and irreplaceable beauty which is associated with him and which contributes to his prestige as a warrior and martyr."[54] To these four virtues should be added another significant aspect of the Indian ethos to which Schuon draws attention:

> The Indian tends towards independence and so towards indifference with regard to the outward world: he surrounds himself with silence as with a magic circle, and this silence is sacred as being the vehicle of the heavenly influences. It is from this silence—of which the natural support is solitude— that the Indian draws his spiritual strength; his ordinary prayer is unvoiced: what is required is not thought but consciousness of the Spirit, and this consciousness is immediate and formless like the vault of heaven.[55]

The smoking of the pipe, as we have seen, is integrated in nearly all of the rituals of the Indians. Of the other three central rites Schuon writes,

> The Sweat Lodge means purification. In it, man renews himself; he becomes a new being. He becomes pure before

his Creator. The solitary Invocation is the highest form of prayer. It is contemplation and union. But it also benefits the whole community, in a subtle and indirect way. . . . This is the highest and most complete form of spiritual life. The Sun Dance is in a sense the prayer of the whole community. For those who dance, it is union with the Great Spirit. The Sun Dance attaches us to the Great Spirit.[56]

Schuon counted the Sun Dance he observed in 1959 as "one of the most powerful things I have ever witnessed," describing it in these terms:

The Sun Dance is a cosmic drama, indeed it is the cosmos itself. It is without beginning and without end: it is the temporal fraction of a timeless and supernatural reality. . . . The Sun Dance is the remembrance of God, purification from the multiple and the outward, union with the One and the Real.[57]

The clear symbolic significance and the elemental convincing power of the Sun Dance are all quite overwhelming. . . . The buffalo is the sacred, primordial power and fecundity of the earth, and the eagle is the light that comes from above, the Revelation; the buffalo is mountain or rock, and the eagle sky and lightning; but the buffalo is also the sun, or the earthly image thereof.[58]

We can bring this discussion of Schuon's writings on the Native Americans to a conclusion with another beautiful passage which recapitulates some of his central themes:

The Indian world signifies first and foremost the reading of the primordial doctrine in the phenomena of Nature . . . and the experiencing of Nature as the holy, primordial Home that everywhere manifests the Great Spirit and everywhere is filled with Him; and this consciousness gives the Red Man his dignity, composed of reverence for Nature and of self-dominion; it also throws light on the singular majesty of his artistically richly-accented appearance, in which eagle and sun combine and which, in the archetypal realm, belongs to the divine prototypes.[59]

Paintings on Indian Themes

From his earliest days Schuon was fascinated by traditional arts. He displayed a preternatural ability to discern in their visible and auditory forms both the celestial imprint of the Revelation from which the tradition in question emerged, and the ethnic genius of the people in question—a kind of collective signature, one might say. Schuon has been acutely sensitive to the role of Beauty in the spiritual life, its "interiorizing alchemy" which brings the soul back to God.[60] Given all this it is not surprising that Schuon himself was an artist and poet as well as a metaphysician. He enjoyed drawing and painting in his childhood years but, by his own reckoning, it was not until after his marriage that his paintings achieved a maturity of style. He produced something in the order of two hundred oil paintings as well as many sketches and drawings.[61]

In 1981 a selection of Schuon's paintings on Indian themes, entitled "Scenes of Plains Indian Life," was exhibited at the Taylor Museum in the Colorado Springs Fine Arts Center. Some of these appeared as plates in *The Feathered Sun: Plains Indians in Art and Philosophy* (1990), while a fuller collection of paintings and drawings, *Images of Primordial and Mystic Beauty*, was published in 1992. While Schuon's artwork has been a secondary and mostly private undertaking, there is no discord between the metaphysical works and the paintings; they are mutually illuminating. It could not be otherwise, for as Schuon wrote to a friend, "my paintings flow forth from the depths of my heart."[62]

Between 1950 and 1965 Schuon's paintings depicted almost exclusively Indian subjects and themes, whilst those from 1965 onwards most often portrayed Celestial Femininity—as the Holy Virgin, or as the White Buffalo Calf Woman of Lakota mythology, or as a manifestation of the *Shakti*, with reminiscences of Lakshmi and Durga, or other Oriental representations of the merciful and bounteous aspects of the Divine Feminine, such as Tara or Kwan-Yin. Thus these paintings draw together certain motifs from the Semitic, Eastern, and primordial mythologies in a synthetic vision which was intensely personal but which reverberated with universal resonances. In her catalogue notes for the 1981 exhibition, Barbara Perry describes Schuon's general approach and style as, "quite simple, spontaneous, and natural, and without any affectation of didactic symbolism. Fundamentally, what he portrays are higher realities as lived through the medium of his own soul."[63]

Schuon's American Indian paintings address their primordial world in all its "sacerdotal hieratism and heroic dignity,"[64] and its sacramental and polysynthetic sense of the theophanic qualities of nature. Schuon himself remarked of his earliest fully realized artwork:

> My first paintings portrayed two Red Indian women, one clothed and the other naked; since then I have more than once repeated this theme, as it signifies the antithesis between sacred form and sacred content, or between the veiling and the unveiling of the holy. Besides purely narrative Indian pictures I often painted the sage—or the masculine nature of wisdom—in the form of an old Indian chief; I often represented him as the center of a council. My paintings of women represented the complement to this, namely beauty, with all the virtues that go with it; my starting point here—in these as in other pictures—was not a deliberate symbolism, but simply a reality that flowed forth from my nature; the meaning was prefigured in my inward being, and did not lie in my conscious intention.[65]

Schuon often also returned to the sacred image of the feathered sun which was found on Indian vestments and tipis, and which he described in these words:

> The Sun is composed of concentric circles formed of stylized eagle feathers; the resulting impression is particularly evocative in that the symbol simultaneously suggests center, radiation, power, and majesty. This symbiosis between the sun and the eagle, which is to be found again in the celebrated headdress of feathers formerly worn by chiefs and great warriors, brings us back to the symbolism of the Sun Dance: here man is spiritually transformed into an eagle soaring towards Heaven and becoming identified with the rays of the Divine Sun.[66]

Over the years and without any intention on his part, the feathered sun became a symbol for Schuon's own spiritual message. Whilst most of Schuon's Indian paintings center on the chief/sage and/or woman, many related motifs and a wealth of visual details pertaining to Indian life give these canvases both vibrancy and poignancy. In recapturing something of the ambience of the ancestral world they serve as an irreplaceable complement to Schuon's writings on the Indians.

The Fate of the Indian Peoples

With the burgeoning interest in the Indians since the 1960s, a great deal has been written about their fate, often lamenting the many injustices that were perpetrated in the name of "civilization" and "progress." There have also been many more accounts of this dismal history as seen from the Indian side, as well as a spate of books about their spiritual traditions. However, many of these accounts are unsatisfactory or, at the least, partial, as they are so often marred by that "unrelieved ignorance of metaphysical principles" which Seyyed Hossein Nasr identified as one of the defining characteristics of the modern outlook.[67] No such reproach can be leveled at Frithjof Schuon, who has not only explicated Indian metaphysics and cosmology with rare authority, but who has explained the deeper significance of the tragic fate of these peoples:

> In order fully to understand the abruptness of the breakup of the Red Indian race one must take account of the fact that this race had lived for thousands of years in a kind of paradise that was practically speaking without limits. . . . Theirs was a rugged paradise to be sure, but one that nevertheless provided an environment full of grandeur and of a sacred character. . . . The Indians identified themselves spiritually and humanly with this inviolate Nature. . . . But as time went on, and concordantly with the development of the "Iron Age" in which passions predominate and wisdom disappears, abuses begin to arise with increasing frequency. . . . The privileged situation of the Indians, on the fringe of "History" and of its crushing urban civilizations, had inevitably to come to an end. There is nothing surprising in the fact that this disintegration of a paradise . . . coincided with modern times.

However, whilst the fate of the Indians had a certain ineluctability, this in no way excuses or extenuates "the villainies of which the Indian has been the victim during several centuries," nor mitigates the pathos of their predicament. ("It must needs be that offences come; but woe to that man by whom the offence cometh!"[68]) The destruction of the Indian peoples and their traditions "remains one of the greatest crimes and most blatant cases of vandalism in all human history."[69]

> The crushing of the Indian race is tragic because in its deepest and most intimate nature this noble people was opposed to

"assimilation"; the red man could only conquer or die; it is the spiritual basis of this alternative that confers on the destiny of the red race an aspect of grandeur and martyrdom. . . . They embodied a character, an idea, a principle, and, being what they were, they could not be unfaithful to themselves. This great drama might be defined as the struggle, not only between a materialistic civilization and another that was chivalrous and spiritual, but also between urban civilization (in the strictly human and pejorative sense of this term, with all its implications of artifice and servility) and the kingdom of Nature considered as the majestic, pure, unlimited apparel of the Divine Spirit. And it is from this idea of the final victory of Nature (final because it is primordial) that those Indians who have remained faithful to their ancestors draw their inexhaustible patience in the face of the misfortunes of their race; Nature, of which they feel themselves to be embodiments, and which at the same time is their sanctuary, will end by conquering this artificial and sacrilegious world, for it is the Garment, the Breath, the very Hand of the Great Spirit.[70]

Conclusion:
The Legacy

If the vision was true and mighty, as I know, it is true and
mighty yet; for such things are of the spirit, and it is in the darkness
of their eyes that men get lost.
Black Elk[1]

And I saw that the sacred hoop of my people was one of many
hoops that made one circle, wide as daylight and as starlight, and in
the center grew one mighty flowering tree to shelter all the
children of one mother and one father.
Black Elk[2]

A century after Black Elk's Great Vision, many young Americans were
in search of alternative ways of understanding themselves, the world,
and the life of the spirit; one of their favored sources was *Black Elk
Speaks*, "a story about the planting and development of native ideas
within the religious imaginations of millions of Americans."[3] The
reasons for the book's popularity have already been canvassed and
there is no point in lengthy recapitulations. But it is useful to recall
Julian Rice's claim that "By conscientiously studying and observing
Lakol wicho'an (traditional Lakota culture) in relation to *Black Elk
Speaks*, a reader might look through both Black Elk and Neihardt to a
Lakota wisdom tradition more profound than any single instrument or
interpreter."[4] By way of a conclusion let us simply recall three of our
inquiry's central themes, concerning the fate of the nomadic peoples,
the Indian metaphysic of nature, and the recovery of Tradition.

The dark fate of the Indians at the hands of the invaders is a story
that has been many times repeated all over the globe. The shameful history of European-Aboriginal relations in my own country, for instance,
furnishes many arresting parallels. The extirpation of indigenous cultures is, *essentially*, not a clash of "races" or even of "civilizations"
but of Tradition and modernity—one which cannot be fully explained
in terms of European imperialism, though in most parts of the world
Europeans have indeed been the agents of destruction. Early in this
study reference was made to the desecration of Tibet, one of the last
bastions of Tradition in the modern world. Consider the words of Lama
Anagarika Govinda, written in the immediate wake of the Chinese
invasion but no less pertinent today than they were half a century ago.

How accurately they describe the fate not only of the Tibetans but of the Native Americans and indeed of many indigenous peoples:

> Why is it that the fate of Tibet has found such a deep echo in the world? There can only be one answer: Tibet has become the symbol of all that present-day humanity is longing for, either because it has been lost or not yet realized or because it is in danger of disappearing from human sight: the stability of a tradition, which has its roots not only in a historical or cultural past, but within the innermost being of man, in whose depth this past is enshrined as an ever-present source of inspiration.

Lama Govinda goes on to stress the symbolism of the struggle between two worlds, the Buddhist world of traditional Tibet and the modern world, in this case represented by a regime which has repudiated its own rich tradition in subservience to the false idols of modernity:

> As on a gigantically raised stage we witness the struggle between two worlds, which may be interpreted, according to the standpoint of the spectator, either as a struggle between the past and the future, between backwardness and progress, belief and science, superstition and knowledge—or as the struggle between spiritual freedom and material power, between the wisdom of the heart and the knowledge of the brain, between the dignity of the human individual and the herd-instinct of the mass, between the faith in the higher destiny of man through inner development and the belief in material prosperity through an ever-increasing production of goods.

As we have seen with the destruction of nomadic cultures everywhere, the infamies of the invaders are justified by the progressivist ideology which underpins the modern outlook:

> We witness the tragedy of a peaceful people without political ambitions and with the sole desire to be left alone, being deprived of its freedom and trampled underfoot by a powerful neighbor in the name of "progress," which as ever must serve as a cover for all the brutalities of the human race.[5]

The parallels between the fate of the Native Americans and other indigenous peoples are too obvious to need accentuating. But perhaps we can pause to consider just one facet of these cultures which fits under Huston Smith's rubric of "what they have that we lack"—a sense of *belonging* in the cosmos, a world of order, beauty, and meaning, so different from modern man's ennui, alienation, and loneliness. Laurens van der Post expressed this sense of belonging in his reflections about the Kalahari people, but he may just as well have been writing of the Native Americans:

> This essence of this being (of the Bushmen), I believe, was his sense of belonging: belonging to nature, the universe, life, and his own humanity. He had committed himself utterly to nature as a fish to the sea. He had no sense of property, owned no animals, and cultivated no land. Life and nature owned all and he accepted without question that, provided he was obedient to the urge of the world within him, the world without, which was not separate in his spirit, would provide. How right he was is proved by the fact that nature was kinder to him by far than civilization ever was. This feeling of belonging set him apart from us on the far side of the deepest divide in the human spirit.[6]

The malignant pseudo-mythology of "progress" is a direct link between the near-extermination of nomadic cultures and the rape of nature. Seyyed Hossein Nasr opened his 1994 Cadbury Lectures with these words: "The Earth is bleeding from wounds inflicted upon it by a humanity no longer in harmony with Heaven and therefore in constant strife with the terrestrial environment."[7] That we are now in a state of "constant strife" is widely recognized, but the root causes of this condition are rarely understood. We witness a plethora of writings on the "ecological crisis," often well-intentioned and carrying fragmentary insights, but fundamentally confused because of an ignorance of those timeless cosmological principles to which the Perennialists recall us. In this respect the contrast between the Indians and ourselves (as "moderns") could hardly be more dramatic. It may well be that the Native Americans' participation in "the supernatural vocation of Nature" could yet have a creative role to play in healing that rupture between Heaven and Earth of which the ecological crisis is but the outer symptom. In the end it is indeed a matter of the state of our consciousness. As the Sufi writer, Abu Bakr Siraj Ed-Din, observed,

"The state of the outer world does not merely correspond to men's souls; it also in a sense depends on that state, since man himself is pontiff of the outer world. Thus the corruption of man must necessarily affect the whole."[8] This understanding has been almost entirely lost in the modern world, with all too obvious consequences. Few people today understand that Nature, in Nasr's words, remains "hungry for our prayers."[9]

A sacramental understanding of Nature is, of course, not confined to the American Indians; on the contrary, it is more or less universal in religious cultures. As Mircea Eliade noted,

> For religious man, nature is never only "natural"; it is always fraught with religious value. This is easy to understand for the cosmos is a divine creation . . . [the gods] manifested the different modalities of the sacred in the very structure of the world and of cosmic phenomena. . . . This divine work always preserves its transparency, that is, it spontaneously reveals the many aspects of the sacred. . . . The cosmos as a whole is an organism at once real, living, and sacred; it simultaneously reveals the modalities of being and of sacrality. Ontophany and hierophany meet.[10]

Even in those traditions, such as the Judeo-Christian, which have been accused of "world-denial," we find countless affirmations of the theophanic sacrality of the natural order. Thus, for example, St Paul: "The invisible things of him from the creation of the world are clearly seen, being understood by the things that are made, even his eternal power and Godhead."[11] Or Mechthild of Magdeburg: "The day of my spiritual awakening was the day I saw, and knew I saw, all things in God and God in all things."[12] Or Meister Eckhart: "Anyone who truly knows creatures may be excused from listening to sermons for every creature is full of God, and is a book."[13] However, the understanding of the transparency of the created order is most immediately and powerfully evident in the primal traditions, in part because their experience is less mediated by the abstractions which inevitably accompany the literate, rational, historicist, and scientific outlook that tyrannizes the modern mind. The mythological, symbolist, and polysynthetic consciousness of the Native Americans is given one of its most lambent expressions in Black Elk's vision and teachings. For those with eyes to see and ears to hear it offers a potent antidote to all those tendencies in modern thought which have left us in a godless and spiritless world, a desacralized universe which remains "opaque, inert, mute."[14] No amount of fashionable concern about the evils of pollution and ecological degradation, no amount of "socially responsible science," nor any sentimental idolization of "nature," can replace the profound spiritual intuition of the sacredness of nature which lies at the heart of the primal traditions. As Schuon insists, for modern man

> this scission between man and the earth—a reflection of the scission between man and God—has borne such bitter fruits that it should not be difficult to admit that, in these days, the timeless message of Nature constitutes a spiritual viaticum of the first importance. . . . It is not a question of projecting a supersaturated and disillusioned individualism into a desecrated Nature—this would be a worldliness like any other—but, on the contrary, of rediscovering in Nature, on the basis of the traditional outlook, the divine substance which is inherent in it; in other words to "see God everywhere."[15]

There are those who tout what has been called "eco-spirituality" which actually amounts to no more than a secular pantheism, if one may be allowed such a term, a materialistic view of the natural world which lays claim to some kind of "spirituality" and "sacredness" while dispensing with a belief in the transcendent, as if night and day could be sundered from the sun, or as if there could be a circle without a center. The notion of "the sacred" bereft of any transcendent dimension is bogus.[16] Equally absurd is the notion of a "secular scientific spirituality": like all such concoctions this kind of naturism is a continental form of idolatry. Moreover, as Philip Sherrard so plainly puts it, "An agnostic and materialistic science of nature is a contradiction in terms. . . . Its findings will necessarily correspond to the living reality as little as a corpse corresponds to the living reality of a human being."[17] What the Native Americans offer is a visionary cosmology in which their beliefs about *Wakan-Tanka*, the natural order, and the human vocation form a seamless web. And here "beliefs" does not refer to a list of abstract propositions and formal creeds, still less to an ideological manifesto about "wilderness values," but to a way of understanding and experiencing the world which is incarnated in their cultural traditions. One need hardly add that their intuitions about nature and the values and attitudes which attend such an understanding stand sharply at odds with modern man's alienation from God, from the creation, from himself. In this context we might usefully recall Emerson's dictum that "the views of nature held by any people determine all their institutions."[18]

The metaphysic of nature which informed the Indian outlook is embodied in the mythology, the rites and indeed, the whole culture, of the Plains Indians. Throughout this study we have seen it manifested in the "polysynthetic" and "symbolist" understanding of the Lakota. However, it may be helpful to some readers to have the *principles* informing the traditional Lakota outlook formulated in more abstract terms, which might allow the correspondences with other traditional perspectives to be more easily discerned. To this end the following rudimentary summation—one which no traditional Indian would make in these terms but which is, I think, in accord with their metaphysical and cosmological understandings—may be useful:

Metaphysical
✧ Reality is One.
✧ Reality is hierarchical: it has many "dimensions," "states of being," "degrees," "worlds," "realms," "divine presences," "levels."
✧ No single "level" can be understood without reference to the rest.
✧ The Real is both transcendent and immanent.

Cosmological
✧ The impermanent material time-space world of flux is created by, or emerges from, the Divine, and bears within itself divine "traces."
✧ The cosmos is pervaded by consciousness, in which man participates.
✧ The terrestrial environment and the visible universe is an intelligible "text" written in the language of symbols and correspondences.
✧ The material world is subject to influences from "above," most immediately from the psychic or animic realm, with which it is in reciprocal relationship; for this reason it can be said that the terrestrial world mirrors man's inner state.

Anthropological
✧ The human is a microcosmic and axial or "amphibious" being who lives in the horizontal dimension of time and space and in the vertical dimension of the Spirit.
✧ Far from being just another "biological organism" involved in the "struggle for survival," humankind has peculiar privileges and responsibilities as the vice-regent, the steward, the pontifex of the natural order; our cosmic responsibilities are fulfilled primarily through worship, prayer, sacrifice, and other rituals.

✣ In a certain sense man "creates" his universe, positively through the ritual re-creation of the acts of the gods, ancestors, sky heroes, spirit beings and such.

✣ "All that lives is holy." Interconnectedness, interdependence, "suchness." *Mitakuye oyasin!*

The implications of these principles for our understanding of the natural order are many, but here are a few: a materialistic science, and the worldview of which it is symptomatic, is one of the root causes of the "environmental crisis" and, in itself, is quite incapable of providing any remedy; "green" naturism is simply the obverse side of one-dimensional scientism, both being ignorant—in principle as well as *de facto*—of the supra-sensorial dimensions of Reality;[19] a holistic and sacramental understanding of nature is the *starting-point* for any "solution," which will necessarily entail prayer, ritual, and sacrifice. In these later days of the present cosmic cycle[20] it would be sanguine, to say the least, to imagine that these principles will find widespread acceptance in the contemporary world. Nonetheless, the fact that these principles and their applications are unintelligible and/or unpalatable to the modern mentality in nowise affects their validity. Nor should those who retain some faith in these principles allow the current state of affairs to provoke a sense of hopelessness. No effort on behalf of the truth is ever in vain. Recall the words of René Guénon pondering the "crisis of the modern world":

> Those who might be tempted to give way to despair should realize that nothing accomplished in this order can ever be lost, that confusion, error, and darkness can win the day only apparently and in a purely ephemeral way, that all partial and transitory disequilibrium must perforce contribute towards the great equilibrium of the whole, and that nothing can ultimately prevail against the power of truth. Their device should be that used formerly by certain initiatory organizations of the West: *Vincit Omnia Veritas.*[21]

The lessons to be derived from the study of a tradition such as that of the Lakota have nothing to do with "turning back the clock" or with a superficial imitation of their modes of living. This is not to say that Native Americans themselves should not preserve and revive their ancestral ways insofar as is possible; indeed, for these people it may well be an existential imperative. As Thomas Yellowtail observed, "In our modern world today, we may seem like drowning men because of the loss of much of our spiritual tradition. As drowning men we should cling to [our] rites as our lifeline and never let go, because this lifeline can save us."[22] But for non-native folk the example and the primordial message of the Indians might most usefully provoke a searching interrogation of the prevailing ideologies of modernity and a renewed interest in the sources of wisdom which are to be found in all traditions. Pondering the legacy of the American Indians, Joseph Brown urged non-natives to look anew at their own spiritual inheritance:

> In spite of the initial attractiveness of Indian traditions, because they are rooted in this land and because of their seeming "mystical" qualities they are nevertheless generally inaccessible to the non-Native American. However, by taking pains to learn what one can from Native American traditions one who is as yet unaffiliated with a true tradition will be aided in knowing what a tradition is in all its complexity, depth, and richness of cultural expressions. It is then possible to undertake the work of rediscovering the roots of what normally, or historically, should be one's own spiritual heritage.[23]

Contrary to the assumptions of many people who are disenchanted with the Judeo-Christian tradition, often for good reason, the perennial wisdom we find in indigenous mythological traditions has also found expression in the great historical religions. No doubt the onslaughts of modernity have left the Occidental traditions in some disarray. Nonetheless, as Schuon reminds us,

> Nothing is more misleading than to pretend, as is so glibly done in our day, that the religions have compromised themselves hopelessly in the course of the centuries or that they are now played out. If one knows what a religion really consists of, one also knows that the religions cannot compromise themselves and they are independent of human doings. . . . As for an exhausting of the religions, one might speak of this if all men had by now become saints or Buddhas.[24]

The religious inclusivism and universalism of many of the Plains Indians can also provide an invaluable lesson for those Christians who for too long have been in the grip of a rigid exclusivism. No one has expressed the basis for this more open and sympathetic attitude better than Yellowtail, a man who, like Black Elk, retained a living connection with the ancestral ways but who also confronted the realities of a religiously pluralistic world:

> You [Acbadadea] have given different ways to different people all over the world. As we know, this earth is round like a wagon wheel. In a wagon wheel all the spokes are set into the center. The circle of the wheel is round, and all spokes come from the center, and the center is You, Acbadadea, the Maker of All Things Above. Each spoke can be considered as a different religion of the world which has been given by You to different peoples and different races. . . . The different paths have been given to us, but they all lead to the same place. We all pray to the same God, to you.[25]

Some final thoughts about Black Elk, the *wicasa wakan*. As John Neihardt observed, Black Elk was a humble and modest man—"modest as a man may be who is sure of what he knows and that what he knows is worth knowing."[26] But he also knew that his visions were a gift from above, that "no good thing can be done by any man alone."[27] His life testifies to the universal truth that, "A man may receive nothing, except it be given him from heaven."[28] Not without reason is *wakan*—"sacred, powerful, mysterious"—one of the most exalted words in Lakota. One litmus test of any traditional civilization is the ubiquitous sense of the sacred, not only in overtly religious matters, but in every aspect of life. Black Elk's life, in all its phases and aspects, is infused with this sense of the sacred—a sense vivified and enriched by his visions but one bequeathed to him by Lakota tradition. Concerning the "sacred" the sovereign metaphysician of our time has written:

> That is sacred which in the first place is attached to the transcendent order, secondly possesses the character of absolute certainty, and thirdly, eludes the comprehension of the ordinary mind. . . . The sacred is the presence of the center in the periphery. . . . The sacred introduces a quality of the absolute into relativities and confers on perishable things a texture of eternity.[29]

With these words in mind it must surely strike us anew how Black Elk's visions, and indeed his whole life, were permeated by the sacred.

The loss or perversion of this spiritual awareness is one of the tokens of modernism. Black Elk and others like him, and more generally the tradition to which he belonged, can perhaps recall us to the sense of the sacred without which no civilization deserves the name. Schuon:

> Civilization only represents a value provided it is supra-human in origin and implies for the "civilized" man a sense of the sacred. . . . A sense of the sacred is fundamental for every civilization because fundamental for man; the sacred—that which is immutable, inviolable, and thus infinitely majestic—is in the very substance of our spirit and of our existence.[30]

Although the present study has ranged over a wide terrain its central concern has been to explore the meaning and significance of the life and teachings of a Lakota *wicasa wakan*, especially as we have them in *Black Elk Speaks*. Here is an assessment by one who has been intimately involved in the Native American renaissance, N. Scott Momaday:

> *Black Elk Speaks* is an extraordinarily human document—and beyond that the record of a profound spiritual journey, the pilgrimage of a people towards their historical fulfillment and culmination, towards the accomplishment of a worthy destiny. That the pilgrimage was in a tragic sense abruptly ended at Wounded Knee in 1890, that Black Elk's words would at last take a tragic turn—"There is no center any longer, and the sacred tree is dead"—is of little consequence in the long run, I believe. For in that sudden and absolute investment in the tragic, in the whole assumption of a tragic sense, there is immeasurable vindication, the achievement of a profound and permanent dignity, an irreducible impression on the records of human history.[31]

In his reflections on the life of Mohandas Gandhi, George Orwell suggested that "saints should always be judged guilty until they are proved innocent, but the tests that have to be applied to them are not, of course, the same in all cases."[32] The test in Black Elk's case must surely be whether he remained faithful to "seeing in a sacred manner the shapes of all things in the spirit," as disclosed to him in the Great Vision. Can we doubt it? Just as Orwell was unable to accumulate more than the most paltry pile of misdemeanors in the Mahatma's life, so too even the most caustic detractors of *Black Elk Speaks* have been unable to file any serious charges against the holy man's character. Here is Joseph Brown writing of Black Elk, his close friend Little Warrior, and other Lakota elders:

> These old men . . . manifested in their being and in every act a nobility, serenity, generosity, concentration, and kindness that we usually associate with the saints of the better-known religions. Indeed it is in these . . . personalities that we have proof of the efficacy and reality of the Indian's spiritual methods and values.[33]

Not long before the death of the holy man, Brown wrote, "It is good being with the saintly old man, for there is much *barakah* [blessing] in his *maqam* [spiritual station], his spiritual poverty, an utter simplicity, a child-like spontaneous quality, his great joy in very small things, and his love to sing and laugh and to make others happy."[34]

Was Black Elk a saint? Possibly, though God alone can judge. But he was, to be sure, a holy man—a visionary mystic, religious leader, a man of noble character, and the narrator of one of the century's most inspiring spiritual documents. Let the *wicasa wakan* himself have the last word, here speaking about *The Sacred Pipe* but also indirectly about *Black Elk Speaks*:

> I have wished to make this book through no other desire than to help my people in understanding the greatness and truth of our own tradition, and also help in bringing peace upon the earth, not only among men, but within men and between the whole of creation.[35]

Appendix I

Excerpts from Letters of Joseph Epes Brown[1]

September 4, 1947, Southwest Harbor, Maine, to Fr. Gall[2] in Belgium
I leave in two days for North & South Dakota. . . . I do not know whether your brother, M. [Frithjof] Schuon, has informed you of my proposed visit to the North American Indians? In any case, I have learned through M. J.A. Cuttat[3] and your brother of your very real interest in the Dakota, and therefore wish to be of assistance in any possible way.

September 30, 1947, Manderson, South Dakota, to Jacques-Albert Cuttat in Lausanne, Switzerland
I have been among the Oglala Sioux of Pine Ridge Agency, S.D. for almost three weeks now, and the way has opened in a most gratifying manner. Most of this time has been spent with Black Elk's family in Manderson. Black Elk's son Benjamin has been invaluable as interpreter, and means of contact. As soon as the nature of this visit was understood, one was received most warmly, and every possible assistance was given. It was stated that this contact was a "Godsend," and was established just in time—for reasons that I shall explain.

Old Black Elk is 85 and shall not live much longer. He is therefore now anxious to reestablish an Order of the Pipe, and is anxious that I record a history of the Sacred Pipe that he shall dictate as part of the process. Before coming here I had spent much time studying the metaphysics of their Pipe, and the accompanying rites, and then realized that in this instrument almost the whole of their ancient doctrine could be preserved.

It shall not be difficult for Black Elk to reestablish this order, for in the first place the original Sacred Pipe is still preserved by a holy man—Elk Head, who lives at Cherry Creek, in the Cheyenne Agency, S.D. (These people are also Oglala, and speak Lakota.) Also in talking with several of the old men here I have found that almost all still keep their pipes, and have never lost their respect for this sacred object. Much of their understanding of it has however, been lost, but it would not be difficult to reestablish this, for they possess all the requirements, and are especially "the poor in spirit," having a most wonderful disregard for the things of this world. . . .

145

When leaving Black Elk, one was presented a sacred red-stone pipe, and a bag of sacred tobacco. This pipe was made long ago by a holy man, Little Deer, and the possession of it I am told shall open the way for me among not only the Sioux but also among the other Plains nations. I mention this only that you may know how well we were received, and that the wheel of these people has not been broken.

October 1, 1947, Manderson, South Dakota, to Fr. Gall in Belgium
I have been among the Oglala Sioux of Pine Ridge Reservation, S.D. for several weeks now, and have been most warmly received by these noble, generous, and patient people. I have been living mostly with Black Elk's family at Manderson, South Dakota—old Black Elk as you know is one of the last of the *wicasa wakan*. His son Benjamin has been to Carlyle School, as well as Catholic mission here, and has thus received a white man's education and all the limitations that that implies. But due to the influence of his father he has just recently awoken to the greatness of his own heritage, and knowing that his father has not much longer to live (he is 85+) wishes to follow in his tracks. We have thus contacted him in time, for the works of Guénon, Coomaraswamy, and your brother [Frithjof Schuon] shall give him the assistance he needs in his work. Benjamin already knows much—in the evenings, using a drum, he sings for me the ancient songs, of the most marvelous beauty—especially the Ghost Dance songs.

. . . Most of the Indians here are Catholic—but of a certain sort— i.e., they recognize the truth wherever they find it, and so know that their ancient way was also the true one.

Old Black Elk is anxious to reestablish an Order of the Pipe— and I believe this to be of the greatest importance, for in this ritual instrument is contained almost the totality of their ancient doctrine— indeed the original [Pipe] is still kept by Elk Head, who lives in Cherry Creek S.D. (I am on my way there to talk with him.) Black Elk would be glad and eager to give you an Indian name, and thus make you a member of the Sioux nation.

October 19, 1947, Wind River, Wyoming, to Whitall Perry in Cairo, Egypt
Up to this time I have been among the Sioux, Assiniboine, Gros Ventre, Crees, & Blackfeet. Among each of these peoples much is still retained of their ancient tradition, although as you know our com-

pulsory schools and the proselytizing furies have made great inroads
& have done tremendous damage. The greatest manifestation of this
seems to be the almost absolute breech between the ages of 50 and
70, & as for the youth, they are as vulgar as any. But those over 70
still follow in their ancient path, know no English, & many are making
efforts to insure the transmission of their wisdom. Whether this can
be done (among the Plains peoples) I am not sure, & doubt it—for
everything is against it—there can be destroyed in one generation
what it took a hundred to create. In each nation I have tried to contact the one who is regarded as the most steadfast in his ancient way
and with those whom I have thought qualified I have left *The Crisis
of the* . . . and AKC's *Am I* . . . ,[4] both of which should do much in
comforting these peoples and in strengthening them in their determination to follow their ancient way. Most of the Old Men with whom
I have talked understand perfectly the true character of the "Modern
World," realize the crisis of the present time, & know that a catas-
trophe of some sort is imminent . . .

October 28, 1947, Julesburg, Colorado, to John Murray in Lausanne, Switzerland

After being with the Blackfeet I understood that one must not be
too hasty in judging the disintegrating influence of the tourist. In the
summer you know they take their lodges and go into the mountains of
the Park, and there sing, dance, and take money for permitting the tourists to take their picture. But several old people told me that although
they earn money from the tourists by doing things at the proper time they
are being paid for living the way they wish to live, in the open, and in
a O [camp circle]; and when they put on their dances, the old people
are conscious of the meaning. In other words, they tolerate the tourists
and take what they can from them. Most of my time here was spent
with an old man, a chief, of the name of Crow Chief Reevis. He lived
far away from town—on a handsome river, and these magnificent
mountains in the background—and there through many evenings we
had long talks. He speaks English when discussing ordinary affairs, but
in discussing doctrine, etc. always uses his own tongue; his daughter-
in-law interpreted very excellently for me. He is a splendid man, was
lodge maker for the Sun Dance last summer, and is one of the most
handsome men I have ever seen. He was most interested in my reason
for being there, was fully conscious of the crisis of the present time,
and said he was trying to impress this on the young people. He said

that he had told as yet no one, but was telling me because he believed it was connected with my being there and with the holy man who had sent me, and that was that he had been having a dream, in which he saw an Ancient Man Above, very old with gray hair, whose eyes were always open, and who was constantly looking, looking everywhere. . . .

It is good to be back with Black Elk; we are now in Julesburg, Colorado, but the harvest shall be over in a few days, when I shall take them all back to Manderson, and there we shall go to work, for you will be pleased to know that the letter from [Frithjof Schuon] has had a tremendous impact on him. His son translated the whole letter to him; he is excellent at this, and you should also know that he is responding and awakening extremely well. . . .

I am sending several strands of braided sweet grass, which the Assiniboine holy man, Medicine Robe, told me to give to [Frithjof Schuon] that he might know that he, Medicine Robe, understands his mission.

November 4, 1947, Manderson, South Dakota, to Jacques-Albert Cuttat in Lausanne, Switzerland

Old Black Elk has been thinking much since I left them a month ago—indeed he has had another vision, and is determined to act on this. It is of course unnecessary to stress the tremendous influence and encouragement this contact with [Frithjof Schuon] has caused. He has needed this stimulus and assistance badly. When we return to Pine Ridge he wishes first that we record the history of the Sacred Pipe, and explaining the metaphysics involved, for he has said that there is no other Sioux who knows this completely. Then he is going to gather together four or five of the qualified old men of Pine Ridge Reservation, and with them as a center he is going to re-establish the Order of the Pipe. In time these men shall take in and instruct the younger men—thus bridging the now broken transmission. And in addition he wishes to visit the other Sioux Reservations, speaking to the holy men there, all of whom he of course knows, and organizing among them this Order of the Pipe.

November 1947 (exact date unknown), Manderson, South Dakota, to Fr. Gall in Belgium

Black Elk received a "vision" when he was very young—and through this was given the power to insure that the hoop of his nation shall not be broken. In a part of this vision it was revealed to him that holy men from the East (i.e., your brother [Frithjof Schuon and], R. Guénon) would help him in this task. Now through the stimulus of this contact, Black Elk is carrying out something which he has felt he must do for some time, but has lacked the necessary encouragement and assistance. This work is to restore the religion of the Pipe—to reconstitute a new order—and thus insure that the spiritual transmission shall not be broken. We are contacting the elderly men of prayer not only in this area, but in the other Sioux reservations, and it is most encouraging to note the manner in which they have responded—and how anxious they are to assist. Just today we have talked with Spotted Crow, Dull Knife, and Red Cloud—son of the great chief. They are splendid men—and these with others shall constitute the center of the Order. . . .

I shall soon send you photographs of your father [Black Elk]. He is a splendid person, and a true holy man—89,[5] and almost blind—sings his ancient sacred songs all the time, and never undertakes anything without first praying. Often I am alone with him—we cannot of course talk, but we sit and smoke, passing the pipe back and forth—this is good and we have no need to talk, for we are of one mind. He loves children, and when they are about they are all over him—he is kindly, gentle, with a most marvelous sense of humor, which is of course characteristic of these people.

November 19, 1947, Manderson, South Dakota, to John Murray in Lausanne, Switzerland

One of the reasons why old Black Elk has been so receptive to us, is the fact that some time ago he had a vision in which he saw that holy men—or representatives of them—would come to him and his people from the East and would help him in his work. A few days ago he told me that he was very happy, for should he die soon, he now knows that his work shall be continued by [Mr. Schuon] and others.

Every few days we take a trip to one of the small settlements about here, and there contact the leading holy men, to whom Black Elk explains his plans, explains why I am here, and has me talk to them a bit. Everywhere there has been great enthusiasm and all have promised him their support, for as you know Black Elk is regarded as their spiritual leader here on the Pine Ridge Reservation; he is also perhaps the oldest of all. It has been a great thing for me to meet these men, precisely the ones we are looking for; probably I could find them no other way. In Pine Ridge we have contacted Spotted

Crow—a splendid old man—Stabber, and Red Cloud (son of the old chief); here at Manderson, Kicking Bear (son of the high priest), and others; at Kyle, American Horse (son of the great chief) and Little Warrior. I cannot praise this latter highly enough; he is as integrated and concentrated a person as I have yet met, quite on a par with Black Elk. . . .

These men, and several more, shall constitute, I believe, the intellectual or spiritual center that we had hoped for. In about three weeks or a month they are all coming to Manderson, and here with many ceremonies the Order of the Pipe shall be established. . . . Also starting tomorrow, we shall begin the work of recording the history of the Sacred Pipe, for Black Elk is the only one who knows it completely. This shall, we hope, be published, so that the followers of this tradition shall have access. . . .

It is often difficult for those who look on the tradition of the American Indians from the outside, or through the "educated" mind, to understand their preoccupation with the animals, and with all things of the Universe, as is shown in their myths and hundreds of songs. But for these people, as of course for all traditional peoples, every created object is important simply because they know the metaphysical correspondence between this world and the real World. No object is for them as it appears to be, but is simply the pale shadow of a Reality, and the instructed Indian understands these correspondences, both horizontal (with the curing rites, etc.) and vertical. Furthermore, they possess a very real hierarchy, and it is for this reason that every created object is *wakan*, holy, or has a power, according to the level of spiritual reality it reflects. . . . Of course, they know that everything in the Universe has its counterpart in the soul of man. Thus Black Elk says that the Spotted Eagle is really within us. The Indian humbles himself before the whole of creation (especially when "lamenting") because all things were created by *Wakan-Tanka* before him, and deserve respect, as they are older than man. However, although the last of created things, man is also first and unique, since he may know *Wakan-Tanka*.

. . . One surely knows that you can never make a white man of an Indian, and that the spirit of these people is still alive, and although slumbering is now most certainly coming to life. . . .

Black Elk has taken a great interest in his son, Fr. Gall; he talks of him often, and is having several things of buckskin made for him. He is also sending him his necklace made of sacred deer hoofs, and we are sending him a pipe and sacred tobacco. It of course means much to Black Elk to have the support of a Christian Father, for the priests here have been continually after Black Elk to give up his heathen practices, and works of the devil, and to participate fully and only in Catholicism. It was not in his book (much to the anger of the Church) that Black Elk was baptized some forty years ago, and was responsible for the "conversion" of many Indians. Black Elk says that he is sorry that his present action shall anger the priests, but that their anger is proof of their ignorance; and in any case *Wakan-Tanka* is happy; for he knows that it is His Will that he does this work.

November 24, 1947 Manderson, South Dakota, to Whitall & Barbara Perry in Cairo, Egypt

[Black Elk] is important to us for several reasons. In the past he had received several visions—in one *Wakan-Tanka*, the Great Spirit, gave him the power to mend the sacred hoop of his nation, the Sioux, to insure that the sacred tree shall not wither. . . .

Our first work is in restoring the religion of the Pipe—a rite and ritual instrument of the very greatest importance, as you may know, containing as it does all the essential of their ancient "religion." Every week we have taken a trip to visit one of the old holy men—to these Black Elk has explained his plans, and it is encouraging to note their eagerness to assist. It is good to know these venerable men, whom I could probably have found in no other way, and these (about 8) shall constitute our center. . . .

In addition to these key men, who shall lead the way, there are 45 others—old men too—who are anxious to help and shall form the bulk—or second rank so to speak. In time the younger people shall be instructed and taken in. . . .

In any case should [the restoration of the Ghost Dance] fail, these people shall still participate in the religion of the Pipe, and this is a great deal. . . . Black Elk wishes to have recorded the history of the Sioux and especially the history of the Sacred Pipe—for his is the only one left who knows all this completely—and he wishes it to be known by his people and especially by those who follow the religion of the Pipe. . . . Soon the old men mentioned above shall gather here and the order of the Pipe shall be "officially established."

. . . Incidentally Little Warrior told me that the only end of the Ghost Dance was to see or be at one with *Wakan-Tanka*!

. . . It is good to be with Black Elk & those like him. He is almost completely blind in the outer eyes, but has said that *Wakan-Tanka* has made clear the eye of his heart, through which he sees all things with the true seeing.

November 27, 1947, Manderson, South Dakota, to John Murray in Lausanne, Switzerland

Black Elk was most pleased to know the dream of the flower,[6] and wishes to tell this woman, that as her sick flower grew and bloomed, so he believes that the once dying tree of his nation shall now also grow and bear fruit; and his people, or at least some of them shall again be walking the Red Road. He has told me (as we know) we have reached the end of a cycle; and leading into the beginning of the next new cycle there is a very narrow bridge. It is his hope that a few of his people—with the holy men of other nations—shall walk across this narrow way.

December 14, 1947, Manderson, South Dakota, to John Murray in Lausanne, Switzerland[7]

You once asked about Elk Head, former keeper of the Sacred Pipe. It seems that he certainly was a qualified person—indeed it was from him that Black Elk received the sacred history, which we are now recording. . . .

Elk Head had two sons, but both were unqualified to be keepers of the Pipe. The Pipe was thus handed down to Elk Head's daughter [Martha], who married a certain Bad Warrior. (Editors' Note 9: *Elk Head's daughter's married name was Martha Bad Warrior.*)

The Pipe then went to Eli Bad Warrior, who had little or no traditional instruction. He does, however, fear the power of the Pipe, and this is good, for it shall keep it from being profaned. I have also recently been told that Bad Warrior is willing to give up the Pipe should the people wish it, and so it seems quite certain that this shall happen in the spring, and Black Elk shall choose a qualified person. . . . (Editors' Note 10: *Martha Bad Warrior passed the original Sacred Pipe to her son, Eli Bad Warrior. Some years after the date of this letter, Eli Bad Warrior passed the Pipe on to his sister, Lucy Bad Warrior. In 1966 Lucy was told in a dream to pass the Pipe to her grandson, Arvol Looking Horse, who was only 12 years old at the time he became the keeper of the Pipe bundle. Arvol Looking Horse is still the keeper of the Pipe bundle and lives near Green Grass on the Cheyenne River Sioux Reservation.*)

Tomorrow I travel to the four quarters and gather up our key leaders: Little Warrior, Good Lance, Red Cloud, Spotted Tail. They shall remain here for three days, during which time our plans shall be laid, and our course of action decided upon. It shall be a great thing to see these venerable old people together again.

December 26, 1947, Manderson, South Dakota, to John Murray in Lausanne, Switzerland

The majority of Indians shall always be poor, for as soon as they get something it is given away. It is of course good, for it keeps them in the lap of Nature from which they gain much strength; for in this period Nature remains in her original purity, uncontaminated by the darkness in men's souls. Indeed many Indians have expressed to me their gratitude to *Wakan-Tanka* for allowing them this privilege.

. . . Crazy Horse and Sitting Bull were the only two chiefs who never compromised with the white man. No man is held in more veneration than Crazy Horse—he is always talked about when any group gathers. His place of burial is still a mystery, and probably always shall be, which is good; but it is believed to be not more than a mile from here.

Little Warrior (Ozuyé jikala) and his wife, daughter of "Yellow Breast" (a nic-name [sic]—Black Elk doesn't remember his true name) who visited Wovoka and brought the Ghost Dance to the Sioux, spent this past week with us. Day and night there were ceremonials, singing, and talks concerning the revival of the religion of the Pipe. In the ʍʍʍʍʍʍ ʍʍ ʍ ʍʍʍ ʍ ʍ ʍ ʍ ʍʍʍʍ ʍʍʍʍʍ ʍ Little Warrior would officiate at the pipe ritual, which as you may know takes on many varied forms, according to the vision of the one who conducts it. In the essentials all ways are the same. . . .

These ceremonials, all different, but all centering around the pipe, went on every night for about five days. Then on the 18th we had the large pipe ceremonial at Manderson. I had sent out notices to all the old Lakota whom we wanted to contact, and perhaps about a hundred came with their teams from all over. . . . This was of course the great day for Black Elk, for his vision was now being realized, and he was as happy and excited as a child. He and Little Warrior painted their faces red, and put on their best clothes, and what Indian clothing they had. Little Warrior wore a handsome black blanket, with beading in white and red on the sides and back, ribbons for the four Quarters hanging from the center of each beaded circle. Never have I seen a priest officiate at a rite with more dignity, confidence and majesty. All—men, women, and children—sat in a large circle, perhaps 50 yards across; the food for the feast was placed in the center. Earth with coals were placed in the center from which the sweet grass was lighted, and all the people purified themselves. Little Warrior constructed the tobacco altar, and Black Elk with dignity and tears said a long prayer. (Some of these prayers I shall soon have translated for you.) The two pipes were laid on the ground stems West (he used the one given to me, for certain reasons) which, with the sacred song, were filled. Black Elk again gave a long prayer, and then Little Warrior held aloft two eagle feathers which he fluttered above and to the four Quarters, doing this slowly and with great majesty—looking much like the eagle himself—with his long arms. The pipes were then lit and passed around sun wise, one starting from the East and one from the West. Each, even the children, took a puff, and as Little Warrior went around with the pipe, he looked precisely as a priest giving the Holy Communion, which it of course is. He then returned the pipe to me and said that now wherever I go I should take his people with me, for they are within this pipe. Many of the old men, strong and handsome, now arose and one by one gave a short speech, each much to the effect that they had neglected the pipe given to them by *Wakan-Tanka*. But it is now a necessity that they use it once again. One said that the civilization of the white men is near to destruction; but it is his hope that a few of his people shall construct a bridge, leading from the end of this period into the next, and this shall be done with the help of the pipe.

December 26, 1947 Manderson, South Dakota, to Fr. Gall (Lakota Ishnala) in Belgium

All day this last Sunday, your father [Black Elk] prayed for you, and had us do so too when we went to church. You were remembered in our grace for Sunday dinner, and all evening he talked of you. Almost miraculously on Monday your letter arrived, and I wish I could convey to you the great joy which it brought to Black Elk. On Christmas Eve we all (except for Black Elk for he was tired) went to midnight Mass. When we returned on Christmas morning your father was sitting up in bed, and seemed extremely happy over something—he told us that he had visited Lakota Ishnala in Belgium, had had a good talk with him, and had just now returned. He said that he had told you that you shall always really be a Lakota, for when you die your body, which is of earth, shall remain with the white men, but your soul shall return to us. He also said that he now sees that he perhaps should have given you a better name: Two Men, for in appearance you are a white man, but in reality you are an Indian.

Note from Joseph Brown added later. It was on this occasion that there was a terrific thunderstorm around the tower where Fr. Gall lives. It was strange to have a thunderstorm at that time of year. Fr. Gall has not said what message he received but he took hold of his pipe and he prayed.

January 8, 1948, Manderson, South Dakota, to John Murray in Lausanne, Switzerland
Most of the Sioux I've met are completely uninterested in any question of their origin. They possess a marvelous freedom from the limiting conditions or consideration of time and place and many remind me of what must have been the condition of soul of primordial man.

January 24, 1948, Manderson, South Dakota, to John Murray in Lausanne, Switzerland
Tomorrow we shall finish the seventh and last rite, completing our history of the Sacred Pipe. I am extremely pleased the way this has turned out. It certainly shall be, as you suggest, a shock to the profane ethnologists, for I have all the material for a complete commentary. It shall take me some time to prepare this for publication, perhaps several months, but this I shall do when I return east and can work with no distraction. It is now time for me to leave, for I believe all has been done that can be at present, and I really think that many here have awakened to the glory of their heritage. All that prevents them from going ahead is their own inertia, which incidentally is very great among the majority of the people. Our work on the book has done Ben much good, for bit by bit he has come to realize the truths that underlie his own rites; he is even now growing his hair long. I leave for Oraibi next week.

Last week, as I had long expected, we received a call from our parish priest, who is also head of the mission school at Pine Ridge. He was quite irate at our pipe ceremonial, and said he did not mind if we merely wanted to put on a show, but if we were serious, it was a terrible thing, for he could not have his people going back to "savagery." At this Ben launched out with quite an oration, defending and pointing out the truths of his own tradition—all the time the priest becoming more and more tense and red in the face. When he finished, old Black Elk started in, and went on for almost half an hour, when the priest looked at his watch and sped off in his automobile in great haste. Black Elk's speech was later explained to me, and it was indeed a magnificent one, although I myself prefer to remain quiet when these things come up, for is not silence the best answer to fools? I might mention that many of the priests here are in great disfavor among the people, due to many acts, which were not exactly straight; but I shall not go into that. The Catholic Church among the Indians in the early days gained many followers, by making catechists of the old men, tempting them with money, good clothes, and a house, and the opportunity to travel. These old men—and Black Elk with them—made hundreds of converts, but now that they have gone, participation in the Church has fallen off, and a vacuum has been left. Let us hope it shall be filled by the renewal of their own way.

January 27, 1948, Manderson, South Dakota, to John Murray in Lausanne, Switzerland

Yesterday Grandfather (Black Elk) and I went to visit Little Warrior again. Two means of action now seem to be well established:

1. In the spring, several holy men from each Sioux reservation shall meet, and then elect the most qualified to be the prospective keeper of the pipe. Then they shall go to the pipe, and it is quite possible that at this time it shall be unveiled, which as you know is possible in a crisis; and a crisis certainly does exist now.

2. It was agreed that the pipe of every old man be handed down to the most worthy of his descendants. This shall be good, for somehow these pipes have a way of getting into the museums, or into the hands of the profane whites.

February 4, 1948, Oraibi, Arizona, to John Murray in Lausanne

The most magnificent Introduction [to *The Sacred Pipe*, written by Frithjof Schuon][8] arrived just a few days before I left Manderson. Yes, it shall be a bitter pill for the ethnologists, but that is just what is needed at this time. Parts of it were read to Black Elk, and he was of course extremely pleased.

March 12, 1948, Aiken, South Carolina, to John Murray in Lausanne, Switzerland

The plunge back to "civilization" was thus something of a jolt, with all its accompanying horrors and complications, but here I have a quiet place, and am starting to work immediately on the book. I hope in two months to have it in decent enough shape to show to a publisher, and get all that arranged—and then the finishing touches, additions, illustrations, etc. can be finished up in Switzerland. I am arranging for passage in June.

March 15, 1948, Aiken, South Carolina, to Whitall Perry in Cairo, Egypt

I enclose some photographs of Little Warrior, & shall try soon to send you some of Black Elk etc. I think it is fairly certain that no photograph was ever taken of Crazy Horse (in spite of the fact that I found one in the Smithsonian files worked with his name—whoever he is it is a splendid figure!). There is great controversy raging about the whole thing.

The commissioner of Indian Affairs—recently visited—stated quite clearly that their policy was neither to encourage nor interfere with those who wish to participate in their own rites, and that at the present time there were no laws prohibiting it—although there could be if enough "pressure" were brought to bear. They would not, however, put their position in writing, until they "had investigated the matter further." Most of the "pressure" incidentally comes from the Catholic Church who wish to stamp out all "works of the devil." But they are so weak at this time—especially among Indians, whose respect they have lost, that it is no very great threat. Things look quite favorable, and it may well be that in the early summer under the guidance of Little Warrior, the "Ghost Dance" shall come to life.

June 17, 1948, Southwest Harbor, Maine, to Fr. Gall in Belgium

Several weeks ago I sent you a rough draft of two of the most important chapters of the book—on the rites of the *Inipi* and the lamenting. This is still rough, and is really just as I copied it from my notes, but I thought you would like to have them even in this shape.

July 8, 1948, Lausanne, Switzerland, to Fr. Gall in Belgium
The long anticipated meeting with your brother is for me a very great event, for he is, and I have long considered him to be, my spiritual master—on a plane even above that of our father Black Elk.

August 26, 1948, Lausanne, Switzerland, to Fr. Gall in Belgium[9]
I wanted to write to you immediately to tell you of the great pleasure I had in the visit, and to express my appreciation for the hospitality which is of course characteristic of your order. I do hope that the few things I was able to tell you, the songs etc. have been a help to you, and have strengthened the very real bonds which unite you to our relatives the Sioux.

October 29, 1948, Lausanne, Switzerland, to Fr. Gall in Belgium
Many thanks for your good letter, and for the most excellent drawing of the Japanese archers. I liked it especially because it illustrated the three phases, the metaphysics of which I mentioned. I wish I could send you a little book I have at home on Japanese archery, by Acker, with many drawings and photographs.[10] He studied with a master in Japan for many years, and completely mastered the art. Strangely enough, the bow is used there, even today, solely as a spiritual discipline—never for hunting. It seems there are still a few guilds which transmit the spiritual instruction. True enough, there are only a few Indians who understand the metaphysics—but even if there is only one, that is a great deal today, and in any case the principles involved cannot be lost. The majority of Indians simply regard the bow as *wakan*, without really understanding why—but even that is much.

November 21, 1948, Lausanne, Switzerland, to Fr. Gall
The first draft of the book is now completed, and there remains only a few notes, corrections, precisions to make. I am preparing a list of Lakota words which I will send to you soon; & trust you will have time to correct them according to ethnological standards, about which I know nothing.

December 17, 1948, Lausanne, Switzerland, to Fr. Gall

I am indeed grateful to you for your fine work on the Lakota words. . . . I think *Inikage* [performance of a sweat lodge ceremony] satisfactory—have written Ben to check on it, along with several other odds and ends. *Hokshichankia* [spiritual influence or seed][11] is a difficult word—Ben and I spent several days struggling over it so do not worry if you cannot locate it![12]

You are quite right—the prayers for the different rites follow certain formulas, a certain flexibility or spontaneity being allowed to the one who prays—in keeping with the whole Indian spirit. It was necessary for Grandfather to repeat certain prayers, and I always noticed that although they were always worded differently, they did follow a certain pattern.

In the question of the rites of the pipe also, there is a certain flexibility according to the occasion.

July 27, 1949, Manderson, South Dakota, to Frithjof Schuon in Lausanne, Switzerland

It is good to see once again our many friends in this sacred country. Old Black Elk I found to be living with another son, some thirty miles south of here. . . . We of course made many smokes and sang many songs, and very frequently I noticed that he mentioned the name of Lakota Ishnala. I found him in fairly good health, yet he is now unable to walk, for the doctors thought it unnecessary to set his broken leg, for because of his age they thought it would never heal. Apparently they do not understand the vitality of these old Indians, for the broken leg did heal very rapidly, but of course painfully crooked, so that now he is not even able to use crutches. His mind is quite clear, yet because of the stroke he has great difficulty in talking, especially on sacred things, for then he gets very excited and the words do not come out. . . .

It is good being with the saintly old man, for there is much *barakah*[13] in his *maqam*, his spiritual poverty, an utter simplicity, a child-like spontaneous quality, his great joy in very small things, and his love to sing and laugh and to make others happy.

July 31, 1949, Custer, South Dakota, to Fr. Gall in Belgium

I am writing this in the sacred Black Hills, seated in my tipi; looking to the east out the door I see tents, camp fires, and passing back and forth, I see these handsome women with their long dresses, black braided hair, and moccasins on their feet. . . .

We have just made a magnificent trip through the Hills, from Custer to Deadwood, some 80 miles. We traveled with about ten wagons and many ponies, taking three days. . . .

Unfortunately, old Black Elk could not be with us, for he is not strong enough to travel. He is staying down in Nebraska. I had several good visits with him. His mind is not quite clear and he has great difficulty in talking. He would, however, mention your name often and I was able to get from him the prayers you wished.[14] They may not go with this letter, for it is difficult now to get Ben still for a few minutes to convert my badly spelt Lakota.

October 8, 1954, Albuquerque, New Mexico, to Frithjof Schuon in Lausanne, Switzerland[15]

It was good to be back at Pine Ridge and to see all the people gathered together for the Dance—some 400 tents. But it was sad to see the way in which the Sun Dance was done and also to note that none of the young Sioux did the dance—only the young Cheyenne led by two old Sioux priests—good men—but not of the quality of a Little Warrior. These Cheyenne had vowed during the war to do the Sun Dance many times should they return safely. They had already done it twice that summer, and would do it once or twice more among other nations. They seemed very pleased after the Dance when I gave them a copy of *The Sacred Pipe*. Even though the Sun Dance was not done well—or rather laxly done—the two days of "social dancing," which consisted largely of the "Omaha" war dance in which almost everybody participated, were very powerful and even now I can still hear those drums (they had five different teams of drummers), and those incredibly strongly beautiful songs and chants. . . .

There is still one more account that I would like to share with you. At Manderson I saw Black Elk's daughter, Mrs. Looks Twice (her husband should have, since he is now in jail for stealing cattle), who seemed to have something on her mind that she wanted to tell me. Finally she explained that before his death they had been worried about Black Elk. Every afternoon at about the same time he would go into something of a trance as if he were talking with some unseen person. Once he scolded his daughter-in-law for entering the house at that time, for he said that she had made the man leave. When they asked him who it was who came to talk with him, (more precisely this person came to pray for Black Elk, saying that he knew that he was soon to die, and he wished to help him in his suffering), he said that it was "a holy man from Europe." His relatives were frightened by these experiences, and Mrs. Looks Twice noticing a large wooden rosary which always hung over his bed—a Moroccan one that I had given him because of his fondness for beads, and for the *barakah*, took this away from him, and according to her after this he did not talk anymore with the "strange man." At Black Elk's death, possibly thinking that it had not been right to do this, she saw that this rosary was buried in the coffin with him.

Our travels of this summer have been of tremendous value to us. For almost two months we heard the powerful rhythms of the big drums almost continually, as we went from one dance to another— and even now I can still hear them, for it seems they have become a part—or more than a part—of me. I know that somehow my lot is tied up with that of the Indians.

Appendix II

Prayer Given to Father Gall by Black Elk, 1949[1]

Lakota wocekiye

Tunkasila Wakan Tanka, o'unkiyapi ye.
Iyotiyekiya oyate unkunpi.
Wayazan na cantesica unkunpi.
O'makiyi yemita oyate kin ob.
Miye mita oyate wacinunniyanpi.

Ina Maka wakanheja.
Tate ouye topa Ina o'wicakiye ye.
Tunka takuya yapi kte.

Tunkasila Wakan Tanka, o'unkiyapi ye.
(Hekaha Sapa heyelo)

Lakota Prayer

Grandfather, Great Spirit, help us.
We, the people, are having a difficult time.
We are in pain and are heartbroken.
Help me, along with my people.
I, with my people, depend on you.

Mother Earth, the children.
Mother, from the Four Winds, help them.
They will be relatives of the Stone.[2]

Grandfather, Great Spirit, help us.
(Thus spake Black Elk)[3]

Appendix III

Selections from Letters of Frithjof Schuon[1]

October 7, 1947, Lausanne, Switzerland, to Ben Black Elk
Most Honored Chief,
In my first letter, which our friend Mr. Brown handed you,[2] I wrote about my brother's and my love for the Indians; now I have learned that you read my letter, and that you explained it to your holy father, and that my brother will be happy. That makes me happy too.

I think Mr. Brown spoke to you about me and my work. I very soon saw the falseness of the modern civilization—the "white man's way"—and I saw it for two reasons: first, I saw with my eyes and with my heart the beauty, grandeur, and spirituality of the other civilizations, and the ugliness and selfishness, the slave-minded materialism of the modern civilization in which I grew up; secondly, I could never believe that one religion alone in the whole world was the true one, and that all other religions were false. As a boy, when I read in books my father gave me about non-Occidental peoples, I could not believe that so many noble and wise men could have been abandoned by God, and that on the other hand so many bad Occidental whites could have received the truth; how is it possible that God, wishing to save every human soul, should have given the saving truth only to one people, and should thus have condemned so many other peoples, who are no worse than these, to remain for centuries and forever in deadly darkness? I even felt that this must be false, and that the holy Truth must have many forms, just as a light may have many colors; God—the Great Spirit—gave that indispensable Truth to every race in a form which is suited to its respective mind. Of course, there have been people who forgot that Truth, as for example, the ancient Europeans to whom God sent Christianity; but He did not send Christianity to all the people in the world, for most people had not forgotten the meaning of their religion. A heathen is a man who worships idols, and who ignores or rejects God; as for the Indians, they never worshiped idols, nor did they ignore or reject God, the Great Spirit. Consequently, the Indians are not heathens, and their religion, though not fully understood by every individual Indian, is a true one, and God is working in it, and gives His Grace in it. This you know best, of course.

When I was older, I saw that the spiritual and contemplative way I was seeking could not be realized on the basis of the very superficial culture of Europe. I wished to live in God. I wished not only to love God, I wished also to know Him, and the Christianity of our time teaches only the love of God, never the knowledge. I knew, moreover, very soon that God would charge me with a mission. And so, with regard to the knowledge of God which I was seeking—because it is a need of my nature, and God wishes to be worshiped by every man according to the nature He gave him—I found this sacred knowledge through a holy man of the Arab people, whose name was Ahmad al-'Alawi. He was a spiritual Master and had many disciples. There I found what I was searching for; the knowledge of God, and the means to realize God. This Master told me: "When man is not like snow in the hands of Truth and does not vanish away in Truth, then Truth is like snow in man's hand and vanishes away." I was then a young man, and I had left Europe for North Africa, where I found my Master. He is dead now; but he is always present in me; he is above life and death; he is one with God.

The Great Spirit gave the indispensable Truth to every race: He gave the Indians their manner of praying, as He gave the Christians and the Muslims and the Hindus and the Yellow peoples their manner of praying. Every old and true religion is a necessary form of the eternal Truth, and a gift from God, the most-high *Wakan-Tanka*. Therefore nothing in the Indian creed is a mere human invention or a senseless thing; every symbol or rite known and practiced by the Indians finds its analogous form and explanation in the traditions of other peoples—in the most direct way, perhaps, in the Hindu tradition, for it is as old as the Indian one, whereas younger traditions are, in a certain sense, more simplified expressions of the same eternal Truth. All the "spirits" or "gods" known and invoked by the Indians—the "Sun," the "Sky," the "Earth," the "Rock," the "Moon," the "Winged-One," the "Wind," the "Mediator," the "Four Winds," and the other cosmic Powers— are universal Principles known to every tradition, whatever may be the form of the symbols; the "Angels" of the Christian, Muslim, and Jewish religions are the same celestial beings as the Indian "Powers" or "Spirits"; the Indian "Thunderbird" is no other than the Muslim "Jibrail" and "Israfil," or the Hindu "Shiva." All Indian rites, such as the most Holy Pipe, or the Sweat Lodge, or fasting and calling to the Great Spirit in search of a vision or a power or an illumination, or the Sun Dance and other rites—all that has without any doubt its deep metaphysical meaning and therefore its spiritual efficacy. Not every rite, of course, has the same central importance, and the fact that the Sun Dance is no longer given in its old form by no means implies that the "holy tree is withered"; for the essential part of every religion is, besides the ritual transmission of a spiritual influence preserved and given by the priests, prayer or invocation of God's Name. This invocation of God, when given in the proper ritual conditions by a traditional priest—a "medicine man" possessing the corresponding authority, function, or power—and accomplished in a good manner, pronounced in the holy language with serious concentration of the mind, in the beginning with fasting, and above all with the confident hope, nay, the faith and certitude of being accepted by God and attaining Him after death or even in this life—this invocation of God, the Great Spirit, is the very essence of every religion.

Before my Master gave me the Holy Name, he gave me the initiation. This same initiation—or transmission of a spiritual seed—was bestowed one thousand three hundred years ago on the Prophet Muhammad. He received this spiritual seed from the highest Angel sent by God, and this seed he put in the hearts of his immediate disciples—not of all his followers. When this spiritual seed, with the help of which the Divine Name purifies and transforms man's heart with time, is bestowed on a new disciple of the order, the Master seizes his hand in the same manner that the Angel seized the Arabian Prophet's hand one thousand three hundred years ago; and in the same moment the Master pronounces a sacred formula, also revealed to the Prophet by the Angel, so that the spiritual seed or power may enter the disciple's heart. Every tradition possesses such an initiation, but often in a very different form, by gestures, speech, looks, and other means, and in certain very exceptional cases even by dreams.

In His Name, God is really present and therefore our heart, when invoking Him, must be present too. Then He purifies us by the grace of His Name; He gives us perfections we had not before; and finally He leads us back to Himself.

There is, besides the invocation aloud, a silent one; I have heard that the Indians often pray silently. This kind of mute prayer is practiced in Asia too: the tongue keeps quiet, but the mind is strongly concentrated on the one divine Reality; man is silent like the sky, not thinking with the head, but contemplating the Great Mystery with the heart, and void of all earthly things. But your holy father knows best.

Thursday, October 9th

One often reads, in so-called "scientific" books, that the word *Wakan-Tanka* does not mean God, any more than other words in the Indian languages, such as *Wakonda, Tirawa, Natosiwa, Manitu, Yastasinan;* it is forgotten—or rather, people are incapable of understanding— that the occidental idea of "God" concerns but the personal aspect of the Divinity, and that the Indian Names of the Great Spirit involve another aspect of the divine Reality. *Wakan-Tanka* is not only God as personal Creator, but also God as impersonal Essence; He is not only God as pure Principle, but also as His own manifestation—or reflected power—within Creation, and even, in a certain sense, God as Creation, insofar as it is possible to speak in this way. *Wakan-Tanka* means not only what is exclusively, but immanently God, in the same manner that the Hindu word *Atma* means not only the divine Reality, but also everything insofar as it is considered as a manifestation of the divine Reality. Though *Wakan-Tanka* can be translated as "Mysterious Power" or otherwise, the expression "Great Spirit," which displeases many "scientists," is certainly the best, for it involves no restriction.

Friday, October 10th

Since Wounded Knee, many Indians could not help thinking that the Great Spirit has been very hard on His red children; many have inferred from the red man's disaster that the white man's way is better than the red man's. They forget that history is not yet ended, and that the white man's punishment, at the end of times, must be far more terrible than the red man's punishment has been; even now, in the last world war, the sufferings of millions of whites have been beyond every possible description, and all this is nothing else but the necessary result of "progress" as it is called, the "white man's way." The white men of the Occident will be punished for their "wickedness"; the Indians were perhaps too proud and sought too much their personal glory instead of the Great Spirit's eternal Glory, but they were not "wicked" like the white man. The whites who see the falseness of the modern civilization do not thereby betray their race; this civilization is false in itself, quite apart from the people, whether they be Japanese or whites, who accept it; the Occidental whites betray themselves insofar as they identify themselves with the modern civilization. A man who states that his family is sick is not a traitor; truth is never a treason, and error never a virtue.

We should realize the truth of Wovoka's vision in ourselves. The ideas of the Ghost Dance were not false, only their too literal interpretation; but Wovoka himself did not understand his visions in this manner. Every religion knows that the "true brother," as the Hopis call the Messiah of the latter days, will come, and every religion gives him a particular name and wishes to possess him for itself; but he will come for all; that is an old and universal prophecy. There must be again holy men among every people; for finally the happy world seen by Wovoka will come even in the outer world, and we must be prepared for it. But before it comes, we are to realize it in ourselves. All that your holy father knows best. He has not waited and suffered in vain, nor have his people: the "holy Tree" will not wither, but it will bloom again and forever.

With my most respectful greetings for Black Elk and with my best wishes for you and your people.

October 31, 1947, Lausanne, Switzerland, to Chief Medicine Robe
Most Honored Chief,
The ways of the Great Spirit are marvelous. It was a great pleasure to me to hear that our friend Mr. Brown found the way to Chief Medicine Robe and the other wise men of the noble Assiniboine people. We, who belong to a sacred community of the East, are happy to learn that the sacred tree of the Indian religion is still alive, and that it will not wither. In our time, which is approaching the end of times, all spiritual forces of mankind must strengthen each other. Therefore it is a joy for us to see that the Indians know this, and we do not doubt that the best among the young men of your people will understand the falsity of the white men's way, which finally abases men to the level of animals; the young men must understand this, as they must understand the grandeur and beauty of the ancient Indian civilization. This Indian civilization gave human life its full meaning, whereas modern civilization kills man's soul; man is no more a free child of the Great Spirit, but a mere slave of human society, and a slave of a deadly materialism; in such a life, man has no longer time to think of God. We should realize in ourselves that which gave the ancient times their grandeur, beauty, and happiness. Every good thing begins in the secret of the heart; outer works mean nothing in themselves; they must be expressions of our inner light. No human soul may encounter the Great Spirit with empty hands. The Great Spirit gave His red children their religion at the beginning of the world, and when He appears at the end, He will ask His red children what they have done with the religion He bestowed on them; and He will ask the same question of every people He has created. Of course, not all Indians will return to the sacred tree of wisdom and virtue they inherited from their fathers; but when in every Indian nation there will be a community of men who pray in the manner of their fathers, and whose hearts are steadily turned towards the Great Spirit, and

who maintain the holy tradition in its inner and outer forms—for the outer forms are very important too—these men will represent before their Creator the whole nation. In our time the ignorant and the wicked govern nearly everywhere, and their loud voices smother the soft voice of truth; but God's is the last word, as after every night the sun comes back again.

November 2

Love of the Indians is a family tradition with us—my brother and myself—and this is why: as a young girl, our paternal grandmother lived in Washington where she became acquainted with an Indian chief who loved her and made a marriage proposal to her. He was called "Singing Swan," and, with many other chiefs, he had come to Washington for a congress. Unfortunately, my grandmother had to go to Europe with her family and could not marry "Singing Swan." He sent her letters in which he called her "my little child"; he also sent her dried flowers from the prairie. The recollection of "Singing Swan" was so vividly impressed on my grandmother's mind that at the age of eighty she still remembered her friend as if she had seen him the day before, and shortly before she died she still spoke of him. When my brother and I were children, she used to talk to us about "Singing Swan"; she pictured to us his beautiful long hair and his buckskin dress of light blue tinge.

Thus we were educated in the love of the Indian peoples, and this was a providential disposition in the plan of the Great Spirit. As I wish to explain to Chief Medicine Robe and his followers the manner in which the Great Spirit led me, I join to these lines my letter to Chief Black Elk's son. As you certainly know, Black Elk is a holy man of the Oglala Sioux.

I have been very happy to hear that Chief Medicine Robe has given Mr. Brown several strands of braided sweet grass for me; I pray every day for him and his wife and their work, and I have told my community to do the same. Now I would be very grateful if you would be so kind as to translate these lines to Chief Medicine Robe and his followers, and also the enclosed letter which I sent to Chief Black Elk's son before Mr. Brown reached the Assiniboine nation.[3]

May the Great Spirit bless all His red children. With my most respectful greetings to Chief Medicine Robe, and with my best wishes for you and the followers of your holy tradition.

October 5, 1977, Pully, Switzerland, to Joseph Epes Brown
My Dear Friend,
I am finally answering your two letters and mailings of documents. I received your "The Question of 'Mysticism' within Native American Traditions," and also "Seeing with a Native Eye," as well as the issue of *Parabola* containing an article by Good Eagle Center; I have just read your article "The Roots of Renewal," which is excellent, and then "On Approaching Native American Religions," which, being a discussion, is very uneven in its contents. Regarding this last text, I would like to make the following remarks:

The difficulties in contacts between whites and Indians are easy to understand. First of all, the white man does not have a sense of the sacred, insofar as he is a modern man, and almost all whites are; if he asks an Indian questions, he does so usually out of curiosity, without realizing that an Indian has no motive for answering interrogations that he considers indiscreet and pointless.

To say that a white man does not have the sense of the sacred, amounts to recognizing that he is full of false ideas; he does not know, intellectually and morally, the axioms of the traditional spirit, or in other words, of spirituality as such; he does not know metaphysics, cosmology, mysticism. Metaphysically, modern man does not know that everything is a manifestation of the Self that is at once transcendent and immanent; he knows nothing of the doctrine of *Atma* and *Maya*, even if he has read some Hindu books, because in that case he believes that these are but concepts holding only historical, psychological, phenomenological interest—in short, things that can be put aside. Cosmologically, he does not know that the world is made of a hierarchical series of regions—beginning with the Self all the way to matter—and that the evolutionist error is but a "horizontal" substitute for "vertical" emanationism that, for its part, unfolds starting from archetypes and through the animic or subtle world. That being the case, modern man knows nothing of the sacred and of its laws, and nothing of the psychology deriving from it and bearing witness to it.

Question: how can one study the metaphysics, cosmology, and spirituality of a people without having any idea of what it means? That is the whole problem. And that is why people go round in circles, indefinitely, while developing, by compensation, subtle or generous considerations that are beside the point. I repeat: the white man does not offer the Indian a sufficient motivation for the questions he asks that is satisfying and acceptable, nor does he offer the mentality that, in the eyes of the Indian, constitutes the qualification required to merit the answers he seeks. From the point of view of any traditional discipline, one does not have the right to speak of sacred things without a sufficient reason, or outside of the master-disciple relationship; or again, there are things that, if discussed without a plausible motive, lose their "power."

Yet there is more: the Indian, apart from the fact that he has no motive for answering questions whose justification he does not perceive, cannot evaluate what the white man's need for logical explanations entails; and if, in spite of this, the Indian answers, he cannot do so by means of the abstract categories of classic European dialectics. He will do so therefore in a symbolic language that the white man, in turn, cannot understand, given that the modern mind does not understand symbolism, or its principles and methods.

If the Indian has gone to a university, there is a very good chance that he will accept without discernment the errors and mental habits of whites and that, because of this, the abstract and differentiated language available to him will be of no avail to him when accounting for the Indian mysteries. In an analogous manner, there are Orientals who think with two separate brains, a traditional one and a modern one, so that their thinking is either impeccable or absurd, depending on the brain with which they are operating. . . .

. . . Returning to symbolism: one could object to my remarks that following the works of Eliade and others . . . academic people who approach the Indians are not so ignorant anymore; I reply that they still remain ignorant and incompetent enough to meet the description I gave above, be it only because they draw no serious conclusions from any real knowledge they have.

Another point I wanted to mention is the following: the "sentimental" or "romantic" character of a type of literature about Indians has an honorable explanation first because of the awareness of the injuries done to the Indians and secondly because of the awareness of their moral and aesthetic values, as well as others; but no writer who supposedly "idealized" the Indians ever thought they were without faults; in any case, the point of view of these authors is something that is so innocuous that it has never constituted an obstacle to the study of the red race. Nothing is more annoying than the contrary viewpoint according to which only the small and banal man is the real man.

At all events, "the Indians as they really are" are only rarely the Indians as they are in their substance and as they were still at the beginning of the twentieth century; first because everything has been done to transform the Indians into cowboys, and then because one wants to attribute to the "authentic Indian" the cowboyism that has been inflicted on him. The aristocratic and more or less primordial simplicity of the Indian is not at all the same thing as the simplifying and democratic mindset of the average American; to be simple and natural is not to be mentally a barbarian. These are remarks that I draw from my own experiences.

October 7

How does one explain to an academic: that Black Elk, in his subtle form, was reabsorbed into the world of the archetypes, passing through the subtle state and stopping at the threshold of the archangelic world; that certitude of the cosmic degrees and all the more so of the Principle resides in the very substance of the Intellect, which inserts itself into the individuality while being universal and in essence principial; that human ignorance derives from both the accidental and providential scission between the Intellect and the ego; that Revelation has for its purpose the actualization of immanent knowledge, hence a knowledge that is connatural with the Intellect; that the goal of spiritual methods is the abolition of the scission between the individual consciousness and the universal Consciousness; how does one explain this to academics, and how can one understand the wisdom of the Indians without knowing all of that?

August 8, 1984, Bloomington, Indiana, to William Stoddart in Windsor, Canada

I received the book *The Sixth Grandfather*, which contains the notes taken by Neihardt during his meetings with Black Elk; it is thus the almost literal dictation—or the rough draft—of *Black Elk Speaks*. Neihardt shortened and simplified things quite a bit; he also inserted a few passages that do not come from Black Elk, but that could come, psychologically speaking, from him. Nonetheless, all of this creates certain problems.

In favor of Neihardt, one can affirm that Black Elk received him, right from the first meeting, with a kind of impatient and surprising fervor, as someone that he had been expecting for a long time; there was thus, on the part of Black Elk, a kind of intuition regarding the American writer's qualification; that is to say, Neihardt's arrival was providential in the eyes of the old Indian. Indeed, Neihardt had certain special gifts; he was like a "medium" of the Indian soul; Black Elk sensed that Neihardt could better express than he himself, Black Elk, could what he intended to say. Quite paradoxically, the American could add a vibration of the Red Indian psychism in instances where the Indian's dictation was completely dry and parsimonious.

But this does not completely excuse the American writer. In both of his prefaces—depending on the edition—he presents his book as a document, without accounting for two points: first, of his literary collaboration, and secondly, of Black Elk's adherence to the Catholic Church; both of those things should have been explained. Correlatively, if Neihardt already had the intention of presenting a document—Black Elk's dictation was a real message—it would have been better, after all, to have renounced all attempts at stylization and amplification; he should have presented his notes as they were. As for the Catholic dimension, it is true that the Indian author did not utter a word about this, and was even evasive when the American asked him a question on this subject; nonetheless, the American should have mentioned this reticence as well as the problem itself.

Like many Indians, including shamans, Black Elk followed both the ancient religion and Christianity, with differences in degree depending on the epochs: in his youth, he was a fervent catechist; toward the end of his life, he inclined more and more toward the ancient religion—*The Sacred Pipe* dictated to Brown is ample proof of this—but he nonetheless died fortified with the rites of the Church. It was the same for his son, whom I knew well.

The reason why so many Indians—including the famous medi-cine-man Fools Crow, whom I met at Wounded Knee—practice both religions at the same time, or rather add the Christian religion to their own—is that the person of the Christ strikes them as an irresistible spiritual reality, and that they see no reason not to integrate him into their religious life; they see no contradiction in this. I am speaking here of the Indians who practice both religions, not of those who are entirely converted to Christianity, nor of those who totally reject it.

Of course, missionaries taught the Indians that everything in the Indian religion is the work of Satan, but many Indians did not believe that; Black Elk never did. Finally, out of weariness, the missionaries ceased insisting too much and at the end, namely nowadays, they have become completely indifferent on this subject. There are even some who participate in the Indian rites, but this is a whole different story.

Some critics of Neihardt's work go so far as to assert that *Black Elk Speaks* offers no doctrinal or scientific reference point; but this is false, because the type of information found in this book is intact, and that is what matters.

P.S. Neihardt felt obliged to simplify the "great vision"—he was always worried about overlong passages and complications—and in that respect future commentators will have no choice but to resort to the original version given in *The Sixth Grandfather*. Be that as it may, *Black Elk Speaks* is above all a biography; for the doctrine one has to refer to *The Sacred Pipe*, all the more as this book is strictly faithful, word for word, to the account given by the Indian author.

August 9

I would like still to emphasize the following point: *Black Elk Speaks* is a providential book, and because of this, it is all that it must be. Black Elk welcomed Neihardt with a kind of prophetic enthusiasm; and this moreover is also how he welcomed Brown. This means that he sensed that these two men were exactly what he needed for his message; *Black Elk Speaks* is one dimension, *The Sacred Pipe* is another.

What caused the ruin, during the nineteenth century and at the beginning of the twentieth, of the red race and of its tradition, was the abrupt alternative between the two notions of the "civilized" and the "savage," each of the terms being taken as an absolute; this made it possible to attribute all possible values to the white man while leaving nothing to the red man; so that, according to this perspective, the latter had no right to exist anymore; that is exactly the conclusion people were seeking. The "noble red man" has been greatly mocked—and this goes on even today; yet this idea is the only one to offer a counterweight to the stupid and criminal alternative which I have just pointed out, and this proves in a certain way the rightness of the idea in question. Nobleness indeed is a value that lies completely outside the alternative mentioned, and it reminds us that man is man before being "civilized" or "savage"; and therefore that any normative human category possesses the dignity of being man, with all the possibilities of value and greatness that this dignity entails.

When the difference between the "civilized" and the "savage" is reduced to normal proportions, one arrives at the complementarity—and the equilibrium—between the "town-dweller" and the "nomad" ... recognizing a positive function for each society within the economy of human possibilities. And this applies also to a situation like that of America where, clearly, each one of the ethnic groups would have something to learn from the other; but this is something, precisely, that the whites were absolutely unwilling to admit. On the side of the Indians, the difficulty was not due to a prejudice of principle; it was due on the one hand from the fact that "civilization" mistreated them, and on the other that the values of this civilization were—and are—mostly compromised by the modern deviation; the whites, too preoccupied with "things," have forgotten what man is, while being "humanists"; but that is exactly why they have forgotten it.

August 30

I will add the following to my reflections from my preceding letter regarding the Indian problem: One could also say that the red man— actually a Mongol who emigrated from Siberia more than ten thousand years ago—has been a victim of the democratic system and of its blind mechanism. Democracy amounts, in practice, to being the tyranny of the majority, and the white majority, in America, had no interest in the existence of the red minority; because of this, the army, which in certain cases should have defended the rights of the Indians—rights that were solemnly guaranteed by treaties—defended the interests of the whites counter to those agreements. To speak of democracy is to speak of demagogy; in such an atmosphere, a popular criminality "in fact" becomes a governmental criminality "by right," at least when the victim finds himself outside the purview of the collectivity included within a specific democratic legality. While it is true that the Indians were not "citizens," they were nonetheless "compatriots," to say the least; their status should have been juridically specified on the basis of that definition. A monarch—or very paradoxically—a military dictator could have ensured interracial justice; a democratic president could not do so; even as fundamentally noble and morally courageous a man as Lincoln, had he been granted the time to take care of the Indians as he intended to, would have been paralyzed in this respect.

At all events, if it is absurd to term a blatant and coordinated genocide a "fatality of history," it is just as absurd to accuse "the Americans"—and them alone—to have killed the red man; because there are no "Americans"; the white inhabitants of the New World are really immigrant Europeans, no less, and it is not those immigrants who invented civilizationism and democracy. The Indian, inasmuch as he embodies virgin nature, the sense of the sacred, and contempt for money, was killed in Europe, in the minds of that culture, quite independently from the American conquest of the new continent; and if the Indian has in Europe defenders and friends, he had some, and much earlier, in America itself.

Notes

Introduction

1. See C.G. Jung, *Mysterium Coniunctionis*, in *The Collected Works of* C.G. *Jung*, vol. 14, 206n.

2. It was published in German as *Ich rufe mein Volk* (I Call My People).

3. R. DeMallie, "John G. Neihardt and Nicholas Black Elk," 242.

4. D. Stover, "A Postcolonial Reading of Black Elk," 127.

5. S. McCluskey, "*Black Elk Speaks*: and So Does John Neihardt," 238-239.

6. John G. Neihardt, "The Book that Would Not Die," 229.

7. For DeMallie's own account of how *The Sixth Grandfather* came to be published see his "John G. Neihardt and Nicholas Black Elk," 248-251.

8. We refer to Joseph Brown's previously unpublished letters written while he was living with Black Elk in 1947 and '48, recently published in the appendix to *The Spiritual Legacy of the American Indian* (2007 edition), and to more correspondence which has since come to light.

9. The terms "spiritual" and "religious" are often used in an imprecise and confused fashion. Here is a short-hand definition: "spiritual": concerning the subjective experience of the sacred; "religious": concerning the forms— myths, rites, art and so on—which help to shape and guide spiritual life.

10. R. DeMallie, "John G. Neihardt's Lakota Legacy," 110.

11. C. Holler, *Reader*, xvi.

12. D. Stover, "A Postcolonial Reading of Black Elk." See also G. Bataille, "Black Elk—New World Prophet."

13. Vine Deloria Jr., Introduction to *Black Elk Speaks* (1979), xiii.

14. Vine Deloria Jr., Introduction to V. Deloria (ed.), *Sender of Words*, 3.

15. C. Holler, *Reader*, xiii.

16. See P. Matthiessen, *In the Spirit of Crazy Horse*, xxxvii. It should be noted that Lame Deer was perhaps reacting against the elevation of one medicine man above others, a practice deplored by many Indians. See W.K. Powers, *Beyond the Vision*, 164. Lame Deer (1903-1976), like Wallace Black Elk (1921-2004, no relation) and the activist Russell Means (1939-2012), belonged to a later generation of Lakota who were bent on disassociating their tradition from Christian influences. *Lame Deer, Seeker of Visions* appeared in 1972 and Wallace Black Elk's *Black Elk: The Sacred Ways of a Lakota* in 1990. The latter's misleading title may well have been a marketing ploy. Black Elk's daughter, Lucy Looks Twice, amongst others, was at some pains to divorce Wallace Black Elk from any connection with her father. See M. Steltenkamp, "A Retrospective," 112-113.

17. W.K. Powers, "When Black Elk Speaks, Everybody Listens," 149.

18. W.K. Powers, "When Black Elk Speaks, Everybody Listens," 148.

19. T. Rozak, *Sources*, 341.

20. S.H. Nasr, *The Need for a Sacred Science*, 124-125.

21. M. Eliade, *The Quest*, 1 (italics mine).

22. *Schuon*, 45
23. F. Schuon, "No Activity without Truth," 36-37.
24. S.H. Nasr, *Sufi Essays*, 126.

Chapter 1: Nomadic Peoples and the Mark of Cain
1. *BES* 122.
2. M. Pallis, review of *The New Religions*, 189-190.
3. R. Guénon, *The Reign of Quantity*, 78.
4. R. Guénon, *The Reign of Quantity*, 180.
5. F. Schuon, *Light on the Ancient Worlds*, 8.
6. La Piana, quoted in *Schuon*, 70n. George La Piana (1879-1971) was a Catholic priest, scholar, and author.
7. Other "signs of the times" included the popularity of the Carlos Casteneda books which claimed to be based on the teachings and drug-induced visions of a Yaqui shaman, Don Juan, and a new cycle of revisionist Western films—*Cheyenne Autumn* (1964, directed John Ford), *Hombre* (1967, Martin Ritt), *Tell Them Willie Boy is Here* (1969, Abraham Polonsky), *Soldier Blue* (1970, Ralph Nelson), *Little Big Man* (1970, Arthur Penn), *A Man Called Horse* (1970, Elliot Silverstein)—in which the Indians were now the "good guys." (The character of Old Lodge Skins in *Little Big Man*, played by Chief Dan George, is clearly based on Black Elk.) Westerns in which Indians were represented with some sympathy and intelligence had appeared sporadically since World War II, amongst them *Devil's Doorway* (1950, Anthony Mann), *Broken Arrow* (1950, Delmer Daves), *The Last Hunt* (1956, Richard Brooks), and *Run of the Arrow* (1957, Sam Fuller). Many other Westerns of the period exposed some of the paradoxes and contradictions inherent in white racism; among the more interesting are John Ford's *The Searchers* (1956) and John Huston's *The Unforgiven* (1960). It hardly need be added that all of these films were directed by non-Native Americans, and in nearly all of them the parts of Indians were performed by non-native actors. It might also be noted that the popular assumption that the white-Indian conflict provided the conventional narrative structure of the Western genre is actually wrong: in the overwhelming majority of Hollywood Westerns in the classical period (c. 1935-1970) the Indians either play only a peripheral role or do not appear at all. The lawman/townspeople vs outlaws and the farmer vs rancher were much more common narrative staples.
8. Sitting Bull's speech, as recorded in W.F. Johnson, *Life of Sitting Bull and History of the Indian War of 1890-1* (1891), has been cited in many histories and anthologies such as *Touch the Earth* (page 77).
9. Helen Hunt Jackson, quoted in *Jackson*, 174. Helen Hunt Jackson (1830-1885) was a poet, novelist, and activist. Her book, *A Century of Dishonor*, from which this passage is taken, was first published in 1881.
10. The events leading up to Crazy Horse's death have been surrounded with uncertainty and controversy. Joe Jackson gives a detailed and even-handed account in *Jackson*, 137-158. He also discusses the various contending theories

about Crazy Horse's burial site; see 161.

11. Teller, quoted in *Holler*, 119-120. Teller was echoing many earlier condemnations of the "medicine-men" as intractable obstacles to the spread of Christianity and "civilization." Thus, for example, Gideon H. Pond in 1854: "Each in particular, and all together as wakan-men, they are not only useless, but a decided and devouring curse to their nation, on whose neck, mentally and morally, they have firmly planted the iron heel of priestly despotism: and until they are put down by the mighty operations of the Divine Spirit, through the word of Christ, they will effectually baffle any effort to elevate and civilize the Dacotas" ("Power and Influence of Dakota Medicine-Men" [1854], quoted in *Holler*, 113).

12. McGillycuddy, quoted in *Holler*, 123.

13. Joe Medicine Crow, quoted in C. Eastman, *Living in Two Worlds*, 130, 133.

14. For a discussion of some of the problems inherent in the use of Indian "autobiographies," including *Black Elk Speaks*, see D. Brumble, *American Indian Autobiography*, M. Castro, *Interpreting the Indian*, R. Heflin, *I Remain Alive*, and M. McAllister, "Native Sources: American Indian Autobiography."

15. E. Zolla, *The Writer and the Shaman*, 3 (italics mine).

16. J.E. Brown, *The Spiritual Legacy*, 22-23.

17. Radin, quoted in H. Smith, *The World's Religions*, 370.

18. H. Smith, *The World's Religions*, 370.

19. Plato, quoted in A. Coomaraswamy, *The Bugbear of Literacy*, 40 (italics mine).

20. A. Coomaraswamy, *The Bugbear of Literacy*, 41.

21. A. Coomaraswamy, *The Bugbear of Literacy*, 35.

22. A. Coomaraswamy, *The Bugbear of Literacy*, 44-45 (italics mine).

23. Lang, quoted in E. Sharpe, *Comparative Religion*, 61.

24. M. Eliade, *Australian Religions*, xiii-xiv.

25. W.E.H. Stanner, "Religion, Totemism and Symbolism," 156.

26. Scholars from various disciplines have canvassed a raft of terms to describe the cultures in question: archaic, indigenous, oral, non-literate, ethnic, tribal, pre-Axial, autochthonous, folk, ethnographic, shamanic, aboriginal. The term "primitive," once favoured by anthropologists, no longer has any currency because of its pejorative associations. I have preferred the term "primal" for reasons outlined by Arvind Sharma; see his *A Primal Perspective on the Philosophy of Religion*, 1-5.

27. V. Frankl, "Reductionism and Nihilism," 398. Frankl made this observation in 1968; it remains as forceful today as it was then.

28. M. Eliade, *Patterns in Comparative Religion*, xiii.

29. "The Rock."

30. S. McCluskey, "*Black Elk Speaks*: and So Does John Neihardt," 233.

31. *Schuon*, 4. As Whitall Perry once observed, "the scientific pursuit of religion puts the saddle on the wrong horse, since it is the domain of religion to evaluate science, and not vice versa" (review of *The Phenomena of Religion*,

127).

32. Walking Buffalo (1871-1967), quoted in T.C. McLuhan, *Touch the Earth*, 23.

33. C. Eastman, *Living in Two Worlds*, 159.

34. Stanley Diamond (1922-1991), in the Franz Boas-Paul Radin lineage, supplies us with one example of an anthropologist who questioned many of the premises of mainstream anthropology. Perhaps it is not without significance that Diamond was also a poet; see his "The Search for the Primitive." To adduce another example, Raymond DeMallie is one of the most well-informed and thoughtful Black Elk scholars.

35. See Sources for some works by these writers.

36. Luther Standing Bear, *Land of the Spotted Eagle*, 250.

37. *S. Pipe*, 1971 edition, xv-xvi.

38. To adduce a few examples one might mention Wilfred Thesiger's work on the Bedouin of Arabia, Laurens van der Post on the Kalahari tribesmen, and James Cowan on the Australian Aborigines.

39. *Sixth G*, 66.

40. W. Paden, *Religious Worlds*, 51. Of course Paden's claim does not mean that diverse religious forms cannot open onto the same supra-formal truth.

Chapter 2: The World of the Lakota

1. F. Schuon, "Holy Silence": www.sophia-perennis.com/silence.htm. A slightly different rendering of this passage can be found in M. Fitzgerald, "Frithjof Schuon's Role in Preserving the Red Indian Spirit," 224.

2. *BES*, 7.

3. The etymology and history of the term "Sioux" is complex, but some Native Americans have rejected it because of various negative associations. To my knowledge there is no satisfactory alternative which encompasses all of the tribes belonging under this canopy. However, it is only used sparingly in the present study. At least one writer has preferred the term "*Oyate*"—people. Research by Douglas R. Parks, David S. Rood, and Raymond J. DeMallie in the late 1970s established that both the Santee and the Yankton referred to themselves by the autonym "Dakota." The name "Nakota" apparently was, and is, the exclusive usage of the Assiniboine and the Stoney, their Canadian relatives. See Douglas R. Parks and Raymond J. DeMallie, "Sioux, Assiniboine, and Stoney Dialects: A Classification"; see also G. Linden, "Dakota Philosophy," 220-221.

4. For an account of this expedition see *Jackson*, 81-85.

5. *Wikipedia* entry: "Lakota people."

6. If it be asked what is meant by the term "sacramental," one can hardly better the traditional Christian formulation that a sacrament is "an outer and visible sign of an inner and invisible grace."

7. See M. Charlesworth, *Religion in Aboriginal Australia*, 13-14.

8. See H. Deakin, "Some Thoughts on Transcendence in Tribal Societies," 95-109. For many striking parallels between the religious cultures and the fates

of the Native Americans and the Australian Aborigines, see A. Smith, "What Hast Thou Done?," and H. Oldmeadow, "Melodies from the Beyond."

9. See M. Eliade, *Australian Religions*, xvff. For an interesting discussion of Sioux conceptions of time and space, see G. Linden, "Dakota Philosophy."

10. On this general subject see M. Eliade, *The Sacred and the Profane*. The phrase "visionary geography" comes from Henri Corbin.

11. *Schuon*, 158.

12. For further explanation of these "defining characteristics," see A.M. Josephy Jr., *The Indian Heritage of America*, chap. 12, 110-123.

13. Luther Standing Bear, *Land of the Spotted Eagle*, 38

14. The most accessible introduction to Eliade's thought is *The Sacred and the Profane* (1959).

15. See, for instance, R.B. Hassrick, *The Sioux: Life and Customs of a Warrior Society*.

16. *S. Pipe*, xx (italics mine). Elsewhere the holy man said, "*Wakan-Tanka*, you are everything, and yet above everything" (J.E. Brown, *The Spiritual Legacy*, 53).

17. Ella Deloria (Yankton Dakota), quoted in J. & M. Fitzgerald, *The Spirit of Indian Women*, 100.

18. *S. Pipe*, 4n.

19. The best account of the place of animals in the spiritual economy of the Lakota is found in J.E. Brown, *Animals of the Soul: Sacred Animals of the Oglala Sioux* (1997). See also Å. Hultkrantz, "Attitudes to Animals in Shoshoni Indian Religion."

20. S.J. Howard, "Incommensurability and Nicholas Black Elk," 114. The term *wakan* has also been translated as "force" and "energy."

21. C. Eastman, *Living in Two Worlds*, 163. Ohiyesa's (1858-1939) father was a Santee Dakota named Many Lightnings. His mother, Great Spirit Woman, was the daughter of Seth Eastman, a white army officer, and Stands Sacred, herself the daughter of Cloud Man, a Santee Dakota chief. Under the name Charles Eastman, Ohiyesa achieved some fame as a physician, writer, and reformer. At the time of the Wounded Knee Massacre he worked as a physician on the Pine Ridge Reservation.

22. Yellowtail, quoted in M. & J. Fitzgerald, *Indian Spirit*, 57.

23. Emerson, quoted in J. &. M. Fitzgerald, *The Sermon of All Creation*, 34.

24. F. Densmore, *Teton Sioux Music*, 85n2.

25. *S. Pipe*, 138.

26. See *Schuon*, 71, 14, and J.E. Brown, *The Spiritual Legacy*, 27.

27. J.E. Brown, *The Spiritual Legacy*, 53.

28. On the traditional symbolism of the circle and the cross, see A. Snodgrass, *Architecture, Time, and Eternity* and R. Guénon, *Symbolism of the Cross* and *Fundamental Symbols*.

29. *BES*, 121.

30. F. Schuon, *Light on the Ancient Worlds* (1965 edition), 84.

31. J.E. Brown, *The Spiritual Legacy*, 27.

32. C. Eastman, *Living in Two Worlds*, 160.

33. The Lakota term closest to our "doctor" is *pejuta wicasa*.

34. On this terminology, see *S. Pipe*, 45n. and M. Steltenkamp, *Nicholas Black Elk*, 45-46.

35. A. Versluis, *Native American Traditions*, 52.

36. M. Eliade, *Shamanism*, 4.

37. M. Eliade, *Shamanism*, xii. The structures and practices of shamanism are remarkably similar across its various geographical locations. The most familiar habitat of shamanism stretches in a vast arc through Siberia and Mongolia and down through both American continents. However, shamanistic practices (not always identified by that term) can be found in many primordial cultures, including those of the Australian Aborigines. The classic anthropological study of Aboriginal "clever men" by A.P. Elkin reveals many striking parallels between the Native American "medicine man" and the Aboriginal *karadji*, "men of high degree" as Elkin termed them. See Elkin's *Aboriginal Men of High Degree*. See also J. Cowan, *Elements of the Aborigine Tradition*, chap. 6. For an anthology of shamanic testimonies, see J. Halifax, *Shamanic Voices*.

38. M. Eliade, *Shamanism*, xix.

39. *Schuon*, 35.

40. The dangers of "black magic" are dramatically illustrated in the Navajo phenomenon of "skinwalkers" or "shape-shifters"—"witches" who have turned their powers to evil and destructive ends.

41. Yellowtail, quoted in M. & J. Fitzgerald, *Indian Spirit*, 3.

42. Abhishiktananda, *The Further Shore*, 105.

43. A. Coomaraswamy, *Hinduism and Buddhism*, quoted in J.E. Brown, *The Spiritual Legacy*, 63. Mythical truth is penultimate because the Truth as such is formless and beyond expression.

44. A. Coomaraswamy, *The Essential Ananda K. Coomaraswamy*, 231.

45. Jung, quoted in A. Jaffe, *The Myth of Meaning*, 15. For some discussion of Jung's religious thought, see H. Oldmeadow, *Mircea Eliade and Carl Jung: "Priests without Surplices?"*

46. J. Campbell, *The Hero with a Thousand Faces*, 3.

47. On the interrelationships of cyclic time, myth, and ritual in Native American traditions see J.E. Brown, *Teaching Spirits*, 9-18.

48. W. Paden, *Religious Worlds*, 120.

49. *S. Pipe*, 4-7.

50. *BES*, 2.

51. *S. Pipe*, 32.

52. *S. Pipe*, 43.

53. *S. Pipe*, 8n. An interesting parallel to the Platonic account of the journeying of the souls in the myth of Er is to be found in the Sioux belief that the released souls of the dead traveled along the Milky Way to a point where they are divided by an old woman, some sent to the right to join *Wakan-Tanka*, some sent to the left to continue in a conditioned state. See *S. Pipe*, 29n.

54. Crowfoot, quoted in M. & J. Fitzgerald, *Indian Spirit*, 85.

55. Thomas Tyon (Oglala), quoted in M. & J. Fitzgerald, *Indian Spirit*, 94. See also the account of Crying for a Vision by Ella Deloria (Yankton Dakota) in J. & M. Fitzgerald, *The Spirit of Indian Women*, 132-134.

56. Ella Deloria, quoted in J. & M. Fitzgerald, *The Spirit of Indian Women*, 97.

57. Fools Crow (Oglala), quoted in M. & J. Fitzgerald, *Indian Spirit* 82.

58. *S. Pipe*, 80.

59. M. Eliade, *The Sacred and the Profane*, 93. This native sense of cosmic responsibility was well captured in an encounter between Carl Jung and a Taos Pueblo elder who was bewildered by the European curtailment of Indian rituals, explaining to the psychologist, "After all, we are a people who live on the roof of the world; we are the sons of Father Sun, and with our religion we daily help our father to go across the sky. *We do this not only for ourselves, but for the whole world.* If we were to cease practicing our religion, in ten years the sun would no longer rise. Then it would be night forever" (quoted in C.G. Jung, *Memories, Dreams, Reflections*, 280 [italics mine]).

60. *Schuon*, 94, 97.

61. *Schuon*, 129-130.

62. *S. Pipe*, 115.

63. *S. Pipe*, 116. For an account from Mourning Dove of the equivalent Salish rite, see J. & M. Fitzgerald, *The Spirit of Indian Women*, 113. The spiritual life of Native American women has until recently been a largely neglected field. This subject lies outside the ambit of the present study, but interested readers will find *The Spirit of Indian Women* a useful starting-point.

64. *S. Pipe*, 127.

Chapter 3: A Sacred Voice is Calling: The Life of Black Elk

1. *BES*, 12. Some scholars take the view that all references to Black Elk's narrative should now draw on the transcript in *The Sixth Grandfather*. I have preferred to use *Black Elk Speaks*. My reasons will become clearer as the study proceeds but they are, in part, explained by Brian Holloway's comments about the use of both transcripts in *Interpreting the Legacy*, 36-37. Readers wishing to juxtapose passages from the two transcripts will find Raymond DeMallie's Concordance helpful; see *Sixth G*, 413-418.

2. *BES*, 1. This well-known passage was actually Neihardt's rendition of what Black Elk *could* have said, rather than a record of his actual words. This, of course, does not preclude the possibility that Neihardt intuitively understood Black Elk's state of mind or recalled him expressing such a sentiment in a conversation that was not recorded by Neihardt's daughter. In any event, he was able to communicate it in these beautiful words.

3. Black Elk's tombstone records his birth year as 1858; on the basis of Black Elk's own accounts, Joseph Brown makes it 1862 and Neihardt 1863; Joe Jackson, Black Elk's most recent biographer, favours 1863, as do Brian Holloway and Sam Wellman; Clyde Holler and Michael Steltenkamp seem to favor 1866. See M. Steltenkamp, *Nicholas Black Elk*, 14-15. The biographical

account in this chapter presents the generally accepted material facts of Black Elk's life, taken from the standard sources by Neihardt, DeMallie, Holler, Steltenkamp, Jackson, and others.

4. Black Elk's mother was also known as Leggings Down. After her conversion to Catholicism she took the Christian name Mary.

5. For an engaging account of this enigmatic figure see L. McMurtry, *Crazy Horse*.

6. Other Lakota bands included the Minneconjous, Brules, Hunkpapas, and Blackfeet. Black Elk's family belonged to one of the northern sub-groups of the Oglala, led by Big Road.

7. The Battle of the Hundred Slain is also known as the Fetterman Fight or Fetterman Massacre, the worst military defeat of the US Army in the Great Plains until the Battle of Little Big Horn ten years later. See D. Brown, *The Fetterman Massacre*. Red Cloud's War is also referred to as the Powder River War and the Bozeman War.

8. Sherman, quoted in *Jackson*, 48.

9. *BES*, 6. The term *wasichu* originally referred to non-native people—in effect, to Europeans, though it carried no reference to skin color. The term gradually took on a new meaning of "people without number, like the stars in the sky, more than can be counted."

10. Red Cloud, quoted in M. & J. Fitzgerald, *Indian Spirit*, 8.

11. DeSmet, quoted in M. Steltenkamp, *Nicholas Black Elk*, 17.

12. *Sixth G*, 3.

13. C. Holler, *Reader*, xxii.

14. *Sixth G*, 183. See also *Jackson*, 116.

15. *BES*, 12.

16. *BES*, 30-31.

17. *Sixth G*, ix.

18. *Sixth G*, 97.

19. *BES*, 127.

20. *BES*, 99.

21. *BES*, 157.

22. M. Eliade, *Shamanism*, 13.

23. *Sixth G*, 6.

24. Luke 2:47, 52.

25. *BES*, 109.

26. For a detailed, chronological account of the preparations and the performance of both the Horse Dance and the Dog Vision Dance, see *Jackson*, chap. 12, 182-189.

27. *Sixth G*, 7.

28. For a brief account of the *yuwipi* ceremony, see J.E. Brown, *The Spiritual Legacy*, 110-111.

29. *BES*, 117.

30. *Schuon*, 88-89.

31. *BES*, 117.

32. *Sixth G*, 245.
33. *BES*, 134.
34. *BES*, 139.
35. *Schuon*, 145.
36. H. Neihardt, *Black Elk and Flaming Rainbow*, 73.
37. *Jackson*, 246.
38. See *Jackson*, 278. Sitting Bull also had great respect for the flamboyant showman because he always kept his word and generally treated the Indians well.
39. *BES*, 145. Wovoka was actually preceded by another millenarian visionary Paiute, Wodzibub, whose teachings triggered the Dance of the Departing Souls, or Ghost Dance, but this movement only lasted a few years. Wodzibub died in 1872 or 1873. See *Jackson*, 288.
40. See P. Steinmetz, *Pipe, Bible, and Peyote Among the Oglala Sioux*, 180-181.
41. *BES*, 148-149. See also *Sixth G*, 257.
42. *Jackson*, 293.
43. Ninety million acres (66%) of all Indian reservation land was taken away and given to non-Indians for free or at subsidized prices during the 47 years of the Dawes Act. Today only 2.3% of all land in the U.S. is on Indian reservations and approximately half of that is owned by non-Indians.
44. *Wikipedia* entry: "The Dawes Act."
45. Sitting Bull's story is told in Robert Utley's *The Lance and the Shield: The Life and Times of Sitting Bull* (1993).
46. R.A. Smith, *Moon of Popping Trees*, 1.
47. The precise number of Indians killed has never been determined. Most estimates put the figure of those who died in the actual massacre at between two and three hundred. Many later died from their wounds.
48. The lack of clarity about Black Elk's changing attitude to the Ghost Dance derives from his own apparent ambivalence, both before and after Wounded Knee, and from the fact that Neihardt slanted Black Elk's account to consolidate his own conviction that the Ghost Dance symbolized "the desperate resistance of the Indians to the tragic inevitability of the destruction of their traditional culture" (C. Holler, "Lakota Religion and Tragedy," 33). See Holler's textual analysis of the passages from *Black Elk Speaks* compared with Enid Neihardt's original transcript, 31-37. On Black Elk's vexed claim that "I started the ghost shirt" (*Sixth G*, 262; omitted from *Black Elk Speaks*), see R. Heflin, "*I Remain Alive*," 183-185.
49. *Jackson*, 329.
50. Black Elk's unedited account of his involvement with the Ghost Dance movement and the massacre at Wounded Knee can be found in Chapter 8 of *Sixth G*, 256-282. It is recounted, with extra material drawn from other sources, in *Jackson*, 316-333.
51. See C. Holler, "Lakota Religion and Tragedy."
52. M. Steltenkamp, *Black Elk: Holy Man of the Oglala*, xxii.
53. The Peyote Cult, after various transmutations, underwent something of a

revival at Pine Ridge in the 1940s, and still persists today as the Native American Church of Jesus Christ. *See Jackson*, 350, 448.

54. *BES*, 169.

55. See S. McCluskey, "*Black Elk Speaks*: and So Does John Neihardt," 238.

56. For the 1973 episode and its aftermath, see P. Matthiessen, *In the Spirit of Crazy Horse*.

57. *Schuon*, 39.

58. Black Elk's son Nicholas died in 1959, Ben in 1973, and Lucy in 1978; these dates are taken from the timeline in M. Steltenkamp, *Nicholas Black Elk*, 235-237.

59. *Jackson*, 283.

60. *Jackson*, 351-352.

61. The account given here of Black Elk's conversion and his work as a catechist is drawn from Michael Steltenkamp's two books and from Joe Jackson's recent biography. Although there has been a great deal of disputation about the meaning and significance of this conversion, the essential facts about Black Elk's outer life now seem to be clearly established.

62. For Lucy's account, see M. Steltenkamp, *Black Elk: Holy Man of the Oglala*, 33-35.

63. See *Sixth G*, 12, and S. Wellman, *Black Elk*, 94.

64. See S. Wellman, *Black Elk*, 95.

65. Jackson suggests that Black Elk may have continued to perform his duties as a *wicasa wakan* secretly, even in the years when he was most actively involved in his work as a catechist (1907-1916). After 1916, when the Jesuits adopted a more tolerant attitude to some of the old ways, Black Elk often publicly performed traditional dances. See *Jackson*, 387-388.

66. For some discussion of Black Elk's choices about language, see R. Heflin, "*I Remain Alive*," 163, and S. Wellman, *Black Elk*, 77.

67. *Sixth G*, 26; *Jackson*, 370.

68. M. Steltenkamp, *Black Elk: Holy Man of the Oglala*, xvii.

69. As Clyde Holler has persuasively argued, Steltenkamp's claims about the extent to which the reservation Lakota remained ignorant of both *Black Elk Speaks* and *The Sacred Pipe* should be treated with some skepticism; see *Holler*, 184-186.

70. T. Mails, *Fools Crow*, 53.

71. Steltenkamp uncovered several different versions of the way in which Black Elk had been partially blinded after an episode with an exploding shell/gunpowder. See M. Steltenkamp, *Nicholas Black Elk*, 26-27. These different accounts can also be found in *Jackson*, 359.

72. For an account of this pageant, see *Jackson*, 441-447.

73. B. Holloway, *Interpreting the Legacy*, 76.

74. B. Holloway, *Interpreting the Legacy*, 78.

75. Letter to Fr. Gall, September 4, 1947, quoted in M. Steltenkamp, *Nicholas Black Elk*, 159.

76. J.E. Brown & E. Cousins, *Teaching Spirits*, 14.

77. M. Fitzgerald, "Frithjof Schuon and the Native Spirit," 17.
78. B. Holloway, *Interpreting the Legacy*, 31.
79. B. Holloway, *Interpreting the Legacy*, 7.
80. On Neihardt's biography see V. Deloria (ed.), *Sender of Words*, H. Neihardt, *Black Elk and Flaming Rainbow*, articles by George Linden and Hilda Neihardt & R. Todd Wise in *Reader*, A.N. Petri, "John G. Neihardt beyond Black Elk," and *Jackson*.
81. Recounted in his book *The River and I*. See also H. Stauffer, "Neihardt's Journey on the Missouri."
82. On the recognition of Neihardt's literary work and the many awards and distinctions he received, see A.N. Petri, "John G. Neihardt beyond Black Elk," 278-279. (Alexis Petri is Neihardt's great-granddaughter.)
83. *A Cycle of the West* incorporated some of his earlier works. For a brief commentary on *Where the Tree Flowered*, see R. DeMallie, "John G. Neihardt's Lakota Legacy," 131-134, and "John G. Neihardt and Nicholas Black Elk," 247-248.
84. See J. Neihardt, "The Book That Would Not Die," 227, and S. McCluskey, "*Black Elk Speaks:* and So Does John Neihardt," 235.
85. H. Neihardt, *Black Elk and Flaming Rainbow*, 38.
86. Hinman was a journalist planning to write a book on Crazy Horse, a project eventually taken up by her friend Mari Sandoz, whose *Crazy Horse: The Strange Man of the Oglalas*, dedicated to Hinman, was published in 1942.
87. *BES*, xxiv (italics mine).
88. R. DeMallie, "John G. Neihardt's Lakota Legacy," 116.
89. See R. DeMallie, "John G. Neihardt and Nicholas Black Elk," 245. See also *Jackson*, 406, and B. Holloway, *Interpreting the Legacy*, 57.
90. R. DeMallie, "John G. Neihardt's Lakota Legacy," 124.
91. L. Utecht, "Neihardt and Black Elk," 284, 285.
92. Neihardt, letter to Julius T. House, August 10, 1930, cited in *Sixth G*, 27. Several scholars have argued that the fact that Black Elk said he was "expect ing" Neihardt does not signify any supra-normal powers on his part, nor does it confer any special status on Neihardt; rather, this was a ritualized form of greeting. See C. Holler, "Lakota Religion and Tragedy," 22.
93. Black Elk, quoted in G. Linden, "John Neihardt and *Black Elk Speaks*," 85.
94. F. Waters, "Neihardt and the Vision of Black Elk," 13. I quote this passage not because I concur with Waters' spiritual evolutionism—on the contrary—but because it introduces an idea to be explored later: that Neihardt, in his role as the mediator between Black Elk and the world of the whites, was an instrument of a power of which he himself may well have been unaware.
95. Black Elk's daughter, Lucy, was upset by the choice of Ben as the translator of her father's words; she had expected this role to be taken by Black Elk's fellow-catechist, Emil Afraid of Hawk. Lucy, herself brought up exclusively as a Catholic, believed that Afraid of Hawk would pay more respect to her father's Catholicism. Ben's role, sanctioned by his father, apparently caused some tension within the family. See *Jackson*, 413.

96. Standing Bear, four years older than Black Elk, had experienced many of the same key events and had also converted to Catholicism, taking the name of the first Christian martyr. While touring Europe with Cody's Wild West show he had been seriously injured. In hospital he fell in love with and later married an Austrian nurse. They returned to Pine Ridge where she was known as "Across the Eastern Water Woman." See *Jackson*, 410-411.

97. C. Eastman, *The Soul of the Indian*, 9.

98. *Sixth G*, 28.

99. *Sixth G*, 31.

100. H. Neihardt, *Black Elk and Flaming Rainbow*, 52.

101. H. Neihardt, *Black Elk and Flaming Rainbow*, 53.

102. B. Holloway, *Interpreting the Legacy*, 17.

103. See G. Linden, "John Neihardt and *Black Elk Speaks*," 79.

104. The interviews which form the basis of *Black Elk Speaks* occurred between May 10 and May 28, 1931.

105. Readers should note that the name of Harney Peak, a significant site in Black Elk's story, was changed on August 11, 2016 to Black Elk Peak. Because it is referred to as Harney Peak by Black Elk himself and by most scholars since, that name is retained in the present work. However, it is a fitting tribute to the holy man that the peak should now be named in his honor.

106. *BES*, 171-172.

107. *Jackson*, 430.

108. See "Biography of Joseph Epes Brown" in J.E Brown, *The Spiritual Legacy*, 127-130.

109. Whitall N. Perry (1920-2005) became a leading voice in the Perennialist school of thought. John M. Murray (1910-1999) was one of Brown's closest friends. Murray moved to Lausanne in 1947 and remained Schuon's neighbor for the remainder of his life, both in Switzerland and America.

110. See M. Fitzgerald, "New Light on Black Elk and *The Sacred Pipe*" for a more detailed account of the intellectual and spiritual paths taken by these four friends.

111. Sally McCluskey, who interviewed Neihardt in April 1971, stated that he was "slightly piqued" by Brown's failure to acknowledge his help in the text of *The Sacred Pipe*; McCluskey adds that Brown did twice write to Neihardt expressing his gratitude and acknowledging that his own literary style could not match the poet's. See "*Black Elk Speaks*: and So Does John Neihardt," 239. For some interesting observations about the diction and style of *Black Elk Speaks* and *The Sacred Pipe* respectively, see B. Holloway, *Interpreting the Legacy*, 22-23.

112. J.E. Brown, *The Spiritual Legacy*, 24.

113. J.E. Brown & E. Cousins, *Teaching Spirits*, 83.

114. Schuon, quoted in M. Fitzgerald, *Frithjof Schuon: Messenger of the Perennial Philosophy*, 91.

115. Brown's other works include *Animals of the Soul* (1992) and, with Emily Cousins, *Teaching Spirits* (2001).

116. On Schuon's life and work, see M. Fitzgerald, *Frithjof Schuon: Messenger of the Perennial Philosophy*, and H. Oldmeadow, *Frithjof Schuon and the Perennial Philosophy*.
117. H. Smith, Foreword to Frithjof Schuon, *The Eye of the Heart*, ix.
118. S. H. Nasr, quoted in R. Fabbri, *Frithjof Schuon: The Shining Realm of the Intellect*, 30n.
119. M. *Steltenkamp, Black Elk: Holy Man of the Oglala*, 132-134.
120. T.M.P. Mahadevan, *Ramana Maharshi*, 77, and *Wikipedia* entry: "Ramana Maharshi."

Chapter 4: The Sacred Hoop and the Flowering Tree: Black Elk's Great Vision
1. *BES*, 26.
2. *BES*, 30-31.
3. The doctrine of archetypes is at least implicit in all religious traditions, explicit in some. In the Hindu and Buddhist traditions it can be found, for example, in theories of the mandala. One might also cite classical Hindu ideas about the Vedas as an earthly reflection of a divine model.
4. Given the popularity of Jung's ideas about "archetypes," it is worth pointing out that these do not constitute a metaphysical doctrine but a hypothesis about certain psychic phenomena.
5. Kung-sun Lung (325-250 BC), quoted in W. Perry, *A Treasury of Traditional Wisdom*, 670.
6. Philo (25 BC AD 50), quoted in W. Perry, *A Treasury of Traditional Wisdom*, 670.
7. Boehme (1154-1191), quoted in W. Perry, *A Treasury of Traditional Wisdom*, 671.
8. Rumi (1207-1273), quoted in *Schuon*, 43.
9. Sendivogius (1566-1636), quoted in J. & M. Fitzgerald, *The Sermon of All Creation*, 75.
10. Suhrawardi (1574-1624), quoted in W. Perry, *A Treasury of Traditional Wisdom*, 673.
11. Eckhart (c. 1260 1328), quoted in W. Perry, *A Treasury of Traditional Wisdom*, 673.
12. R. Guénon, *Spiritual Authority and Temporal Power*, 12.
13. Abu Bakr Siraj Ed-Din, *The Book of Certainty*, 50. This book gives an account of the doctrine of archetypes and of the multiple states of being from a Sufic perspective. See also René Guénon's *The Multiple States of Being*.
14. R. Guénon, *Spiritual Authority and Temporal Power*, 12.
15. F. Schuon, *Art from the Sacred to the Profane*, 4.
16. *BES*, 53.
17. See, for instance, J. Rice, *Black Elk's Story*, 27.
18. *BES*, 105. (The 2014 complete edition misprints the "I" in the last sentence as "It.")
19. R. Guénon, *East and West*, 37.

20. A. Govinda, *Creative Meditation and Multi-Dimensional Consciousness*, 102.

21. See M. Eliade, "Methodological Remarks on the Study of Religious Symbolism," 95.

22. C.G. Jung, C.G. *Jung: The Collected Works*, Vol. 6, (from *Psychological Types*), 2534.

23. S.H. Nasr, *Sufi Essays*, 88 (italics mine). For a particularly lucid exposition of the nature of traditional symbolism, see A. Snodgrass, *The Symbolism of the Stupa*, 1-10. See also G. Eaton, *The Richest Vein*, 186ff., M. Pallis, *A Buddhist Spectrum*, 144-163, and T. Scott, "Understanding 'Symbol.'"

24. See F. Schuon, *Gnosis: Divine Wisdom*, 106-121, and S.H. Nasr, *Man and Nature*, 131.

25. F. Schuon, "Foundations of an Integral Aesthetics," 135n. See also C. Isherwood, *Ramakrishna and His Disciples*, 61ff.

26. M. Eliade, *The Sacred and the Profane*, 12, 178.

27. O. von Simson, *The Gothic Cathedral*, xvi.

28. Coleridge, quoted in T. Roszak, *Where the Wasteland Ends*, 353.

29. M. Eliade, *The Sacred and the Profane*, 12-13.

30. F. Schuon, *From the Divine to the Human*, 87.

31. T. Merton, *Ishi Means Man*, 17.

32. See *Sixth G*, 84. White Bull (1849-1947) was the principal informant of Stanley Vestal, author of *Sitting Bull: Champion of the Sioux* (1932).

33. T. Merton, *Ishi Means Man*, 22.

34. *S. Pipe*, 44.

35. M. Fitzgerald, *Yellowtail*, 115.

36. J.E. Brown, *The Spiritual Legacy*, 11.

37. C. Lévi-Strauss, *Totemism*, 97-98. As Huston Smith has remarked, Lévi-Strauss actually took "surprisingly little interest in what myths meant to the peoples who lived by them"; he was too intent on constructing his structuralist theory. See H. Smith, "What They Have That We Lack," 89.

38. C. Eastman, *Living in Two Worlds*, 162.

39. *S. Pipe*, 45n.

40. *Schuon*, 30-31.

41. *Schuon*, 31.

42. *BES*, 14. All of the direct quotes that follow in the next few pages, unless otherwise indicated, come from *BES*, chap. 3, 13-29.

43. *BES*, 19.

44. "Drought" is rendered as "drouth" in *BES*. I have preferred the "drought" of earlier editions.

45. *BES*, 26.

46. *BES*, 26.

47. Neihardt's controversial editorial omissions in Black Elk's account include passages dealing with the "soldier weed" with which Black Elk was to destroy the whites; see *Sixth G*, 135-137, and R. DeMallie, "John G. Neihardt and Nicholas Black Elk," 260-261.

48. *BES*, 28.
49. See J. Rice, "*Akicita* of the Thunder," and R. Sayre, "Vision and Experience in *Black Elk Speaks*."
50. F. Waters, "Neihardt and the Vision of Black Elk," 20.
51. R. Todd Wise, "The Great Vision of Black Elk as Literary Ritual," 253. Works by the authors mentioned can be found in the list of Sources.
52. *Sixth G*, 52-53.
53. Neihardt lecture, quoted in B. Holloway, *Interpreting the Legacy*, 25.
54. F. Schuon, *Spiritual Perspectives and Human Facts*, 119 (italics mine).
55. W. James, *Varieties of Religious Experience*, 305.
56. Rudolf Otto's *The Idea of the Holy* (1917) still provides one of the more fertile models of mystical experience. There are many points of convergence between Black Elk's Great Vision and the numinous experience theorized by the German theologian.
57. Keats, in a letter to his brothers, December 21,1817; *Wikipedia* entry: "Negative capability."
58. F. Schuon, *Understanding Islam*, 40-41.
59. M. Eliade, *The Quest*, 62 (italics mine).
60. Barth, quoted in T. Merton, *Opening the Bible*, 26.
61. Abhishiktananda, *Hindu-Christian Meeting Point*, 112.
62. Schuon distinguishes this kind of certitude from one that is merely mental by describing it as "quasi-ontological certitude"; see *To Have a Center*, 56.
63. *Schuon*, 14, 71. Schuon recalls that this symbolism was explained to him by Ben Black Elk.
64. See also A. Snodgrass, *Architecture, Time, and Eternity*, Vol. 2, 425-431. Snodgrass explicates the spatio-temporal relationships of the four Winds and the directions, as well as the symbolic significances of Lakota "architecture."
65. *Sixth G*, 86. Robert Sayre had made this point much earlier when he wrote that everything in the Great Vision was "very consistent with the myths of Sioux and plains culture" ("Vision and Experience in *Black Elk Speaks*," 347). David Trumble observed that "almost everything that [Black Elk] tells us about himself is explicitly or implicitly related to the history of the tribe. . . . Even the Great Vision, which dominates the book just as it dominated Black Elk's life, has to do with Black Elk's relation to the tribe and its well-being" (D. Trumble, *American Indian Autobiography*, 169).
66. *Sixth G*, 49.

Chapter 5: Preserving Black Elk's Legacy: John G. Neihardt, Joseph Epes Brown, and Their Critics

1. R. DeMallie, "John Neihardt's Lakota Legacy," 85.
2. Nasr, quoted in "Biography of Joseph Epes Brown," in the commemorative edition of *The Spiritual Legacy* (2007), 130.
3. C. Holler, *Reader*, xiii (italics mine). For a critique of Holler's own "construction" of Black Elk, see D. Stover's review of *Black Elk's Religion: The Sun Dance and Lakota Catholicism*.

4. Quoted in E. Zolla, *The Writer and the Shaman*, 262.

5. B. Whitney, *John G. Neihardt*, 86.

6. E. Zolla, *The Writer and the Shaman*, 264-265.

7. Zane Grey's best-selling novel, *The Vanishing Indian*, was published in 1925 after first appearing in serial form in *Ladies' Home Journal*.

8. C. Holler, "Lakota Religion and Tragedy," 36.

9. C. Holler, "Lakota Religion and Tragedy," 41.

10. *BES*, 169.

11. *Sixth G*, 56.

12. G.T. Couser, "*Black Elk Speaks* with Forked Tongue," 85.

13. W.K. Powers, "When Black Elks Speaks, Everybody Listens," 9.

14. J. Rice, *Black Elk's Story*, 14.

15. S. Wellman, *Black Elk*, front-piece, 112, 113, 115. Wellman seems quite impervious to the fact that his own biography would certainly not have been possible without Neihardt's work. We might also note in passing that Mari Sandoz owed a good deal to Neihardt in her work *Crazy Horse: The Strange Man of the Oglalas* (1942). For Neihardt's literary influence on Sandoz, see B. Holloway, *Interpreting the Legacy*, 182-184.

16. J. Rice, *Black Elk's Story*, x. Rice also makes a good deal of the influence of German Romanticism on Neihardt's outlook. For a heartfelt riposte to Rice's charges against Neihardt, see G. Linden, "John Neihardt and *Black Elk Speaks*," especially 82-84.

17. For some discussion of this kind of critique, see R. Todd Wise, "*Black Elk Speaks* as Testimonial Literature," 24-25.

18. W.K. Powers, "When Black Elk Speaks, Everybody Listens," 137.

19. W.K. Powers, "When Black Elk Speaks, Everybody Listens," 149, 136.

20. M. Steltenkamp, *Nicholas Black Elk*, 143. In the same letter (September 1934), the old man complained that Neihardt had promised him half the profits of the book but was now claiming that he had not made a cent on the book. DeMallie raises the possibility that Lucy Looks Twice was actually the author of the letter in question. See *Sixth G*, 62.

21. G.T. Couser, "*Black Elk Speaks* with Forked Tongue," 76.

22. Means, quoted in G. Fields, "*Inipi*, the Purification Rite (Sweat Lodge) and Black Elk," 171.

23. D. Stover, "A Postcolonial Reading of Black Elk," 130.

24. G.T. Couser, "*Black Elk Speaks* with Forked Tongue," 79.

25. See *Sixth G*, 135-137.

26. See C. Holler, "Lakota Religion and Tragedy," 29-31.

27. C. Holler, "Lakota Religion and Tragedy," 31.

28. Frithjof Schuon letter to William Stoddart, August 8, 1984, contained in its entirety in Appendix III.

29. Frithjof Schuon letter to William Stoddart, August 8, 1984. Another example that falls into this category is Neihardt's failure to mention Black Elk's relationship to the Catholic Church. Frithjof Schuon discusses this criticism in the aforementioned 1984 letter to Stoddart.

30. B. Holloway, *Interpreting the Legacy*, 22. It might also be noted that Brown's prose is more poetic in *The Sacred Pipe* than in his other works where his style, while always functional, is sometimes quite pedestrian.

31. *BES*, 169.

32. *BES*, 171-172.

33. Neihardt, quoted in *Jackson*, 453.

34. B. Holloway, *Interpreting the Legacy*, 36.

35. B. Holloway, *Interpreting the Legacy*, 36. Holloway's book contains many reproductions of Enid Neihardt's stenographic notes, the original handwritten transcripts, and John Neihardt's handwritten manuscripts.

36. B. Holloway, *Interpreting the Legacy*, 3.

37. From the Foreword to the 1979 edition of *Black Elk Speaks*, xiv. Clyde Holler has outlined the reasons why he finds Deloria's attitude unsatisfactory; see "Lakota Religion and Tragedy," 40-41.

38. *Schuon*, 77.

39. E. Zolla, *The Writer and the Shaman*, 264.

40. E. Zolla, *The Writer and the Shaman*, 271.

41. M. McAllister, "Native Sources: American Indian Autobiography," 15.

42. Neihardt, quoted in McCluskey, "*Black Elk Speaks*: and So Does John Neihardt," 238-239.

43. E. Zolla, *The Writer and the Shaman*, 264.

44. S. McCluskey, "*Black Elk Speaks*: and So Does John Neihardt," 235.

45. H. Neihardt, *Black Elk and Flaming Rainbow*, 77 (italics mine). A slightly different rendition of this passage can be found in *Sixth G*, 40-41.

46. H. Neihardt, *Black Elk and Flaming Rainbow*, 68.

47. R. DeMallie, "John G. Neihardt's Lakota Legacy," 111.

48. S. McCluskey, "*Black Elk Speaks*: and So Does John Neihardt," 238.

49. S. McCluskey, "*Black Elk Speaks*: and So Does John Neihardt," 241.

50. R. Heflin, "*I Remain Alive*," 161.

51. N.S. Momaday, "To Save a Great Vision," 36-37

52. M. Castro, *Interpreting the Indian*, 90-91.

53. Shorthand draft of a letter in the Neihardt Collection, quoted by R. DeMallie, "John G. Neihardt's Lakota Legacy," 123 (italics mine).

54. Neihardt lecture, quoted in B. Holloway, *Interpreting the Legacy*, 25.

55. R. DeMallie, "John G. Neihardt's Lakota Legacy," 133.

56. From the cover of *Teaching Spirits* (2001).

57. Fitzgerald is referring to the research work and recordings he undertook for his subsequent book, *Yellowtail: Crow Medicine Man and Sun Dance Chief* (1991).

58. Unpublished correspondence from Michael Fitzgerald to Marina Weatherly Brown, November 19, 2016.

59. Letter of March 12, 1948 to John Murray in Lausanne.

60. Letter of June 17, 1948, Southwest Harbor, Maine, to Fr. Gall in Belgium.

61. Letter of November 21, 1948, Lausanne, Switzerland, to Fr. Gall in Belgium. In a margin note Brown adds, "(Am enclosing now—some are not too

important, but I check the ones that are especially important. You will of course add all the inflections, etc.).''

62. Letter of December 17, 1948, Lausanne, Switzerland, to Fr. Gall in Belgium.

63. Fitzgerald offered the following remarks about the translation of *Inikage* and *Hokshichankia*: "*Inikage* is the performance of a sweat lodge ceremony. *Hokshichankia* is spiritual influence or seed. This is the definition used by Brown in the chapter entitled 'The Releasing of the Soul' in *The Sacred Pipe*" (personal correspondence, December 10, 2016).

64. Personal conversation between M. Fitzgerald and C. Schuon, February 2017.

65. E. Zolla, *The Writer and the Shaman*, 272. For an early review of *The Sacred Pipe* see G. Hewes in *American Anthropologist* and P. Olson in *Great Plains Quarterly* (see Sources for details).

66. J. Rice, *Black Elk's Story*, xi.

67. J. Rice, *Black Elk's Story*, 4 (italics mine).

68. *Holler*, 183n.

69. See, for example, *Holler*, 141.

70. *Jackson*, 459.

71. See M. Fitzgerald, "New Light on Black Elk and *The Sacred Pipe*." Elsewhere in his account Jackson recognizes that the *heyoka* ceremony was only for a few rare individuals, but in the discussion just mentioned he seems to have forgotten the fact.

72. *Interpreting the Legacy*, 16.

73. M. Steltenkamp, *Black Elk: Holy Man of the Oglala*, xv.

74. G. Fields, "*Inipi*, the Purification Rite (Sweat Lodge) and Black Elk," 173.

75. The most detailed accounts of the Sun Dance are to be found in the classic works by James Walker, reproduced in *Lakota Belief and Ritual*, Frances Densmore, *Teton Sioux Music* or *World of the Teton Sioux Indians*, Thomas Mails, *Sundancing at Rosebud and Pine Ridge*, and Clyde Holler, *Black Elk's Religion: The Sun Dance and Lakota Catholicism*.

76. H. Smith, "What They Have That We Lack," 93. This encomium, welcome as it is, ignores Schuon's work in the same vein.

77. The State of South Dakota tourism website: "[Ben Black Elk] is known as the 'fifth face on the mountain' for his dedicated service at Mount Rushmore. But Ben Black Elk's work to preserve the Lakota culture stretched far beyond the national monument. That makes him one of South Dakota's Great Faces. . . . Each year the South Dakota Office of Tourism gives out the Ben Black Elk Award, which recognizes an individual who has made tireless and outstanding contributions to the state's visitor industry" (www.travelsouthdakota.com. newsroom/press-releases/south-dakotas-great-faces/ben-black-elk).

78. *Jackson*, 468.

79. Personal correspondence from Michael Fitzgerald, April 2016. In 1971 Fitzgerald was the Associate Instructor for Joseph Brown's Indiana University class and Brown's neighbor.

80. Sixteen of Brown's letters to Fr. Gall, written in the years 1947-49, have been preserved. Erich Schuon was born in Basle in 1906 and became a Trappist monk at the age of fifteen, spending the rest of his life in a Belgian monastery. He died in 1991.

81. Letter of July 8, 1948 to Fr. Gall in Belgium. As Fitzgerald has recently made clear, Joe Jackson's conjecture that "at some point [Brown] seems to have disengaged from Schuon" (458) is not supported by the facts. Brown continued to correspond with Schuon until at least the mid-1980s, and visited him in Bloomington in 1981 and 1984. It was only the onset of Alzheimer's in the late 1980s that produced whatever "disengagement" there may have been. See M. Fitzgerald, "New Light on Black Elk and *The Sacred Pipe.*"

82. Jackson speculates that Black Elk may mistakenly have imagined that Erich Schuon (later "Fr. Gall") might be his own son, conceived during his relationship with a French woman during his touring days. As Jackson points out, this was quite impossible as any such child, if there was one, would have been born in 1890, not 1906 (Erich's birth year).

83. Letter of December 26, 1947, Manderson, South Dakota, to Fr. Gall in Belgium; a fuller excerpt of the letter can be found in *The Spiritual Legacy*, 113.

Chapter 6: Lakota Traditionalist and/or Catholic Catechist?

1. *Sixth G*, 59.
2. H. Neihardt, *Black Elk and Flaming Rainbow*, 119.
3. M. Steltenkamp, *Black Elk: Holy Man of the Oglala*, xx.
4. Clyde Holler was one of the first scholars to examine Black Elk's problematic relationship to Christianity in "Black Elk's Relationship to Christianity" (1984). However, it was Steltenkamp's book which brought this issue center stage.
5. See, for example, D. Stover, "A Postcolonial Reading of Black Elk," 127-141.
6. *Jackson*, 361.
7. P. Steinmetz, *Pipe, Bible, and Peyote Among the Oglala Sioux*, 182.
8. See R. DeMallie, "John G. Neihardt and Nicholas Black Elk," 265.
9. J. Rice, *Black Elk's Story*, xi.
10. G.T. Couser, "*Black Elk Speaks* with Forked Tongue," 80.
11. H. Neihardt, *Black Elk and Flaming Rainbow*, 88.
12. M. Steltenkamp, *Black Elk: Holy Man of the Oglala*, 94-111 and M. Steltenkamp, *Nicholas Black Elk*, 115-117. Amongst the symbols and images which Steltenkamp finds in both the Great Vision and the Two Roads Map: "Thunder-beings, flying men, a daybreak star, a rainbow, tree imagery, circled villages, a black road, a red road, friendly wings, a blue man in flames, people mourning, a history of the people, and a young man appearing to be ill" (M. Steltenkamp, *Nicholas Black Elk*, 117).
13. M. Steltenkamp, *Nicholas Black Elk*, 117.
14. *Sixth G*, 21.

15. *Sixth G*, 59-60.

16. *Sixth G*, 59.

17. *Sixth G*, 58 (italics mine).

18. See *Sixth G*, 62.

19. *Jackson*, 439-440.

20. Quoted in S.J. Howard, "Incommensurability and Nicholas Black Elk," 118 (Howard's italics).

21. Fools Crow, quoted in S.J. Howard, "Incommensurability and Nicholas Black Elk," 111.

22. See *Sixth G*, 72.

23. H. Neihardt, *Black Elk and Flaming Rainbow*, 119.

24. For an even-handed discussion of these issues, see *Holler*, 209ff.

25. S.J. Howard, "Incommensurability and Nicholas Black Elk," 121.

26. M. Steltenkamp, *Nicholas Black Elk*, 223.

27. See Schuon's August 8, 1984 letter to William Stoddart in Appendix III.

28. W.K. Powers, *Beyond the Vision*, 102 (italics mine).

29. W.K. Powers, *Beyond the Vision*, 109.

30. Personal recollection of Catherine Schuon. Elva One Feather (1915-2000) is the mother of Gerald One Feather, an Oglala Lakota Tribal President and the founder of the Oglala Lakota College. Elva's husband, Jackson One Feather, held several different positions in the Oglala Lakota tribal government.

31. W.K. Powers, *Beyond the Vision*, 124.

32. See W.K. Powers, "When Black Elk Speaks, Everybody Listens" and *Beyond the Vision*, 164. For some judicious criticisms of Powers' model see *Holler*, 208-214.

33. *Holler*, 215, 217.

34. *Holler*, 35-36.

35. *Holler*, 215.

36. Letter of August 10, 1930 to Julius T. House, cited in *Sixth G*, 27.

37. *Holler*, 182.

38. *Holler*, 223.

39. Postcolonialism "is an academic discipline featuring methods of intellectual discourse that analyze, explain, and respond to the cultural legacies of colonialism and imperialism" (*Wikipedia* entry: "Postcolonialism").

40. See D. Costello, *Black Elk: Colonialism and Lakota Catholicism*, 15-21.

41. M. Fitzgerald, "Frithjof Schuon and the Native Spirit," 21.

42. J-B. Aymard & P. Laude, *Frithjof Schuon: Life and Teachings*, 93.

43. B. Bäumer, "Swami Abhishiktananda." See also H. Oldmeadow, *A Christian Pilgrim in India: The Spiritual Journey of Swami Abhishiktananda* (Henri Le Saux), especially chap. 9.

44. Paul Steinmetz provides an account of the funeral of Ben Black Elk, which he describes as "the most significant celebration of the bringing together of the Lakota and Christian religious traditions" (*Pipe, Bible, and Peyote Among the Oglala Sioux*, 38-39).

45. Joe Medicine Crow, quoted in C. Eastman, *Living in Two Worlds*, 133

(italics mine).

46. M. Fitzgerald, "Frithjof Schuon and the Native Spirit," 22.

47. *Schuon*, 159.

48. C. Eastman, *Living in Two Worlds*, 158. "It is my personal belief, after thirty-five years' experience of it, that there is no such thing as 'Christian civilization.' I believe that Christianity and modern civilization are opposed and irreconcilable, and that the spirit of Christianity and of our ancient religion is essentially the same" (C. Eastman, *The Soul of the Indian*, 24).

49. C. Eastman, *Living in Two Worlds*, 159.

50. J.E. Brown, *The Spiritual Legacy*, 20. In her extended essay on nomadic peoples and cultures, Robyn Davidson concludes that nomadic peoples "do not focus on long-term goals so much as continually accommodate themselves to change. . . . Theirs are Aristotelian values of 'practical wisdom' and balance. Adaptability, flexibility, mental agility, the ability to cope with flux." (*No Fixed Address*, 49).

51. I refer to several letters from Brown to his friend Fr. Gall (Erich Schuon), to Frithjof Schuon, and to others. Excerpts from this correspondence are provided in Appendix I of the present study. These letters complement those found in the 2007 edition of *The Spiritual Legacy* and confirm Black Elk's commitment to the revival of the traditional rites.

52. For instance, Brown also describes in some detail a *yuwipi* ceremony in which Black Elk and other elders participated. See letter of December 26, 1947, *The Spiritual Legacy*, 108-113. He also recounts an occasion where Black Elk, feeling soiled by the city, conducted a sweat ceremony in a grimy Denver hotel room (letter of October 28, 1947, *The Spiritual Legacy*, 102-103).

53. Letter of November 19, 1947, *The Spiritual Legacy*, 103-105. Michael Fitzgerald has suggested that a more appropriate term than "Order of the Pipe" might be "Society of the Pipe," in accordance with the nomenclature used on most Indian reservations.

54. Letter to Fr. Gall, October 1, 1947.

55. Quoted by M. Fitzgerald, "Frithjof Schuon and the Native Spirit," 25.

56. J.E. Brown, *The Spiritual Legacy*, 111-112. Joe Jackson overstates the case in claiming that Black Elk's efforts in regard to the "Order of the Pipe" were largely motivated by a concern with the protection of the original Sacred Calf Pipe Bundle (see *Jackson*, 458-460). The evidence we have—by way of Brown's letters and Black Elk's own testimony—suggest that the holy man's *primary* concern was always the preservation of the ancient rites. As Michael Fitzgerald has recently demonstrated, Jackson's explanation of the fate of the original Sacred Pipe Bundle is quite misleading and fails to take into account plentiful evidence in the very sources which he cites, including letters from Brown which were first made public in 2007. As Fitzgerald observes, "The first problem with this assessment is that Jackson provides readers no additional information about the subsequent fate of the Sacred Pipe Bundle so readers are left to ponder what appears to be a problematic and uncertain fate

of this all-important sacred object of the Sioux people." See Brown's letter dated December 14, 1947 in Appendix I. Fitzgerald explains the recent history of the transmission of the Sacred Pipe Bundle and states that since 1966 this sacred object has been in the safekeeping of Arvol Looking Horse, "a well-recognized and respected spiritual leader" who lives on the Cheyenne River Sioux Reservation. See M. Fitzgerald, "New Light on Black Elk and *The Sacred Pipe.*"

57. Joseph Brown letter of January 27, 1948 from Manderson, South Dakota to John Murray.

58. See Joseph Brown letter dated January 24, 1948 in Appendix I.

59. Letter of November 19, 1947, *The Spiritual Legacy*, 105. See Appendix I for additional information about Black Elk's rebuke of the local Catholic priest.

60. J.E. Brown, *The Spiritual Legacy*, x-xi.

61. For a detailed history of the Lakota Sun Dance since 1866 see *Holler,* of special interest in the present context is the chapter "The Sun Dance Under Ban, 1883-1934/1952," 110-138.

62. See F. Densmore, *World of the Teton Sioux*, 28. Jackson quotes Will H. Spindler's *Tragedy Strikes at Wounded Knee*, 36, in which the 1881 ceremony is called "the last great Sun Dance." See Jackson, 206, 525.

63. R. Utley, *Last Days of the Sioux Nation*, 33. See also H.W. Paige, *Songs of the Teton Sioux*, 120.

64. See *Holler*, 136

65. See P. Steinmetz, *Pipe, Bible, and Peyote among the Oglala Lakota*, 28. See also Holler, 136-137, and *Jackson*, 351, 448.

66. T. Mails, *Sundancing at Rosebud and Pine Ridge*, 10.

67. T. Mails, *Fools Crow*, 119.

68. Fitzgerald believes Joe Jackson "paint[s] a portrait of Lakota cultural renewal that is unnecessarily harsh." Fitzgerald provides persuasive evidence to support his conclusion that "Black Elk's quest to save the spiritual traditions of his people was successful in large part. All seven sacred rites are preserved and four of those rites are in widespread use by Sioux traditionalists. Even the Sioux language is undergoing revitalization" (M. Fitzgerald, "New Light on Black Elk and *The Sacred Pipe*").

69. Vine Deloria, Jr., Introduction to *Black Elk Speaks* (1979 ed.), xiii.

70. For a discussion of the ways in which Black Elk *reinterpreted* the Sun Dance, see *Holler*, 179-203 and Holler, "Black Elk's Relationship to Christianity."

71. The *Wikipedia* entry for Black Elk simply states the conclusion that "Lakota traditionalists now follow his [Black Elk's] version of the dance." This observation is documented by Mails' comprehensive works, including *Sundancing at Rosebud and Pine Ridge*. It is also endorsed by Michael Fitzgerald, who has attended approximately thirty Lakota Sun Dance and sweat lodge ceremonies on five different reservations.

72. Fools Crow is honored by a bronze life-sized bust outside the Visitor Cen-

ter at Bear Butte State Park, one of the holiest places for the Sioux people. He is also one of the few Indian spiritual leaders to give an opening prayer before the U.S. Senate (September 5, 1975).

73. T. Mails, *Fools Crow*, 119.

Chapter 7: The Holy Man from the East

1. Quoted in M. Fitzgerald, *Frithjof Schuon: Messenger of the Perennial Philosophy*, 91.

2. *Schuon*, 158.

3. See the following works by M. Fitzgerald, "Frithjof Schuon's Role in Preserving the Red Indian Spirit"; "Frithjof Schuon and the Native Spirit: Interview with Michael Fitzgerald"; *Frithjof Schuon: Messenger of the Perennial Philosophy*, especially chap. 16, 84-94; and "New Light on Black Elk and *The Sacred Pipe*."

4. Letter of Frithjof Schuon to Chief Medicine Robe, October 31, 1947, Lausanne; see Appendix III.

5. See C. Schuon, "Frithjof Schuon: Memories and Anecdotes," 41. The dates on the relevant letters establish that Schuon asked Murray to find books on authentic American Indians in 1946 and that in early 1947 Schuon read *Black Elk Speaks* and wrote to Murray asking him or one of his friends to find Black Elk.

6. Personal recollection of Catherine Schuon. Catherine Schuon's recollection disarms the fanciful suggestion by Joe Jackson that Schuon may have first encountered the Lakota sage by way of Carl Jung's copy of *Black Elk Speaks* (See *Jackson*, 457). Whilst Joe Jackson's book is, generally, built on careful and thorough research, his references to Schuon and to Brown's relation to him betray some misunderstanding. Two of Jackson's statements cannot be allowed to stand unchallenged. Firstly: "If there is one part of Brown's life that seems ambiguous, it is this early fascination with Schuon. . . . Though Brown was not one to publicly denounce a past mentor, at some point he seemed to have disengaged from the man" (457-458). Brown was actually a disciple of Frithjof Schuon and remained in contact with him until his later years, when Brown was afflicted with Alzheimer's disease (See M. Fitzgerald, "New Light on Black Elk and *The Sacred Pipe*"). Secondly: "With Schuon's entry we see the first sign of the New Age frenzy that would envelop everything related to *Black Elk Speaks* in a warm and fuzzy nimbus" (458). Anyone who has actually read Schuon's writings on the Indians would understand that it is his achieved purpose to reaffirm the validity of traditional Lakotan modes and to *disassociate* them from the "warm and fuzzy nimbus" created by the "New Age frenzy" which he deplored. It might also be observed in passing that Jackson seemingly has not the least understanding of why the late Huston Smith should call Schuon "the greatest religious thinker" of the last century.

7. Brown had a similar experience when a Blackfoot chief "said that he had told as yet no one, but was telling me [about Blackfoot doctrine] because he believed it was connected with my being there and with the Holy Man who

had sent me, and that was that he had been having a dream, in which he saw an Ancient Man Above, very old with gray hair, whose eyes were always open, and who was constantly looking, looking everywhere." See Brown's letters to Fr. Gall in Appendix I dated October 28, 1947, November 19, 1947, and mid-November, 1947.

8. See Brown's letter dated October 8, 1954 in Appendix I, M. Fitzgerald, "Frithjof Schuon and the Native Spirit," 18-19, and *Frithjof Schuon: Messenger of the Perennial Philosophy*, 37-38.

9. Personal correspondence, 2017.

10. See the account by Lucy Looks Twice in M. Steltenkamp, *Black Elk: Holy Man of the Oglala*, 128-129. Frithjof Schuon's travel journal contains the following account of his visit to Black Elk's grave with Lucy Looks Twice: "July 3, 1963, Manderson. We then all went together to the grave, which lay on a hill among other graves; we stood there for a while and prayed, each on his own; it was the occasion of much blessing. As we went down the hill, Mrs. Looks Twice told us that during the time before Black Elk's death a holy man from the East had come to him from across the sea every day at three o'clock in the afternoon; this man had previously sent him a kind of necklace. It was a Moroccan rosary. 'Do you come from overseas?' she asked. Deeply affected, we took our leave of the old Indian woman, after we had exchanged gifts."

11. Brown letter dated February 4, 1948, Oraibi, Arizona to John Murray in Appendix I and M. Fitzgerald, *Frithjof Schuon: Messenger of the Perennial Philosophy*, 91. See also M. Fitzgerald, "New Light on Black Elk and *The Sacred Pipe*."

12. *Black Elk Speaks* was first published in French as *Héhaka Sapa. La Grande vision: Histoire d'un prophète sioux telle qu'elle a été contée à John G. Neihardt* in 1969 by Éditions traditionnelles. Their translation was subsequently published by Le Mail in 1987 (new edition in 2014 by O.D. editions) as *Elan noir parle: La vie d'un saint-homme des sioux Oglalas*.

13. Personal recollection of Catherine Schuon: "Schuon encouraged, whomever he talked with, to stay faithful to their own tradition, and he distributed widely his 'Message on Indian Religion.'" Schuon's travel journal for his first trip to the American West ends with this postscript: "Two months after our return home from America, Reginald Laubin wrote me the following lines: 'In September a few of our Arapaho and Sioux friends came over to put on a *yuwipi* ceremony for us. In the sweat tipi they said prayers for their friends and they included Mr. Schuon, for help and guidance in his wonderful work in bringing about an understanding and realization that so many religions are alike. We never dreamed that they knew of you, so you can imagine our surprise and delight when they mentioned your name and even had a copy of your splendid article on Indian religion. They were very much impressed by your good words.' And all help is from God alone!" (M. Fitzgerald, *Frithjof Schuon: Messenger of the Perennial Philosophy*, 205).

14. See M. Fitzgerald, "Frithjof Schuon's Role in Preserving the Red Indian Spirit," 220-222.

15. Letter quoted in M. Fitzgerald, *Frithjof Schuon: Messenger of the Perennial Philosophy*, 40.

16. From Schuon's unpublished *Memories and Meditations*, quoted in M. Fitzgerald, "Frithjof Schuon and the Native Spirit," 28.

17. See M. Fitzgerald, "Frithjof Schuon and the Native Spirit," 30-31n.

18. J-P. Aymard & P. Laude, *Frithjof Schuon: Life and Teachings*, 100. Here "Self" is to be understood not in any narrow psychological sense but in the full amplitude of the Hindu term *Atman*.

19. J-P. Aymard & P. Laude, *Frithjof Schuon: Life and Teachings*, 100.

20. B. Perry, "Frithjof Schuon: Metaphysician and Artist" (no pagination).

21. See *Schuon*, 92-93.

22. F. Schuon, *Treasures of Buddhism*, 177-178.

23. F. Schuon, *Treasures of Buddhism*, 177.

24. *Schuon*, 102.

25. F. Schuon, *Understanding Islam*, 183.

26. F. Schuon, *Understanding Islam*, 133.

27. S. H. Nasr, *Ideals and Realities of Islam*, 21.

28. J.E. Brown, *The Spiritual Legacy*, 53.

29. *Schuon*, 20.

30. *Schuon*, 6.

31. Dante, quoted in G. Eaton, *The Richest Vein*, 187.

32. *Schuon*, 68. This echoes the old Rabbinic dictum that "The world is not the dwelling place of God: God is the dwelling-place of the world."

33. *S. Pipe*, xx (italics mine).

34. Luther Standing Bear, *Land of the Spotted Eagle*, 197.

35. *Schuon*, 105.

36. *Schuon*, 154.

37. *Schuon*, 20.

38. *Schuon*, 9. Schuon also points out that obviously not "every individual belonging to a collectivity of symbolist or contemplative mentality is himself fully conscious of all that the symbols mean" (*Schuon*, 10).

39. *S. Pipe*, 115.

40. *Schuon*, 46.

41. Plotinus, quoted in E.F. Schumacher, *A Guide for the Perplexed*, 49.

42. Aquinas in his "Commentary on the First Book of the Sentences of Peter Lombard, Distinction III, Question 1, Article 1" (http://www.aquinasonline. com, [accessed February 11, 2017]).

43. *Schuon*, 30.

44. *Schuon*, 47.

45. *Schuon*, 9-10 (italics mine).

46. *Schuon*, 34-35, 31.

47. *Schuon*, 44.

48. *Schuon*, 71.

49. See *Schuon*, 14. For further reading, see A. Snodgrass, *Architecture, Time, and Eternity*, Vol. 2, 425-449. Snodgrass elaborates the spatio-temporal rela-

tionships of the four Winds and the directions, as well as the symbolic significances of Lakota "architecture."

50. *BES*, 2.

51. *Schuon*, 106.

52. On the generosity of the Indians, see the excerpt in Appendix I from Joseph Brown's letter to Frithjof Schuon, dated December 26, 1947.

53. For another perspective on the virtues exalted by the Sioux, see G. Linden, "Dakota Philosophy," 232-240.

54. F. Schuon, *Light on the Ancient Worlds*, 71.

55. *Schuon*, 64.

56. *Schuon*, 106.

57. *Schuon*, 129, 135, and 134.

58. *Schuon*, 134.

59. *Schuon*, 158.

60. The archetype of Beauty, writes Schuon, "is the superabundance and equilibrium of Divine qualities, and at the same time the overflowing of the existential potentialities in Pure Being" (*Logic and Transcendence*, 241). Marsilio Ficino, the Renaissance Platonist, aptly defined Beauty as "that ray which parting from the visage of God, penetrates into all things" (quoted in R.J. Clements, *Michelangelo's Theory of Art*, 5).

61. Schuon himself made no claims for his art, insisting that his essential message was conveyed in his metaphysical writings: "I am not a painter with an interest in metaphysics, but a metaphysician who from time to time produces a painting" (quoted in the Foreword to *Songs for a Spiritual Traveler*, viii). When approached about the possibility of exhibiting some of his paintings—this fairly late in his life—he was reluctant, but acceded because his paintings too carried a spiritual message.

62. Schuon, letter to Leo Schaya, August 28, 1985, quoted in M. Fitzgerald, *Frithjof Schuon: Messenger of the Perennial Philosophy*, 101.

63. B. Perry, "Frithjof Schuon: Metaphysician and Artist" (no pagination).

64. J-B. Aymard & P. Laude, *Frithjof Schuon: Life and Teachings*, 117.

65. Schuon, quoted in M. Pollack, Introduction to *Images of Primordial and Mystic Beauty*, 3-4.

66. *Schuon*, 100.

67. See S.H. Nasr, "Reflections on Islam and Modern Thought."

68. Luke 17:1.

69. *Schuon*, 41-42.

70. *Schuon*, 70.

Conclusion: The Legacy

1. *BES*, 1.

2. *BES*, 28.

3. A. Porterfield, "Black Elk's Significance in American Culture," 45.

4. J. Rice, "*Akicita* of the Thunder," 75.

5. The three passages cited come from A. Govinda, *The Way of the White*

Clouds, xxi-xxiii.

6. L. van der Post, *Testament to the Bushmen*, quoted in K. Raine, "The Underlying Order," 185.

7. S.H. Nasr, *Religion and the Order of Nature*, 3. For a wide-ranging analysis of the spiritual crisis of modernity, and of the ways in which the "environmental crisis" is a symptom of this deeper malaise, see also S.H. Nasr, *Man and Nature*.

8. Abu Bakr Siraj Ed-Din, *The Book of Certainty*, 33.

9. The phrase comes from S.H. Nasr, *Spiritual and Religious Dimensions of the Environmental Crisis*, 13.

10. M. Eliade, *The Sacred and the Profane*, 116-117.

11. Romans 1:20. For an anthology of Christian affirmations in this vein, see *The Sermon of All Creation*, ed. J. & M. Fitzgerald. On the implication of the Christian churches in the environmental crisis, see W. Berry, "Christianity and the Survival of Creation," in *Sex, Economy, Freedom, and Community*, 93-116. For a discussion of cross-cultural religious understandings of nature, see H. Oldmeadow, "The Firmament Sheweth His Handiwork" and other essays in *Seeing God Everywhere*, ed. B. McDonald.

12. Mechthild of Magdeburg (1210-1297), quoted in J. & M. Fitzgerald, *The Sermon of all Creation*, 22.

13. Meister Eckhart (1260-1328), quoted in J. & M. Fitzgerald, *The Sermon of All Creation*, 61.

14. M. Eliade, *The Sacred and the Profane*, 178.

15. *Schuon*, 13.

16. As Rudolf Otto, the great theorist of religion, put it, "Holiness [i.e., sacredness] is a category peculiar to religion . . . it is perfectly *sui generis* and irreducible to any other" (*The Idea of the Holy*, 7).

17. P. Sherrard, *Christianity: Lineaments of a Sacred Tradition*, 219. See also Sherrard's *The Rape of Man and Nature*.

18. Emerson, quoted in T.C. McLuhan, *Cathedrals of the Spirit*, 211.

19. It might, however, be added that "environmentalism," unlike scientism, is often fuelled by a vague but potent intuition that the natural order has a qualitative significance and value. From this point of view "environmentalism" is vastly preferable to a rigidly materialistic understanding of "nature."

20. For some reference to the ways in which the Plains Indians understood cosmic cycles, and the Four Ages, see S. Pipe, 9n, and *Schuon*, 113-114. For some exposition of the traditional doctrine of cycles, see H. Oldmeadow, *Frithjof Schuon and the Perennial Philosophy*, 201-213.

21. These are the concluding words of René Guénon's *Crisis of the Modern World* (1927). This translation is taken from the *Vincit Omnia Veritas* website: http://www.religioperennis.org/ruh.religioperennis.org/index.html.

22. M. Fitzgerald, *Yellowtail*, 121.

23. J.E. Brown, *The Spiritual Legacy*, 86. See also J.E. Brown, "Becoming Part of It."

24. F. Schuon, "No Activity without Truth," 29.

25. M. Fitzgerald, *Yellowtail*, 198.
26. Neihardt, letter to Julius T. House, August 10, 1930, cited in *Sixth G*, 27.
27. *BES*, 1.
28. John 3:27.
29. F. Schuon, *Understanding Islam*, 45.
30. F. Schuon, *Understanding Islam*, 26.
31. N.S. Momaday, "To Save a Great Vision," 31.
32. G. Orwell, "Reflections on Gandhi," 523.
33. J.E. Brown, *The Spiritual Legacy*, 24.
34. Letter to Frithjof Schuon, July 27, 1949.
35. *S. Pipe*, xx.

Appendix I: Excerpts from Letters of Joseph Epes Brown

1. Joseph Brown's surviving letters from the late 1940s and early 1950s were preserved by three of his friends: Frithjof Schuon, Fr. Gall, and John Murray. Frithjof Schuon contemporaneously archived fourteen of Brown's letters. Michael Fitzgerald gave copies of those letters to Brown's wife, Elenita, in 2001. Excerpts from these letters were published in the 2007 commemorative edition of Brown's *The Spiritual Legacy of the American Indian*. Fifteen letters from Brown to Fr. Gall (who died in 1991) were made available to Fitzgerald in December 2016 by Fr. Gall's close friend Paul Verbeeren, who lives in Belgium. Late in 2016 Joseph Fitzgerald, researching the life of Whitall Perry for a forthcoming book, uncovered another six letters from Brown to Perry, and a further two written by Perry himself that pertain to Joseph Brown. Michael Fitzgerald gave copies of these more recently discovered letters to Brown's daughter, Marina Weatherly Brown who, since the death of her mother in August 2016, represents the Brown family. I am indebted to Michael and Joseph Fitzgerald, Elenita Brown, Paul Verbeeren, and Clyde Holler for their help in accessing these letters. I am deeply grateful to Michael Fitzgerald for his generous assistance in the preparation of all three Appendices.
2. On Fr. Gall (Erich Schuon) see the last section of chap. 5 of the present book.
3. Jacques-Albert Cuttat (1909-1989) was a Swiss diplomat and scholar with a deep interest in comparative religion.
4. These references are to René Guénon's *The Crisis of the Modern World* and Ananda K. Coomaraswamy's *Am I My Brother's Keeper?*
5. Brown's references to Black Elk's age are speculative and sometimes contradictory. For instance, in his letter of September 30, 1947 he writes that Black Elk is 85, but now, just over two years later, he gives the old man's age as 89. The problem of establishing Black Elk's precise date of birth was discussed in chap. 3.
6. This reference is to a lady's dream about a withered flower that appeared to be dead but then miraculously grew and bloomed.
7. Editors' Notes from *The Spiritual Legacy*, 107, are shown in italics.
8. The Introduction was later published, with minor variations, as the chapter

"The Sacred Pipe" in Schuon's *The Feathered Sun.*

9. This letter was written shortly after Joseph Brown's first meeting with Fr. Gall, which took place in Belgium.

10. *Japanese Archery* by William R.B. Acker, first published in 1937.

11. This is the definition used by Brown in the chapter entitled "The Releasing of the Soul" in *The Sacred Pipe.*

12. This excerpt reveals Joseph Brown's concern to be as accurate as possible in his use of Lakota terms, seeking help from Fr. Gall and having Ben Back Elk review the whole *Inipi* chapter and other parts of the book during his final editing process.

13. *Barakah* is Arabic for blessing or grace; in Islam, it refers to a spiritual influence or energy emanating originally from God, but often attached to sacred objects and spiritual persons; *maqam* is Arabic for a "permanent spiritual station."

14. It is probable that this is a reference to the Lakota prayer from Black Elk to Fr. Gall, which is presented in Appendix II.

15. After a summer during which Brown traveled to several different American Indian reservations.

Appendix II: Prayer Given to Fr. Gall by Black Elk

1. Made available by Paul Verbeeren.

2. Michael Fitzgerald has commented as follows: "I believe 'the Stone' likely refers to the Sacred Stones that are the basis for chap. 7 ("Sacred Stones") of Frances Densmore's classic *Teton Sioux Music.* I believe Black Elk is asking *Wakan-Tanka* to use the power of the four winds to help the children become relatives of the Sacred Stones, and in so doing assimilate the qualities and powers of the Sacred Stones. The kinship of all creation is part of the meaning of the phrase *mitakuye oyasin*—'we are all related' or 'all things are related.' It might be more accurate to say that Black Elk prays that the children will come to realize that they are relatives of the Stone Man, but even the Lakota metaphysic already recognizes that 'all things are related.'" (personal correspondence, December 8, 2016). And Clyde Holler: ". . . given that we're all related, by calling attention to a particular one of the relatives, Black Elk means to call attention to its qualities or its powers. In other words, stone endures. In this particular lived situation, Black Elk wants to call the young Lakota's attention to the task, and/or the ability to endure, to maintain one's identity. Or perhaps, better said, to instill in them the quality of endurance. In other words, this is a prayer for the endurance of the people, which I think entails the idea of cultural endurance" (personal correspondence, December 9, 2016).

3. Translated by Ben Black Bear, Jr.

Appendix III: Selections from Letters of Frithjof Schuon

1. Made available by the Estate of Frithjof Schuon.

2. Frithjof Schuon is referring to a letter that he wrote to the Black Elks,

which Joseph Brown hand-delivered shortly after his arrival in September, 1947. We do not have a copy of that letter.

3. The letter to Chief Medicine Robe was written in care of his grandson, Mark Flying.

Sources

Abhishiktananda. *The Further Shore*. Delhi: ISPCK, 1975.

———. *Hindu-Christian Meeting Point*. Delhi: ISPCK, 1976.

Aymard, Jean-Baptiste & Patrick Laude. *Frithjof Schuon: Life and Teachings*. Albany: SUNY, 2005.

Bataille, Gretchen M. "Black Elk—New World Prophet." In *Sender of Words: Essays in Memory of John G. Neihardt*, ed. Vine Deloria Jr., 135-142.

Bäumer, Bettina. "Swami Abhishiktananda/Henri Le Saux OSB, Pilgrim and Hermit: A Bridge between Hinduism and Christianity." http:www. monasticdialog. com/bulletins/72/baumer.htm. (accessed in 2008; this site has since disappeared).

Berry, Wendell. *Sex, Economy, Freedom & Community*. New York: Pantheon, 1993.

Brown, Dee. *Bury My Heart at Wounded Knee*. London: Pan, 1972.

———. *The Fetterman Massacre*. London: Pan Books, 1974.

———. "The Power of John Neihardt." In *Sender of Words: Essays in Memory of John G. Neihardt*, ed. Vine Deloria Jr., 5-11.

Brown, Joseph Epes. *The Sacred Pipe: Black Elk's Account of the Seven Rites of the Oglala Sioux* (1971). Norman: University of Oklahoma, 1989.

———. *The Spiritual Legacy of the American Indian: With Letters While Living with Black Elk* (1982). Edited by Marina Brown Weatherly, Elenita Brown & Michael O. Fitzgerald. Bloomington: World Wisdom, 2007.

———. *Animals of the Soul: Sacred Animals of the Oglala Sioux*. Rockport: Element, 1993.

——— & Emily Cousins. *Teaching Spirits: Understanding Native American Religious Traditions*. New York: Oxford University, 2001.

———. "The Persistence of Essential Values among North American Plains Indians." *Studies in Comparative Religion* 3:4, Autumn, 1969 (can be accessed at: http://www.worldwisdom.com/public/authors/Joseph-Epes-Brown.aspx).

———. "The Unlikely Associates: A Study in Oglala Sioux Magic and Metaphysic." *Studies in Comparative Religion* 4:3, Summer, 1970 (can be accessed at: http://www.worldwisdom.com/public/authors/Joseph-Epes-Brown.aspx).

———. "Becoming Part of It." In *Seeing God Everywhere*, ed. Barry McDonald, 269-277.

———. "On Being Human." In *Every Branch of Me*, ed. B. McDonald, 207-212.

———. Introduction to *The North American Indians: Photographs by Edward S. Curtis*. New York: Aperture Books, 1972, no pagination.

Brumble, David. *American Indian Autobiography*. Berkeley: University of California, 1988.

Campbell, Joseph. *The Hero with a Thousand Faces.* Princeton: Princeton University, Bollingen Series, 1949.

Capps, Walter H. (ed.). *Seeing with a Native Eye: Essays on Native American Religion.* New York: Harper & Row, 1976.

Castro, Michael. *Interpreting the Indian: Twentieth Century Poets and the Native American.* Santa Fe: University of New Mexico, 1983.

Charlesworth, Max (ed.). *Religion in Aboriginal Australia.* St. Lucia: University of Queensland, 1984.

Clements, Robert J. *Michelangelo's Theory of Art.* New York: New York University, 1961.

Coomaraswamy, Ananda K. *The Transformation of Nature in Art.* New York: Dover, 1956.

————. *Selected Papers, I: Traditional Art and Symbolism.* Edited by Roger Lipsey. Princeton: Princeton University, Bollingen Series, 1977.

————. *Selected Papers, II: Metaphysics.* Edited by Roger Lipsey. Princeton: Princeton University, Bollingen Series, 1977.

————. *The Bugbear of Literacy.* London: Perennial Books, 1979.

————. *The Essential Ananda K. Coomaraswamy.* Edited by Rama P. Coomaraswamy. Bloomington: World Wisdom, 2003.

Couser, G. Thomas. "*Black Elk Speaks* with Forked Tongue." In *Studies in Autobiography*, ed. James Olner, 73-88.

Costello, Damian. *Black Elk: Colonialism and Lakota Catholicism.* Maryknoll: Orbis Books, 2005.

Cowan, James. *Mysteries of the Dream-Time: The Spiritual Life of Australian Aborigines.* Bridport: Prism, 1992.

————. *The Elements of the Aborigine Tradition.* Shaftesbury, Dorset: Element, 1992.

————. *Two Men Dreaming: A Memoir, A Journey.* Sydney: Brandl & Schlesinger, 1995.

Davidson, Robyn. "No Fixed Address: Nomads and the Fate of the Planet." *Quarterly Essay* 24. Melbourne: Black Inc., 2006.

Deakin, Hilton. "Some Thoughts on Transcendence in Tribal Societies." In *Ways of Transcendence: Insights from Major Religions and Modern Thought*, ed. E. Dowdy, 95-109.

Deloria Jr., Vine. "Introduction" to *Black Elk Speaks.* Lincoln: University of Nebraska, 1979, xi-xiv.

———— (ed.). *Sender of Words: Essays in Memory of John G. Neihardt* (1984). Lincoln: University of Nebraska, 2005.

DeMallie, Raymond J. *The Sixth Grandfather: Black Elk's Teachings Given to John G. Neihardt.* Lincoln: University of Nebraska, 1984.

————. "John G. Neihardt's Lakota Legacy." In *Sender of Words: Essays in Memory of John G. Neihardt*, ed. Vine Deloria Jr., 110-134.

————. "John G. Neihardt and Nicholas Black Elk." Appendix 6 in *Black Elk Speaks: The Complete Edition*, 242-266.

Densmore, Frances. *Teton Sioux Music* (1918). New York: Da Capo, 1972.

————. *World of the Teton Sioux Indians: Their Music, Life & Culture.* Edited by Joseph A. Fitzgerald. Bloomington: World Wisdom, 2016.

Diamond, Stanley. "In Search of the Primitive." In *Sources,* ed. Theodore Roszak, 212-236.

Dowdy, E. (ed.). *Ways of Transcendence: Insights from Major Religions and Modern Thought.* Adelaide: Association for the Study of Religion, 1992.

Dunsmore, Roger. "Nicolas Black Elk: Holy Man in History." In *Sender of Words: Essays in Memory of John G. Neihardt,* ed. Vine Deloria Jr., 143-158.

Eaton, Gai. *The Richest Vein.* London: Faber & Faber, 1949.

Eastman, Charles (Ohiyesa). *The Soul of the Indian* (1911). New York: Dover, 2003.

————. *Light on the Indian World.* Edited by Michael Oren Fitzgerald. Bloomington: World Wisdom, 2002.

————. *The Essential Charles Eastman* (Ohiyesa). Edited by Michael Oren Fitzgerald. Bloomington: World Wisdom, 2007.

Eliade, Mircea. *Patterns in Comparative Religion.* New York: Sheed & Ward, 1958.

————. *The Sacred and the Profane.* New York: Harcourt Brace Jovanovich, 1959.

————. *The Quest: History and Meaning in Religion.* Chicago: University of Chicago, 1969.

————. *Australian Religions.* Ithaca: Cornell University, 1973.

————. *Shamanism: Archaic Techniques of Ecstasy.* Princeton: Princeton University, Bollingen Series, 1974.

————. "Methodological Remarks on the Study of Religious Symbolism." In *The History of Religions: Essays in Methodology,* ed. Mircea Eliade & Joseph Kitagawa, 86-107.

————— & Joseph Kitagawa (eds.), *The History of Religions: Essays in Methodology.* Chicago: University of Chicago, 1959.

Elkin, A.P. *Aboriginal Men of High Degree.* St Lucia: University of Queensland, 1977.

Fabbri, Renaud. *Frithjof Schuon: The Shining Realm of the Pure Intellect.* Miami University, M.A. dissertation, 2007.

————— & Tim Scott (eds.) *Vincit Omnia Veritas: Collected Essays.* Bendigo: La Trobe University, 2008.

Fields, Gregory P. "*Inipi,* the Purification Rite (Sweat Lodge), and Black Elk." In *The Black Elk Reader,* ed. Clyde Holler, 188-205.

Fitzgerald, Michael. *Yellowtail: Crow Medicine Man and Sundance Chief.* Norman: University of Oklahoma, 1991.

————. *Frithjof Schuon: Messenger of the Perennial Philosophy.* Bloomington: World Wisdom, 2010.

————. *Living in Two Worlds: The American Indian Experience.* Bloomington: World Wisdom, 2010.

————. "Frithjof Schuon's Role in Preserving the Red Indian Spirit." *Sophia*

4:2, 1998, 220-232.

———. "Frithjof Schuon and the Native Spirit: Interview with Michael Fitzgerald." In *Vincit Omnia Veritas: Collected Essays*, eds. Renaud Fabbri & Tim Scott, 7-33 (originally published in the Religio Perennis online journal, *Vincit Omnia Veritas* 3:2, 2007).

———. "New Light on Black Elk and *The Sacred Pipe*." *American Indian Culture and Research Journal* 41:4, 2017.

Fitzgerald, Judith & Michael. *The Sermon of All Creation: Christians on Nature*. Bloomington: World Wisdom, 2005.

———. *The Spirit of Indian Women*. Bloomington: World Wisdom, 2005.

———. *Indian Spirit*. Bloomington: World Wisdom, 2006.

Frankl, Victor. "Reductionism and Nihilism." In *Beyond Reductionism: New Perspectives in the Life Sciences*, ed. A. Koestler & J.R. Smythies, 396-408.

Govinda, Anagarika. *The Way of the White Clouds*. Boulder: Shambhala, 1970.

———. *Creative Meditation and Multi-Dimensional Consciousness*. Wheaton: Quest, 1976.

Guénon, René. *East and West* (1924). Hillsdale: Sophia Perennis, 2001.

———. *Spiritual Authority and Temporal Power* (1929). Hillsdale: Sophia Perennis, 2001.

———. *The Symbolism of the Cross* (1931). London: Luzac, 1975.

———. *The Multiple States of Being* (1932). New York: Larson, 1984.

———. *The Reign of Quantity & the Signs of the Times* (1945). Ghent: Sophia Perennis et Universalis, 1995.

———. *Fundamental Symbols: The Universal Language of Sacred Science*. Cambridge, UK: Quinta Essentia, 1995.

Halifax, Joan (ed.). *Shamanic Voices: The Shaman as Seer, Poet, and Healer*. New York: Penguin, 1979.

Hassrick, Royal B. *The Sioux: Life and Customs of a Warrior Society*. Norman: University of Oklahoma, 1964.

Heflin, Ruth J. (ed.). *"I Remain Alive": The Sioux Literary Renaissance*. Syracuse: Syracuse University Press, 2000.

———. "Black Elk Passes on the Power of the Earth." In *The Black Elk Reader*, ed. C. Holler, 3-18.

Hewes, Gordon. Review of Joseph Epes Brown, *The Sacred Pipe*. *American Anthropologist* 56, 1954, 907-908.

Holler, Clyde. *Black Elk's Religion: The Sun Dance and Lakota Catholicism*. Syracuse: Syracuse University, 1995.

———. "Black Elk's Relationship to Christianity." *American Indian Quarterly* 8:1, Winter 1984, 37-49.

———. "Lakota Religion and Tragedy: The Theology of *Black Elk Speaks*." *Journal of the American Academy of Religion* LII:1, 1984, 19-45.

———. "Black Elk, Nicholas (1866-1950)." *Encyclopaedia of the Great Plains* (http://plainshumanities.uni.edu/encyclopedia/).

——— (ed.). *The Black Elk Reader*. Syracuse: Syracuse University, 2000.

Holloway, Brian. *Interpreting the Legacy: John Neihardt and "Black Elk*

Speaks." Boulder: University Press of Colorado, 2003.

Howard, Scott J. "Incommensurability and Nicholas Black Elk: An Exploration." *American Indian Culture and Research Journal* 23:1, 1999, 111-136.

Hultkrantz, Åke. *The Religions of the American Indian.* Berkeley: University of California, 1979.

———. "Attitudes to Animals in Shoshoni Indian Religion." *Studies in Comparative Religion* 4:2, Spring 1970, 70-79.

———. Introduction to Joseph Epes Brown, *The Spiritual Legacy of the American Indian: With Letters While Living with Black Elk*, eds. Marina Brown Weatherly, Elenita Brown & Michael O. Fitzgerald. Bloomington: World Wisdom, 2007, xvii-xxiv.

Irwin, Lee. Review of Michael Steltenkamp, *Black Elk: Holy Man of the Oglala. Great Plains Research* 4.2, 1994, 342-344.

Isherwood, Christopher. *Ramakrishna and His Disciples.* Calcutta: Advaita Ashram, 1963.

Iverson, Peter. "Neihardt, Collier, and the Continuity of Indian Life." In *Sender of Words: Essays in Memory of John G. Neihardt*, ed. Vine Deloria Jr., 100-109.

Jackson, Joe. *Black Elk: The Life of an American Visionary.* New York: Farrar, Straus & Giroux, 2016.

Jaffé, Aniela. *The Myth of Meaning.* Baltimore: Penguin, 1975.

James, William. *Varieties of Religious Experience.* London: Fontana, 1961.

Josephy Jr., Alvin M. *The Indian Heritage of America.* New York: Knopf, 1968.

———. "The Poet Beyond Black Elk." In *Sender of Words: Essays in Memory of John G. Neihardt*, ed. Vine Deloria Jr., 25-29.

Jung, Carl J. *Memories, Dreams, Reflections.* London: Fontana/Collins, 1983.

——— *C.G. Jung: Collected Works, Vol. 6; Psychological Types* (1921), ed. H. Read, M. Fordham & G. Adler. London: Routledge, 2014.

———. *The Collected Works of C.G. Jung, Vol. 14: Mysterium Coniunctionis* (1955). Princeton: Princeton University, 1963.

Kaye, Frances M. "Just What is Cultural Appropriation, Anyway?" In *The Black Elk Reader*, ed. C. Holler, 147-168.

Koestler, Arthur & J.R. Smythies (eds.). *Beyond Reductionism: New Perspectives in the Life Sciences.* London: Hutchinson, 1969.

Kroeber, Theodora. *Ishi in Two Worlds.* Berkeley: University of California, 1961.

Lame Deer, John Fire & Richard Erdoes. *Lame Deer: Seeker of Visions.* New York: Washington Square Press, 1972.

Laubin, Reginald & Gladys. *The Indian Tipi* (1957). New York: Ballantine Books, 1971.

Lévi-Strauss, Claude, *Totemism* (1962). London: Merlin Press, 1991.

Linden, George W. "Dakota Philosophy." In *The Black Elk Reader*, ed. Clyde Holler, 209-240.

————. "John Neihardt and *Black Elk Speaks*: A Personal Reminiscence." In *The Black Elk Reader*, ed. Clyde Holler, 79-86.

Matthiessen, Peter. *In the Spirit of Crazy Horse.* New York: Viking Press, 1983.

————. *Indian Country.* London: Fontana, 1985.

Mahadevan, T.M.P. *Ramana Maharshi: The Sage of Arunacala.* London: Allen & Unwin, 1977.

Mails, Thomas E. *Fools Crow: Wisdom and Power.* Lincoln: University of Nebraska, 1979. _

————. *Sundancing at Rosebud and Pine Ridge.* Sioux Falls: The Center for Western Studies, 1978.

McAllister, Mick. "Native Sources: American Indian Autobiography." *Western American Literature* 32, 1997, 3-23.

McCluskey, Sally. "*Black Elk Speaks*: And So Does John Neihardt." *Western American Literature* 6:4, Winter 1972, 231-242.

McDonald, Barry (ed.). *Seeing God Everywhere: Essays on Nature and the Sacred.* Bloomington: World Wisdom, 2003.

———— (ed.). *Every Branch of Me: Essays on the Meaning of Man.* Bloomington: World Wisdom, 2002.

McLuhan, T.C. (ed.). *Touch the Earth.* London: Abacus, 1973.

———— (ed.). *Cathedrals of the Spirit: The Message of Sacred Places.* Toronto: HarperCollins, 1996.

McMurtry, Larry. *Crazy Horse.* London: Weidenfeld & Nicolson, 1999.

Merton, Thomas. *Opening the Bible.* London: Allen & Unwin, 1972.

————. *Ishi Means Man.* Greensboro: Unicorn Press, 1973.

Momaday, N. Scott. "To Save a Great Vision." In *Sender of Words: Essays in Memory of John G. Neihardt*, ed. Vine Deloria Jr., 30-38.

Nabokov, Peter (ed.). *Two Leggings: The Making of a Crow Warrior.* New York: Thomas Crowell, 1967.

Nasr, Seyyed Hossein. *Ideals and Realities of Islam.* London: Allen & Unwin, 1966.

————. *Man and Nature: The Spiritual Crisis of Modern Man.* London: Allen & Unwin, 1968.

————. *Sufi Essays.* London: Allen & Unwin, 1972.

————. *The Need for a Sacred Science.* Albany: SUNY, 1993.

————. *Religion and the Order of Nature.* New York: Oxford University, 1996.

————. *The Spiritual and Religious Dimension of the Environmental Crisis.* London: Temenos Academy, 1999.

————. "Reflections on Islam and Modern Thought." *The Islamic Quarterly* 23:3, 1979, 119-131.

———— & Katherine O'Brien (eds.). *The Essential Sophia.* Bloomington: World Wisdom, 2006.

Needleman, Jacob (ed.). *The Sword of Gnosis.* Baltimore: Penguin, 1974.

Neihardt, Hilda. *Black Elk and Flaming Rainbow: Personal Memories of the Lakota Holy Man and John Neihardt.* Lincoln: University of Nebraska,

1995.

———— & R. Todd Wise. "Black Elk and John G. Neihardt." In *The Black Elk Reader*, ed. Clyde Holler, 87-103.

———— & Lori Utecht (eds.). *Black Elk Lives: Conversations with the Black Elk Family*. Lincoln: University of Nebraska, 2000.

Neihardt, John G. *Black Elk Speaks: The Complete Edition*. Introduced by Philip J. Deloria, annotated by Raymond J. DeMallie. Lincoln: University of Nebraska, 2014. Originally published as *Black Elk Speaks: Being the Life Story of a Holy Man of the Oglala Sioux*. New York: William Morrow & Company, 1932. Reference has also been made to the 1961, 1972, 1979, and 1988 editions.

————. "The Book That Would Not Die." *Western American Literature* 6:4, Winter 1972, 227-230. (This also appeared as the Introduction to the 1972 Pocket edition of *Black Elk Speaks*.)

Oldmeadow, Harry. *Mircea Eliade and Carl Jung: "Priests without Surplices"?* Bendigo: La Trobe University, 1995.

————. *A Christian Pilgrim in India: The Spiritual Journey of Swami Abhishiktananda (Henri Le Saux)*. Bloomington: World Wisdom, 2008.

————. *Frithjof Schuon and the Perennial Philosophy*. Bloomington: World Wisdom, 2010.

————. *Touchstones of the Spirit: Essays on Religion, Tradition, and Modernity*. Bloomington: World Wisdom, 2012.

————. "'The Firmament Sheweth His Handiwork': Reawakening a Religious Sense of the Natural Order." In *Seeing God Everywhere*, ed. Barry McDonald, 29-50.

————. "Melodies from the Beyond." In Harry Oldmeadow, *Touchstones of the Spirit*, 3-22.

———— (ed.). *The Betrayal of Tradition: Essays on the Spiritual Crisis of Modernity*. Bloomington: World Wisdom, 2005.

———— (ed.). *Light from the East: Eastern Wisdom for the Modern West*. Bloomington: World Wisdom, 2007.

———— (ed.). *Crossing Religious Frontiers*. Bloomington: World Wisdom, 2010.

Olney, James (ed.). *Studies in Autobiography*. New York: Oxford University, 1988.

Olson, Paul. Review of Joseph Epes Brown, *The Sacred Pipe*. *Great Plains Quarterly* Summer 1983, 187-188.

Orwell, George. "Reflections on Gandhi." In *The Collected Essays, Vol 4: In Front of Your Nose*. Harmondsworth: Penguin, 1970.

Otto, Rudolf. *The Idea of the Holy* (1917). London: Oxford University, 1958.

Paden, William. *Religious Worlds: The Comparative Study of Religion*. Boston: Beacon Press, 1988.

Paige, Harry W. *Songs of the Teton Sioux*. Los Angeles: Westernlore Press, 1970.

Pallis, Marco. *A Buddhist Spectrum*. London: Allen & Unwin, 1980.

————. Review of *The New Religions*, ed. Jacob Needleman. *Studies in Comparative Religion* 5:3, 1971, 189-190.

Parks, Douglas R. & Raymond J. DeMallie. "Sioux, Assiniboine, and Stoney Dialects: A Classification." *Anthropological Linguistics* 34:1/4 (Spring-Winter, 1992), 233-255.

Perry, Barbara. "Frithjof Schuon: Metaphysician and Artist." Bloomington: World Wisdom, 1981.

Perry, Whitall (ed.). *A Treasury of Traditional Wisdom*. London: Allen & Unwin, 1971.

————. Review of Ninian Smart, *The Phenomena of Religion*. *Studies in Comparative Religion* 7:2, 1973, 127.

————. "Corrigendum." *Studies in Comparative Religion* 15:3-4, 1983, 141.

Petri, Alexis N. "John G. Neihardt beyond Black Elk." Appendix 7 in *Black Elk Speaks: The Complete Edition*, 267-281.

Pollack, Michael. Introduction to *Images of Primordial and Mystic Beauty: Paintings by Frithjof Schuon*, 1-4.

Porterfield, Amanda. "Black Elk's Significance in American Culture." In *The Black Elk Reader*, ed. Clyde Holler, 39-58.

Powers, William K., *Beyond the Vision: Essays on American Indian Culture*. Norman: Oklahoma University, 1987.

————. "When Black Elks Speaks, Everybody Listens." In *Religion in Native North America*, ed. Christopher Vecsey, 136-151.

Raine, Kathleen. "The Underlying Order: Nature and the Imagination." In *Seeing God Everywhere*, ed. Barry McDonald, 171-190.

Rice, Julian. *Black Elk's Story: Distinguishing Its Lakota Purpose*. Albuquerque: University of New Mexico, 1991.

————. "*Akicita* of the Thunder: Horses in Black Elk's Vision." In *The Black Elk Reader*, ed. Clyde Holler, 59-76.

Roszak, Theodore. *The Making of a Counter-Culture: Reflections on the Technocratic Society and Its Youthful Opposition*. London: Routledge, 1970.

————. *Where the Wasteland Ends*. New York: Doubleday, 1972.

———— (ed.). *Sources: An Anthology of Contemporary Materials Useful for Preserving Personal Sanity While Braving the Great Technological Wilderness*. New York: Harper & Row, 1972.

Sandoz, Mari. *Crazy Horse: The Strange Man of the Oglalas* (1942). Lincoln: University of Nebraska, 1961.

Sayre, Robert. "Vision and Experience in *Black Elk Speaks*." *College English* 32:5, February 1971, 509-535.

Schumacher, E.F. *A Guide for the Perplexed*. London: Jonathan Cape, 1977.

Schuon, Catherine. "Frithjof Schuon: Memories and Anecdotes." *Sacred Web* 8, 2001, 35-60.

Schuon, Frithjof. *Spiritual Perspectives and Human Facts* (1954). Bloomington: World Wisdom, 2007.

————. *Language of the Self* (1959). Bloomington: World Wisdom, 1999.

————. *Gnosis: Divine Wisdom* (1959). Bloomington: World Wisdom, 2006.

————. *Understanding Islam* (1963). Bloomington: World Wisdom, 1998.

————. *Light on the Ancient Worlds* (1965). Bloomington: World Wisdom, 2006.

————. *Logic and Transcendence* (1975). Bloomington: World Wisdom, 1984.

————. *Esoterism as Principle and as Way*. Bloomington: World Wisdom, 1981.

————. *From the Divine to the Human* (1982). Bloomington: World Wisdom, 2013.

————. *To Have a Center* (1990). Bloomington: World Wisdom, 2015.

————. *The Feathered Sun: Plains Indians in Art and Philosophy*. Bloomington: World Wisdom, 1990.

————. *Images of Primordial and Mystic Beauty: Paintings by Frithjof Schuon*. Bloomington: Abodes, 1992.

————. *Treasures of Buddhism*. Bloomington: World Wisdom, 1993.

————. *The Eye of the Heart: Metaphysics, Cosmology, Spiritual Life*. Bloomington: World Wisdom, 1997.

————. *Songs for a Spiritual Traveler*. Bloomington: World Wisdom, 2002.

————. *Art from the Sacred to the Profane: East and West*. Edited by Catherine Schuon. Bloomington: World Wisdom, 2007.

————. "No Activity Without Truth." In *The Sword of Gnosis*, ed. Jacob Needleman, 27-39.

————. "Foundations of an Integral Aesthetics." *Studies in Comparative Religion* 10:3, 1976.

Scott, Tim. "Understanding 'Symbol'." *Sacred Web* 6, Winter, 2000 (sacredweb.com/online_articles/sw6_scott.html).

Sharma. Arvind. *A Primal Perspective on the Philosophy of Religion*. Dordrecht: Springer, 2006.

———— (ed.). *Fragments of Infinity: Essays in Religion and Philosophy*. Bridport. Prism, 1991.

Sharpe, Eric. *Comparative Religion*. London: Duckworth, 1975.

Sherrard, Philip. *The Rape of Man and Nature*. Colombo: Sri Lanka Institute of Traditional Studies, 1987.

————. *Christianity: Lineaments of a Sacred Tradition*. Brookline, Mass.: Holy Cross Orthodox Press, 1998.

Simson, Otto von. *The Gothic Cathedral*. Princeton: Bollingen Series, 1974.

Siraj Ed-Din, Abu Bakr. *The Book of Certainty*. New York: Samuel Weiser, 1974.

Smith, Aminah. "'What Hast Thou Done?': The Australian Aborigines and the Fate of the Nomads." In *Crossing Religious Frontiers*, ed. Harry Oldmeadow, 50-59.

Smith, Rex Alan. *Moon of Popping Trees: The Tragedy at Wounded Knee and the End of the Indian Wars*. Lincoln: University of Nebraska, 1981.

Smith, Huston, *The World's Religions*. New York: HarperCollins, 1991.

————. "What They Have That We Lack: A Tribute to the Native Americans via Joseph Epes Brown." In *The Essential Sophia*, eds. Seyyed Hossein Nasr & Katherine O'Brien, 85-95.

————. Foreword to Frithjof Schuon, *The Eye of the Heart: Metaphysics, Cosmology, Spiritual Life*, ix-xi.

Snodgrass, Adrian. *The Symbolism of the Stupa.* Delhi: Motilal Banarsidass, 1992.

————. *Architecture, Time, and Eternity: Studies in the Stellar and Temporal Symbolism of Traditional Buildings*, 2 vols. New Delhi: P.K. Goel/Aditya Prakasan, 1990.

Standing Bear, Luther. *My People the Sioux* (1928). Lincoln: University of Nebraska, 1975.

————. *Land of the Spotted Eagle* (1933). Lincoln: University of Nebraska, 1978.

Stanner, W.E.H. "Religion, Totemism, and Symbolism." In *Religion in Aboriginal Australia*, ed. Max Charlesworth, 137-172.

Stauffer, Helen. "Neihardt's Journey on the Missouri." In *Sender of Words: Essays in Memory of John G. Neihardt*, ed. Vine Deloria Jr., 59-71.

Steinmetz, Paul B. *Pipe, Bible, and Peyote among the Oglala Lakota: A Study in Religious Identity.* Knoxville: University of Tennessee, 1990.

————. *The Sacred Pipe: An Archetypal Theology.* Syracuse: Syracuse University, 1998.

Steltenkamp, Michael F. *Black Elk: Holy Man of the Oglala.* Norman: University of Oklahoma, 1993.

————. *Nicholas Black Elk: Medicine Man, Missionary, Mystic.* Norman: University of Oklahoma, 2009.

————. "A Retrospective on *Black Elk: Holy Man of the Oglala.*" In *The Black Elk Reader*, ed. Clyde Holler, 104-126.

————. "American Indian Sainthood and the Catholic Church." *American Catholic Studies* 124:1, Spring 2013, 93-104.

Stover, Dale. Review of Clyde Holler, *Black Elk's Religion: The Sun Dance and Lakota Catholicism*, n.p. (www.aril.org; accessed 6th February, 2017).

————. "A Postcolonial Reading of Black Elk." In *The Black Elk Reader*, ed. Clyde Holler, 127-146.

Thesiger, Wilfred. *Arabian Sands.* Harmondsworth: Penguin, 1964.

Utecht, Lori. "Neihardt and Black Elk." Appendix 8 in *Black Elk Speaks: The Complete Edition*, 282-290.

Utley, Robert. *The Last Days of the Sioux Nation.* New Haven: Yale University, 1966.

————. *The Lance and the Shield: The Life and Times of Sitting Bull.* London: Pimlico, 1993.

Van der Post, Laurens. *The Lost World of the Kalahari.* London: Hogarth Press, 1958.

Vecsey, Christopher (ed.). *Religion in Native North America.* Moscow: University of Idaho, 1990.

Versluis, Arthur. *The Song of the Cosmos*. Bridport: Prism, 1991.

———. *The Elements of Native American Traditions*. Shaftesbury, Dorset: Element, 1993.

Vestal, Stanley. *Sitting Bull: Champion of the Sioux*. Norman: University of Oklahoma, 1932.

Walker, James. *Lakota Belief and Ritual* (1980). Edited by Raymond DeMallie & Elaine Jahner. Lincoln: University of Nebraska, 1991,

Waters, Frank. "Neihardt and the Vision of Black Elk." In *Sender of Words: Essays in Memory of John G. Neihardt*, ed. Vine Deloria Jr., 12-24.

Wellman, Sam. *Black Elk: The Complete Story*. North Newton: Wild Centuries Press, 2014.

Wikipedia entries: "Dawes Act"; "*Black Elk Speaks*"; "Lakota People"; "Postcolonialism"; "Ramana Maharshi" (all accessed 6th February, 2017).

Whitney, Blair. *John G. Neihardt*. New York: Twayne, 1976.

Wise, R. Todd. "*Black Elk Speaks* as Testimonial Literature." In *The Black Elk Reader*, ed. Clyde Holler, 19-38.

———. "The Great Vision of Black Elk as Literary Ritual." In *The Black Elk Reader*, ed. Clyde Holler, 241-261.

Young, Quentin H. *Mystic Visions: Black Elk's Great Vision Clarified*. Marble: World Branch Publishing, 2015.

Zolla, Elémire. *The Writer and the Shaman: A Morphology of the American Indian*. New York: Harcourt Brace Jovanovich, 1973.

Acknowledgments

For material, moral, and intellectual support, my heartfelt thanks to:

Ben Black Bear, Jr.
Marina Brown Weatherly
Anne Cox
Michael & Judith Fitzgerald
Joseph Fitzgerald
Clyde Holler
Coralie Hughes
Stephen Maber
Rose Mazza
Alex Minchinton
Clinton Minnaar
Neihardt Foundation
Maurie & Marcia Nestor
Peter & Wendy Oldmeadow
Charlie Rose
Catherine Schuon
The State Historical Society of Missouri
William Stoddart
Dale Stover
Charles Trimble
Chief James Trosper
Paul Verbeeren
Paul Weeks

This book is dedicated to Michael Fitzgerald,
friend and benefactor of the Plains Indians.

The royalties from this book will be donated to
the Lakota Language Consortium.

Index

Abhishiktananda, Swami, 71, 108, 180, 189, 194
Abu Bakr Siraj Ed-Din, 58, 135, 187, 201
Ahmad al-'Alawi, Shaykh, 164
Anagarika Govinda, Lama, 133, 134
animism, polysynthetic, 64, 120, 124
Anna Brings White, 43
Aquinas, St. Thomas, 54, 73, 123, 199
Arabian Prophet (Muhammad), the, 165
archetypes, the, 57, 58, 59, 73, 169, 171, 187
assimilation (of Indians into white culture), 4, 5, 47, 132
Atma, 166, 169

Battle of Little Big Horn, the, xiii, 4, 35, 182
Benjamin Black Elk, xviii, 20, 43, 50, 51, 55, 76, 91, 92, 93, 96, 99, 103, 104, 109, 116, 145, 146, 155, 159, 160, 163, 184, 185, 189, 192, 194, 203
Big Foot's band, 41
Black Elk, *passim*
Black Elk Speaks (Neihardt), xi, xiii, xiv, xv, xvi, xviii, 2, 6, 24, 26, 31, 39, 42, 45, 47, 48, 50, 51, 52, 53, 54, 68, 70, 75, 76, 77, 78, 79, 80, 81, 82, 83, 84, 85, 86, 87, 88, 90, 92, 95, 96, 99, 101, 102, 103, 111, 112, 113, 116, 117, 133, 142, 143, 171, 172, 173, 175, 177, 181, 183, 184, 185, 186, 189, 190, 191, 193, 194, 196, 197, 198
Black Hills, the, 15, 40, 42, 51, 159
Brown, Dee, 2, 43, 85
Brown, Joseph Epes, xii, xiv, xv,

xvi, xviii, xix, 2, 7, 12, 13, 19, 31, 43, 46, 47, 52, 53, 54, 55, 56, 62, 63, 75, 79, 81, 84, 85, 89, 90, 91, 92, 93, 94, 95, 96, 97, 98, 99, 100, 101, 104, 105, 107, 110, 111, 112, 113, 115, 116, 117, 121, 124, 140, 143, 155, 163, 167, 168, 169, 172, 173, 175, 177, 179, 180, 181, 182, 184, 186, 188, 189, 191, 192, 193, 195, 196, 197, 198, 199, 200, 201, 202, 203, 204. See also *Sacred Pipe, The*
"Buffalo Bill" Cody, 39, 40, 44, 46
Burckhardt, Titus, xviii, 118

Cain, 176; and Abel, 1, 2
Castro, Michael , 87
Catholic Church, the, 102, 156, 157, 172, 190, 214
Catholicism, xv, xvi, xviii, 44, 45, 46, 79, 80, 93, 94, 95, 100, 102, 104, 105, 107, 151, 182, 185, 186, 189, 192, 194
Celestial Femininity, 128
Chevilliat, Jacques, 117
Chief Joseph, xiii, 3
Chief Seattle, 3
Christ, 100, 102, 109, 172, 177, 184
Christianity, xv, 46, 72, 75, 93, 94, 100, 101, 103, 105, 106, 107, 108, 109, 110, 163, 164, 172, 177, 193, 195, 196, 201
civilizationism, 174
Coleridge, 60, 122, 188
conversion, xv, 44, 46, 79, 93, 95, 99, 100, 101, 103, 104, 105, 110, 151, 182, 184
Coomaraswamy, Ananda K., xii, xviii, 9, 25, 52, 53, 146, 177, 180, 202
Costello, Damien, 68, 69, 100, 107

217

For a glossary of all key foreign words used in books published by World Wisdom, including metaphysical terms in English, consult: www.DictionaryofSpiritualTerms.org.
This on-line Dictionary of Spiritual Terms provides extensive definitions, examples, and related terms in other languages.

Biographical Notes

Harry Oldmeadow was, until his retirement in 2012, Coordinator of Philosophy and Religious Studies at La Trobe University Bendigo in south-eastern Australia. He spent his childhood in India where his parents were missionaries. He studied at the Australian National University, Sydney University, St John's College Oxford, the University of Canberra and La Trobe University, and has degrees in history, religious studies and cinema studies.

Recognized as one of the leading scholarly authorities on the Perennialist school, his publications include *Traditionalism: Religion in the light of the Perennial Philosophy* (2000), *Frithjof Schuon and the Perennial Philosophy* (2010) and *Touchstones of the Spirit: Essays on Religion, Tradition and Modernity* (2012).

Oldmeadow has visited the sub-continent many times and written extensively on the spiritual encounter of East and West in *Journeys East: 20th Century Encounters with Eastern Religious Traditions* (2004) and *A Christian Pilgrim in India: the Spiritual Journey of Swami Abhishiktananda* (2008).

He has contributed to many journals, including *Sophia*, *Sacred Web*, and *The Temenos Academy Review*, edited several anthologies for World Wisdom, including *The Betrayal of Tradition* and *Light from the East*, and edited and annotated new translations of three of Frithjof Schuon's books, *In the Face of the Absolute*, *To Have a Center*, and *Treasures of Buddhism*.

Harry Oldmeadow has a long-standing interest in the spiritual traditions of nomadic peoples, especially the Australian Aborigines and the American Plains Indians. He has attended traditional Sun Dances in the American West, participated in Sweat Lodge ceremonies, and met with people of several different tribes. He lives with his wife and a small dog in Bendigo, Australia.

Charles "Chuck" Trimble was born and raised on the Pine Ridge Indian Reservation in South Dakota and is an enrolled member of the Oglala Sioux Tribe. He received his elementary and high school education at the Holy Rosary Mission Indian School in Pine Ridge, South Dakota and his B.F.A. degree from the University of South Dakota in 1957.

In 1969 Trimble was principal founder of the American Indian Press Association, and served as the organization's Executive Director for three years. In 1972 he was elected Executive Director of the National Congress of American Indians (NCAI). During his tenure, the NCAI is generally credited with having lobbied for enactment of the Indian Financing Act, the Indian Health Care Improvement Act, the Indian Self Determination Act, the Indian Religious Freedom Act, the Indian Child Welfare Act, and an unprecedented return of land to Indian tribes.

Trimble was actively involved in international affairs for protection of indigenous rights and human rights in general and has represented the United States at many conferences around the world.

He taught courses on Native American affairs at Fort Lewis College in Durango, Colorado, and at the University of Nebraska-Omaha College of Continuing Studies. He has also taught in the Nebraska State Historical Society's Nebraska Institute for Teachers. As president of the John G. Neihardt Foundation, Trimble established the Institute for Vision and Learning, a summer workshop in literature and writing for Native American high school students. He was also Director of the Institute of American Indian Studies at the University of South Dakota for the 2004-2007 academic years.

Trimble's numerous awards include the Pioneer Award from the Nebraskaland Foundation and Distinguished Alumni Awards from both the University of South Dakota and Cameron University. He was awarded an honorary degree in Lakota Leadership from Oglala Lakota College and has received honorary Doctorate degrees from Creighton University, Wayne State College, and the University of South Dakota, his alma mater.

Chuck Trimble was inducted into the South Dakota Hall of Fame in 2013. The author of *Iyeska*, he is now retired and lives in Omaha, Nebraska, with his wife, Anne.

Other American Indian Titles

All Our Relatives: Traditional Native American Thoughts about Nature
compiled and illustrated by Paul Goble, 2005

The Boy and His Mud Horses: And Other Stories from the Tipi
compiled and illustrated by Paul Goble, 2010

The Cheyenne Indians: Their History and Lifeways
by George Bird Grinnell, edited by Joseph A. Fitzgerald, 2008

Children of the Tipi: Life in the Buffalo Days
edited by Michael Oren Fitzgerald, 2013

Custer's Last Battle: Red Hawk's Account of the Battle of the Little Bighorn
compiled and illustrated by Paul Goble, 2013

The Earth Made New: Plains Indian Stories of Creation
compiled and illustrated by Paul Goble, 2009

The Essential Charles Eastman (Ohiyesa)
edited by Michael Oren Fitzgerald, 2007

The Feathered Sun: Plains Indians in Art and Philosophy
by Frithjof Schuon, 1990

The Gospel of the Redman: Commemorative Edition
compiled by Ernest Thompson Seton and Julia M. Seton, 2005

Horse Raid: The Making of a Warrior
compiled and illustrated by Paul Goble, 2014

The Hunter's Promise
by Joseph Bruchac, illustrated by Bill Farnsworth, 2015

The Image Taker:
The Selected Stories and Photographs of Edward S. Curtis
edited by Gerald Hasuman and Bob Kapoun, 2009

Indian Boyhood: The True Story of a Sioux Upbringing
by Charles Eastman, adapted by Michael Oren Fitzgerald,
illustrated by Heidi M. Rasch, 2016

Indian Spirit: Revised and Enlarged
edited by Judith and Michael Oren Fitzgerald, 2006

Living in Two Worlds: The American Indian Experience
by Charles Eastman, edited by Michael Oren Fitzgerald, 2010

The Man Who Dreamed of Elk-Dogs: & Other Stories from the Tipi
compiled and illustrated by Paul Goble, 2012

Native Spirit: The Sun Dance Way
by Thomas Yellowtail, edited by Michael Oren Fitzgerald, 2007

The Otter, the Spotted Frog, and the Great Flood
by Gerald Hausman, illustrated by Ramon Shiloh, 2013

Red Cloud's War: Brave Eagle's Account of the Fetterman Fight
compiled and illustrated by Paul Goble, 2015

The Spirit of Indian Women
edited by Judith and Michael Oren Fitzgerald, 2005

Spirit of the Earth: Indian Voices on Nature
edited by Joseph and Michael Oren Fitzgerald, 2017

The Spiritual Legacy of the American Indian: Commemorative Edition
with Letters While Living with Black Elk
by Joseph Epes Brown, 2007

The Thunder Egg
by Tim Myers, illustrated by Winfield Coleman, 2015

Tipi: Home of the Nomadic Buffalo Hunters
compiled and illustrated by Paul Goble, 2007

Whispers of the Wolf by Pauline Ts'o, 2015

The Women who Lived with Wolves: And Other Stories from the Tipi
compiled and illustrated by Paul Goble, 2011

World of the Teton Sioux Indians: Their Music, Life, and Culture
by Frances Densmore, edited by Joseph A. Fitzgerald, 2016

Films about American Indian Spirituality

Native Spirit & The Sun Dance Way
produced by Michael Oren Fitzgerald, directed by Jennifer Casey, 2007